Teaching and Targets

Teachers, school managers and governors are now more publicly accountable than ever. They are expected to know how their school is performing and how to improve that performance. Target-setting is a key tool in the drive to raise standards, and has been implemented at every level of the education system.

This book explains target-setting from both the teacher's and pupil's viewpoint, and investigates the role of assessment in successful teaching and learning. It shows that it is possible to develop a whole-school target-setting policy, co-ordinating the use of targets for individual pupils, subject departments and teams, and whole-school-improvement plans. In this way, targets can be used positively for the benefit of pupils, teachers and managers.

This book will be important reading for all teachers, headteachers, senior management teams, assessment co-ordinators and subject leaders in schools, and will also be of interest to governors, LEA advisors and providers of initial teacher training.

John Blanchard is a freelance education consultant, inspector and governor trainer. He has also worked as a teacher and senior LEA advisor for assessment, and on initial teacher training and continuing professional development courses for several universities.

Teaching and Targets
Self-evaluation and school improvement

John Blanchard

London and New York

First published 2002
by RoutledgeFalmer
11 New Fetter Lane, London EC4P 4EE

Simultaneously published in the USA and Canada
by RoutledgeFalmer
29 West 35th Street, New York, NY 10001

RoutledgeFalmer is an imprint of the Taylor & Francis Group

© 2002 John Blanchard

Typeset in Goudy by M Rules
Printed and bound in Great Britain by
MPG Books Ltd, Bodmin

British Library Cataloguing in Publication Data
A catalogue record for this book is available from the British Library

Library of Congress Cataloging in Publication Data
A catalog record has been requested

ISBN 0–415–28438–4

For Jacky
with love

Contents

Acknowledgements

I am grateful to many friends and colleagues for the help they have given over many years. I especially want to record how strong is the legacy of my conversations with Bill Brookes, and thank him for his care and wisdom. I wish to thank also: Fran Ashworth, Tim Balmforth, Susi Bancroft, Shirley Clarke, Les Cowling, Rita Horner, Betty Port, Keith Pugh, Norman Schamroth, David Rees, Sally Thorne, Sue Swaffield (President) and the Association for Assessment Inspectors and Advisers, and many colleagues in the Dorset School Improvement Service, especially Celia Stacey, my assistant for many years. Crucially too thanks to the headteachers and staffs of the following schools:

All Saints CE VSA School, Weymouth, Dorset
Archbishop Wake CE VC First School, Blandford, Dorset
Ashdown Secondary School, Poole
Bicknell School, Bournemouth
The Blandford VC Comprehensive School, Blandford, Dorset
Christ the King Roman Catholic Primary School, Amesbury, Wiltshire
The Dorchester (Thomas Hardye) VA Comprehensive School,
 Dorchester, Dorset
Gillingham Wyke Primary School, Dorset
Holbrook Primary School, Trowbridge, Wiltshire
Linwood School, Bournemouth
Lytchett Minster Comprehensive School, Dorset
Lytchett Matravers Primary School, Dorset
Marchant-Holliday School, Wincanton, Somerset
Milldown CE VC First School, Blandford, Dorset
Milldown CE VC Middle School, Blandford, Dorset
Motcombe CE VA First School, Shaftesbury, Dorset
Mountjoy School, Bridport, Dorset
Pokesdown Primary School, Bournemouth
The Purbeck Comprehensive School, Wareham, Dorset
St James' CE VC First School, Alderholt, Dorset
St James' CE VA Primary School, Bournemouth
St Leonard's Middle School, Blandford, Dorset

Swanage Middle School, Dorset
Twynham Comprehensive School, Christchurch, Dorset
Wyke Regis Junior School, Dorset
Wyvern School, Weymouth, Dorset.

I am grateful to the British Education Research Association, whose academic secretary, Michael Bassey, convened a seminar, chaired by Professor Peter Mortimore, on 9 May 2001 at the Institute of Education, London University, to critique the Hay/McBer work on teacher effectiveness.

A note about audience and context especially for colleagues in further and higher education

I have based my writing on the language and frames of reference commonly used in schools. I realise that in primary schools we usually refer to 'children', in secondary schools to 'pupils' and 'students', and in further and higher education to 'students'. Throughout this book, I write about 'pupils', 'teachers', 'school' and 'headteacher', rather than 'students', 'lecturers', 'college' and 'principal'. But I hope very much that colleagues in further and higher education will be able to recognise their own realities in what I write.

The bulk of my material is taken from research and experience in education 4 to 19 and from maintained schools. I hope colleagues in other contexts will not be too irritated by having to convert terminology and detail. Chapter 11, 'Monitoring and evaluation', and Appendix 3, 'Consistency in assessment', for example, can be used in colleges of further education without much translation, and they were written with post-16 education as much in mind as Key Stages 1 to 4. Chapter 8, 'Subject teams and targets', is especially relevant to 16-plus educational contexts. Appendix 4, 'Statistical techniques', applies across all phases of education.

Perhaps the main differences between compulsory education and sixth form college, further and higher education are in scale and the nature of the learners. Most colleges are bigger than schools, and this means that management delegation and communication take particular forms that may not be required in many schools. The students do not have to be there, and their lives and concerns can involve challenges that do not so often preoccupy children up to the age of 16.

Nevertheless I suggest that the central arguments and materials of this book can be applied beyond compulsory schooling. Further research, I realise, needs to be done in these fields, for example, relating to retention-rate targets and the use of GCSE grades in target-setting for foundation, intermediate and advanced students at 16-plus. But the core concepts of institutional targets, subject team targets, performance-management objectives for individual members of staff, and individual students' targets, I believe, retain their relevance across different contexts of college and school. These are what I explore in this book.

Introduction

Why should we be so concerned with targets? Part of the reason is the government's conviction that targets help raise standards in schools. Legislation, based on this belief, passed in recent years, means that targets are used at every level of the education system. Year groups of pupils have targets set for them as an indicator of schools' effectiveness. Headteachers, deputy headteachers and teachers have objectives set as part of their performance management. Individual pupils have targets. School governors are responsible for publishing whole-school attainment targets. School-improvement planning focuses on targets, and all specialist colleges have to set annual targets.

Targets and the raising of standards are now so rhetorically linked that merely setting targets might seem sufficient to raise standards. But saying something should happen does not bring it about. And let us not forget that large-scale whole-school targets depend on smaller-scale targets for teachers and pupils. A school does not hit a target. Neither does a cohort of pupils. Everything depends on the individual pupils who hit or miss their targets.

Whether or not school targets are hit hinges on what teachers and pupils feel, think and do. If targets exist independently of teachers and pupils, if they are the province only of managers, administrators and politicians, targets can only have a negligible or negative effect on what teachers and pupils feel, think and do, and so do little to enhance what pupils experience and achieve.

This book explores how as teachers, managers and governors you can use targets to have a beneficial effect on your school's performance. Crucial will be the relationship between whole-school targets and targets that teachers and pupils aim for. The intention is to help you to:

- establish a coherent policy for all the different kinds of target and objective that are used in school;
- set targets that are sufficiently clear and specific to provide motivation and direction;
- make sure that using targets is meaningful for the people involved and does not degenerate into bureaucratic routine.

It will be vital to recognise the primacy of pupils' motivations, perceptions and achievements. However much teachers, managers and others beyond the school may concern themselves with targets, ultimately it is the pupils who determine a school's performance. Interestingly, several of the entries to the *Guardian* newspaper's competition 'The school I'd like' (published on 22 May and 5 June 2001) emphasise being listened to, conversation, having reasons for tasks, being recognised as an individual, and leaving something to be remembered by.

These are key questions: *What are you trying to achieve? How are you doing? What have you achieved?* The more aware pupils are of these questions and of their own answers to them, the more focused will be their efforts, the greater their sense of satisfaction, and the more successful their application of what they have learned to new and different situations. As teachers and school managers you face the same questions about your purpose, job satisfaction and development.

Teaching is designed to stimulate and help pupils to learn. The management of teaching is designed to organise, resource and support teaching. Teaching is all about having intentions and reflecting on what happens when those intentions are pursued. The same can be said about managing teaching.

Whether you are a pupil, teacher, manager, or governor, knowing what you are trying to achieve helps you prepare, resource, guide, sustain, monitor and evaluate your efforts. What you were trying to achieve at the outset becomes at last the measure of how well you have done. For teachers, school managers and governors, all of this has become a technical, politicised and often statutory matter. The jargon is plentiful and ever changing:

- *What are you trying to achieve?* = intentions, plans, objectives, goals, aims, mission, vision, development, project, targets, initiative, improvement.
- *How are you doing?* = formative assessment, monitoring, progress, (self-) review, interim reporting, reflective practice, feedback.
- *What have you achieved?* = summative assessment, progress, outcomes, results, achievements, attainments, (self-) review, reporting, (self-) evaluation, audit.

As teachers and managers you answer those questions individually in the first instance. But because education is a social pursuit, the answers have also to be shared.

'What are you trying to achieve?' joins up with 'What are *we* trying to achieve?' 'How are you doing?' becomes 'How are *we* doing?' 'What have you achieved?' leads to 'What have *we* achieved?' As teachers and school managers you have to find explicit and collective answers to questions about your intentions, progress and effectiveness. You could not otherwise do your jobs as members of teams or as a whole school.

In part because education is publicly governed and funded, teachers and managers are held to account by their colleagues, their governing body, and local or foundation authority, and community. Being accountable means more than being answerable for performance. It means having to try to improve.

When as teachers and managers you try to improve your effectiveness, you address these questions: 'How do we express what we are trying to achieve?' 'How do we check how we are doing?' 'How do we measure what we have achieved?' And when being inspected, you compare your own answers with the judgements made by outsiders. You could not otherwise be seen to be doing your job.

And since 1990 the stakes have been raised: schools are now expected to be more purposeful, more effective, and more accountable. In the last decade of the twentieth century all of the following were introduced in England and Wales:

- the National Curriculum;
- statutory testing and the publication of league tables;
- Ofsted inspection and public reporting;
- national standards for teacher qualification, headship, and other roles;
- reporting by school governing bodies of results and targets;
- performance management for headteachers and teaching staff.

Each of those has played a part in bringing about the present situation whereby everyone in education now has targets. Pupils have them. Teachers have them. Schools have them. This book concerns all of those, and only indirectly touches on the kinds of target that both LEAs and the DfES have, though the targets that the DfES sets help to determine LEAs' targets which in turn help to determine the whole-school targets that LEA advisers and headteachers negotiate.

It was in 1998 that formal, public targets were set for the first time in relation to pupils' attainment. Their results were seen in 2000. Chapter 1 of this book addresses schools' initial experience of using performance targets for pupils' attainment. We will consider the impressions of some headteachers and deputy headteachers.

Targets are intended to benefit teaching and learning. Central to any effort to raise standards in schools must be what happens in the classroom. Chapter 2 presents the findings of my research into pupils' perceptions, carried out over the summer term 2000 in nine schools, primary, secondary and special, covering four LEAs. I also refer to the results of a similar exercise, carried out by a deputy headteacher in a middle school.

Chapter 3, 'Ethos, teaching and targets', remains in the classroom, and takes a research-based look at the use of targets as a means of promoting successful learning in school. We begin with a list of different kinds of target which might be used by individual pupils. We go on to consider in detail seven features of effective teaching which characterise subject teaching and occasions when teacher and pupil 'take time out' to discuss progress, difficulties and targets.

Chapter 4, 'Formative assessment and targets', also set in the classroom, explores what research has to tell us about pupils' taking initiative in and control over their learning. We will consider different purposes and kinds of assessment and the role that targets might play within them. We will examine how targets can be broken down and supported by specific steps to be taken. We will take note of the important difference between things that affect pupils socially and things that affect pupils personally in school. We will consider what makes a good target, and I present a draft policy for the use of targets as a way of promoting pupils' learning.

Targets were given prominence by the government's commitment to raising standards in schools. The context that generally receives public attention is macro rather than micro. Whole-school performance and development take the lime-light rather than the classroom, though the classroom is the prime field of action and the determinant of what a school achieves. Chapter 5, 'Whole-school targets and improvement', looks at what teachers and their managers can do to improve their school's performance. Chapter 6 pays particular attention to special educational needs, an area sometimes ill-served by the first versions of new legislation. We will explore the many different kinds of whole-school target that are possible, and consider how best they might be used in a special school to promote the pupils' welfare and learning most effectively.

Chapter 7 continues the whole-school theme and reminds us that there is more to school than academic work. Personal and social aspects of provision, for example, may be vital for a school to attend to. And inclusion is central to government's efforts to improve schooling by focusing on ethos and attitudes and their effect on pupils' learning.

Chapter 8 moves to the work of management, teaching and care teams. How teams use targets provides a crucial link between pupils' targets and whole-school targets and improvement.

Next we turn to the question of targets as they apply to individual headteachers and members of staff. Chapter 9, 'Performance management and objectives', deals with the process that prompts teachers, headteachers and their deputies time to review and focus their efforts within procedures introduced in 2000–1 to replace the appraisal system in England and Wales. My concern is to find ways of bringing coherence to whole-school improvement, teams' and individuals' continuing professional development. The chapter includes a lesson observation framework and protocol, which might be used as part of teachers' performance management. This section tackles the sensitive issue of how to handle critical judgements about teaching.

Strategic responsibility for what takes place in school is statutorily borne by school governors. Chapter 10 looks at the role governors have to play in the use of targets and objectives. The intention will be to enable constructive partnership between governors and professionals with regard to strategy, monitoring and performance management.

Chapter 11 picks up the implications of all that has gone before. Keeping track of progress is sometimes neglected. Targets are set and objectives defined; then the business of teaching or management becomes so absorbing, self-generating, and tiring that time is not found for critical reflection. This chapter will offer frameworks so that development activity might be seen through to evaluation, experience might be learned from and lessons applied in subsequent endeavour.

Appendix 1 contains the detail of what was summarised in Chapter 2, from my interviews of pupils. You can read here what the pupils said in answer to my questions about their experience of school and targets.

Appendix 2 presents guidance relating to the reviewing or making of policy for marking. This links with Chapters 3 and 4.

Appendix 3 deals with the crucial issue of consistency in assessment. Teachers' use of targets is only as good as the accuracy, validity and dependability of their assessments of pupils' progress and achievement.

Appendix 4 explains some essential statistical techniques, now commonly used in performance data analysis and target-setting. Line of best fit, value added, and chances charts are explained, for example.

Appendix 5 presents a case study of how using targets was developed in a primary school, Appendix 6 a case study of a secondary school.

Appendices 7 and 8 follow up Chapter 5 and provide guidance for schools' assessment policy and practice. Appendix 7 presents a model calendar for school self-review and target-setting. Appendix 8 contains a checklist for policy and practice in assessment and the use of targets.

There is a bibliography, followed finally by a glossary of technical terms and acronyms. And there is an index.

At the outset, we need to make some distinctions. It is a problem in education, acutely felt, for example by school governors, that the language we use is sometimes ambiguous and misleading. Sometimes a word such as 'target' is used in a very specific, technical sense, at other times more casually in ordinary conversation. It is possible for governors to listen to professionals and not be at all clear about what targets are being discussed.

We need to distinguish between statutory **targets for whole-school improvement** and **targets for individual pupils**. Whole-school targets are designed to bring about changes in a school's culture, resources, teaching, or systems, so that large numbers of pupils will benefit in their learning and achievement.

Statutory targets for school improvement	*Targets for individual pupils*
state what a school is aiming for in terms of year groups' attainment in tests or exams;	indicate what one or more pupils will, if successful, learn, i.e. learn to do or be;
are determined by the headteacher, LEA representative and governors on the basis of comparisons with similar schools' performance;	are determined by the teacher, or by the pupil, or by both in consultation with one another; they may take into consideration projected attainment on the basis of previously assessed performance;
consist of the percentage of a year group of pupils to attain a given level, grade, or specific quality of performance, at a given stage in their schooling;	consist of a description of the knowledge, skill or understanding aimed for by the individual pupil;

have to be set for the end of Key Stages 2, 3 and 4;	are voluntary;
have uniform time-scales or fixed end-points;	are set for a lesson, a half day, a day, a number of days, a week, or longer;
cannot be altered;	can be changed at any time;
have to be published by the school's governing body;	are between the teacher and the pupil, but are not generally confidential and may be made known to the pupil's parents or carers;
are part of the data against which the school may be held accountable;	play no direct part in summary judgements about the school's effectiveness;
can only have an indirect bearing on pupils' learning.	have a direct bearing on the pupil's learning.

Coherence between the two levels of targeting, the macro and the micro, seems the main challenge.

Coherence depends on clarity. There is a further important distinction to make between **task** and **target** as far as individual pupils are concerned. A task is what a pupil has to do. The notion of an individual's target should be reserved for the learning an individual's task is designed to bring about. The two may in practice sometimes overlap. For example, when a pupil has to write a story with a beginning, a middle and an end, task and target might appear synonymous. But the target stresses the **learning**, and the task stresses the **doing**. The task may be to walk the length of this beam, while the target will be to learn about balance and trust. I believe a school's, a team's and a teacher's effectiveness depends on their being crystal clear about the difference between what a pupil is doing and what a pupil is learning.

A task is a vehicle for the learning; it answers the question *What are you doing?* A target gives the reason for the task and the activity; it answers the question *Why are you doing that?* And it gives a particularly personal answer. Asked *Why are you doing that?* a pupil might point to the lesson objective or to the topic or unit the class is working on, but a target gives the reason in terms that are meaningful to the individual pupil.

It is possible for more than one pupil to have the same target. Some teachers set class targets. And lesson objectives and pupils' targets can overlap and sometimes even be identical. But while a pupil can be indifferent towards certain lesson objectives, it makes no sense to say a pupil takes no interest in her/his targets. A pupil can be said to have a target only if s/he has some commitment towards achieving it. A lesson objective begins, and may end, as the teacher's responsibility. An individual pupil's target has as soon as possible to become, and must end as, the pupil's responsibility. The bottom line is that lesson objectives are primarily the teachers' concern, however much they want the pupils to 'own' them. Targets have to be the personal concern of the individual pupils.

We can, then, distinguish between **lesson objectives** and **pupils' targets**.

Lesson objectives	*Pupils' targets*
guide the teacher, and, when passed on, tell the class the purpose or aim of lesson activities;	tell the pupils what aspects of their performance to try to focus on and improve;
are usually for a class;	are usually for individual pupils;
usually last for a lesson;	may last for less than a lesson or much longer;
may be recorded as a part of monitoring in order to satisfy co-ordinators, managers, or inspectors about the quality of the teachers' lesson planning;	may be recorded in order to inform dialogue between teacher and pupil; may also be recorded to support Individual Education Planning for pupils experiencing Special Educational Needs;
are almost always set by teachers;	may be set by the teacher, or by the pupil, or be devised jointly by teacher and pupil;
give feedback to the teacher, and to the class too if the teacher wishes, measuring what has been achieved against the original intention;	are a reference point for evaluative feedback available to the individual pupil;
have no enduring practical value for the teacher or class beyond the lesson, each lesson objective being one part of the medium- and long-term-planning and scheme-of-work jigsaw.	serve as a focus of attention for as long as the target remains valid, and, as targets are hit, plot a record of personal achievement.

The use of targets is a fast-moving aspect of education. Performance management and school self-review became concerns in 2000, and help make it possible now to draw together all the different manifestations of targets that there are in a school into something resembling a coherent whole. Pupils' targets; clear and explicit lesson objectives; each teacher's personal objectives for improved performance and continuing professional development; subject and care teams' development plans and activities; senior managers' objectives; the whole-school improvement plan; targets for pupils' attainment at the end of key stages negotiated with LEA consultants – all of these can be made to serve the welfare and learning of pupils, and the increased effectiveness of teachers, managers and governors. Coherence in matters of planning, targeting, teaching, managing, monitoring and evaluating will be our focus.

The argument I wish to make at the core of this book is that coherence is to be achieved through the painstaking acknowledgement of the different dynamics that are peculiar and appropriate to the different fields of targeting activity that now exist in schools. Account has to be taken of the three essential phases of using targets: target-setting; the monitoring of progress towards target achievement; and the evaluation of outcomes. And this has to be done for:

- the pupils' use of targets;
- the use of targets by teaching, pastoral, and management teams;
- every teacher's and manager's use of targets, or 'objectives', as part of their performance management;
- the use of targets as part of whole-school improvement.

When those four planes are crossed by the three phases of using targets, twelve fields are shown. Coherence is to be looked for by means of cross-checking between them. We can identify how each of the fields is accessed and checked:

Target used	*Setting*	*Monitoring*	*Evaluation*
by Pupils	Teacher–pupil negotiation, exercise book, folder, wall display, card system . . .	Ditto, with assessments by self, peers, teacher, classroom assistant . . .	Ditto; plus testimony by any audience or participant at school or at home; and process accreditation (e.g. IiP), inspection . . .
Teams	Subject/Year/ Key Stage/ SMT development planning	By the team itself; by colleagues outside the team; or by others commissioned for the purpose	Ditto; process accreditation (e.g. IiP), inspection . . .
PM for HT and staff	PM annual meeting with external adviser and governors in the case of the headteacher, and with Team Leader in all other cases	By parties to PM, and anyone else by agreement; observation and scrutiny of ongoing work	PM annual meeting which draws together and summarises all available evidence of performance

Whole school	Processes involving SMT, staff, governors, LEA/diocese representative/ finance partners, leading to SIP	Ditto with possible input from inspection, commissioned work . . .	Ditto

While each phase is being attended to within a given plane, some notice can be taken of what is known about the targeting that is occurring in other planes. It is the case, however, that the targeting that occurs in each plane has also to be self-sufficient and take its own course. The targets that emerge as useful for individual pupils have to stand as valid in themselves. And the same is true for the targets that the teams use, that individual members of staff and management use in their performance management, and that are adopted by whole-school planning. Integrity across the different forms of target has to rest first of all on the integrity of the targeting within each plane. Beyond that, overall integrity derives from the dynamic interplay between the planes.

If contradictions are found between targets that emerge from those different fields of activity, they have to be confronted and resolved. Correspondence between different forms of target has to be sought and worked for. What you cannot expect is that targets defined in one plane will determine the targets used in another. In other words, whole-school targets cannot produce individual pupils' targets. Neither can individual pupils' targets be computed into whole-school targets. Each has to take account of the other, without losing its own integrity. Each has creatively to reinforce the other. (See Appendix 8 for an assessment and targets policy, which illustrates the kind of coherence I have tried to define.)

1 Schools' initial experience of using performance targets for pupils' attainment

Statutory targets were set in English schools for the first time in the year 1998–9. Summer 2000 saw the results for those Years 6 and 11 cohorts. The targets which governing bodies had by law to publish at that time were:

at Key Stage 2:   percentage of pupils to attain National Curriculum level
(for 11-year-olds)   4 or above in English and mathematics;

at Key Stage 4:   percentage of pupils to gain five or more A* to C grades
(for 16-year-olds)   at GCSE or their equivalent;
                      percentage of pupils to gain one or more A* to G grades
at GCSE or their equivalent;
average pupil total point score at GCSE or their
equivalent.

From 2000 an additional set of targets had to be published:

at Key Stage 3:   percentage of pupils to attain National Curriculum level
(for 14-year-olds)   5 or above in English, mathematics and science.

Further, from 2001 the target for the percentage of pupils gaining one or more A* to G grades at GCSE or their equivalent is replaced by this target:

at Key Stage 4:   percentage of pupils to gain five or more A* to G grades
(for 16-year-olds)   at GCSE or their equivalent.

Finally, from 2001 special schools have to use P-scales or their equivalent in setting whole-school targets. These are performance scales, designed to promote learning in pupils whose capabilities are not initially represented by National Curriculum level 1.

In the autumn term 2000 I wanted to find out what colleagues in school felt about using cohort targets. I surveyed a dozen headteachers and deputy headteachers in my locality. What follows is based on their responses to these questions:

- What has your school learned about the use of performance targets?
- What have been the benefits of using performance targets for pupils' attainment?
- How could the system be improved?

Here, first, is a summary of the views expressed.

1   Colleagues in the schools I contacted felt they had learned from the first two years of having to set targets for cohorts' attainment. They were aware of the core problem of needing to relate macro-targets to micro-targets: connecting whole-school targets with individual teachers' and pupils' targets.

2   Colleagues in school saw in the use of targets a clear benefit to the monitoring of pupils' progress: planning could be better informed and focused on what pupils needed to do to bring about further progress. Schools were developing the use of more sophisticated planning and assessment techniques. Some, for example, had introduced P-scales and usually found them helpful. These elaborate skills and understandings required by pupils in performing simple tasks, as a foundation for National Curriculum programmes of study.

3   Progress and value-added measures should be emphasised rather than raw attainment measures.

4   The myth of 'continual improvement' needed to be exploded: year groups differ.

5   The status and value of teacher assessment needed to be raised in the public mind: test results dominate, are simplistic, and need to be treated with greater caution.

6   There was a danger of the 'Hawthorn effect' distorting perceptions and the allocation of resources. Teachers were succeeding in raising standards, but there were problems associated with forcing the progress of selected pupils. Pupils might produce what is required on demand, but not consolidate their learning and then apparently regress. And it seemed unfair to concentrate resources and attention on certain pupils, perhaps at the expense of others.

7   Some pupils' results appear inflated as a result of the 'extra' teaching or coaching they have received: what problems are we storing up by misleading pupils, parents, and fellow professionals about pupils' capabilities? A pupil's being able to perform a certain task on a given day is no guarantee that s/he can apply the skill, knowledge or understanding on other occasions and in other contexts.

8   There could be greater flexibility in the timing of when cohort targets are formally set: schools are developing their own cycles of planning and reviewing, and account needs to be taken of this.

Those arguments and points are elaborated below.

Colleagues were well aware that there are many different kinds of target in a wide range of contexts. Though the media and politicians highlight one kind of indicator of schools' performance, headteachers and staffs are now familiar with lots of different forms of data and target. There are targets that focus on individual pupils' efforts. There are targets that focus on the attainments of groups of pupils or pupil cohorts. As part of performance management, and as part of the work of management, teaching and care teams, there are objectives which give direction to headteachers' and teachers' work for the year.

Colleagues spoke most positively about targets set for individual pupils and groups of pupils where setting targets was thought to have a direct impact on classroom planning and activity. Least valued were the statutory, published cohort targets for attainment at the end of key stages. These targets seemed too distant, too abstract, too generalised, too bureaucratic and too susceptible to the vagaries of cohort fluctuations in ability, unlikely to have great meaning. Their role in overall accountability was recognised, but more enlightened and enlightening uses of data and targets were being developed and needed to be recognised.

Having to set and publish targets had encouraged senior management teams and teachers to look carefully at their pupils' performance, to track their progress, and to project likely future outcomes with a degree of challenge. There was universal agreement that rigorous assessment and having challenging expectations positively help school performance and development.

As a result perhaps of focusing on assessment and tracking, colleagues are now quick to distinguish between targets relating to attainment and targets relating to progress. Raw attainment is now thought to be a relatively weak indicator of performance. Colleagues have become much more interested in measuring pupils' progress. Some, for example, would favour a development in the use of targets which specify percentages of pupils whose attainment is predicted to rise by one level, two levels, three levels, and so on. And using levels subdivided into three, targets could be expressed in terms of points increases, aggregated and averaged for the cohort.

Colleagues in school did not have a problem with valid and consistent assessment, monitoring of pupils' progress, and reasoned yet ambitious projection of attainment to aim for. They were committed to such activity, and were keen to develop further techniques and strategies accordingly. They were concerned, however, that some people could still unhinge performance targets from that painstaking focus on the individual pupil and her/his teaching. Targets should not lose touch with assessments of individual pupils' progress and prospects. Colleagues thought it folly to think that results could show year-on-year improvement. Attention to individuals' histories, needs and capabilities consistently showed variation between year groups. Cohorts vary, and perpetual improvement is a chimera.

The colleagues I spoke to seemed to agree that the further you move away from the individual pupils, the less meaningful data become. Quartiles, PANDA reports and autumn packages provide a background, but only a background against which teachers can view the more specific data they collect about their own pupils. Teacher assessments are valued within schools, but tests dominate the public mind. Overall, the politicisation of assessment and performance data is felt to be a problem, distorting and distracting attention from schools' main purposes and actual achievements.

Colleagues appreciated their LEA's performance data services and the support provided by school consultants. Some would have liked more help, for example, in the shape of detailed suggestions about graphic presentation and analyses of data. Others were concerned that there should be greater consistency in the approach that consultants take in their work with schools.

Some primary colleagues reported that the experience of using targets had taught them how the effect of booster classes might be underestimated. Where teachers had additional resources to support specific pupils' performance in National Curriculum tests, the results were often striking. A note of caution had to be sounded though. Carefully targeted pupils could raise their performance in tests because they were taught to succeed in the tests. Several colleagues were not sure that these pupils were being better educated, and were worried that the breadth and balance of their curriculum was being disturbed by the emphasis on English and mathematics to the detriment of other subjects, particularly the arts. Some colleagues have agreed to award a level only after the pupil has shown the particular set of capabilities on a number of occasions in different contexts. This is done, for example, in the primary school whose case study I present in Appendix 5. Teachers there at December School have to observe the necessary skills, understandings and knowledge on at least three occasions before they record that the pupil has achieved that level.

A further concern was that the results could, therefore, be inflated. Some pupils, for example, were transferring to secondary school with levels 4 and 5 that the teachers did not fully trust. The test results were not necessarily thought to be the fairest reflection of the pupils' overall capability. A clear illustration of this was science, where results were outstripping those in English and mathematics. Both primary and secondary colleagues were unhappy about how this could mislead pupils, and parents and carers, and cause confusion about what could reasonably be aimed for, say, in GCSE examinations.

Some colleagues would like the timetable for target-setting to be reviewed, and would prefer to be able to choose themselves how to run their cycle. For example, one secondary school colleague reported that his staff set targets in the February of Year 10, so that the first five or six months of the GCSE courses can be used as an indicator of potential and prospect. The setting of targets was all the more reliable for that.

So, to sum up . . .

There were shifts in school managers' and teachers' perceptions and practices during the first years of using formal and public targets. Colleagues became more conscious of their accountability and of the range of available measures to plot progress and attainment. Teachers became more aware of how they might over-estimate or underestimate their pupils' potential. Finding time to talk individually with pupils about their progress and needs was, if anything, an increasing problem, but there was more pressure than ever to try to build in quality one-to-one time.

2 What pupils think of targets

Targets have a considerable impact on life in schools. The issue is much more complex than some discussions allow, and pupils' perceptions are not always taken into account. This chapter looks at what pupils think of the part that targets might play in their learning. I shall report findings from my research carried out between March and July 2000 in nine schools, covering four LEAs. Finally I shall refer to the results of a similar exercise, carried out by a deputy headteacher in a middle school, during the autumn of 1998.

Rationale and method

I visited nine schools across the age range 5 to 18 to find out what pupils think about targets. The schools were primary, middle, secondary and special, in four different LEAs, two urban unitaries and two counties. In all I visited forty-three classes, taught by forty-one teachers. My research was framed by the question: What sense do pupils have of the part that targets play in their learning?

I wrote to headteachers with whom I had had some professional contact or to whom I had been recommended, so that they would at least recognise my name and perhaps not be surprised by my request to visit their schools in order to find out about how targets were being used in the classroom.

The headteachers put me in touch with teachers who volunteered to take part. I told them I would give them feedback on my visit and send them a report afterwards, letting them know what their pupils had said and adding any suggestions I might have had about the use of targets. My visits usually lasted a full day, and I would visit between two and six classes, depending on what suited the school. Where it seemed appropriate, I met pupils in groups of four outside the classroom. Sometimes I joined in the lesson and put my questions to pairs of pupils and individuals, occasionally to the whole class.

I had asked the teachers not to tell the pupils that I was interested in targets. Generally pupils were told that I wanted to find out about how they learn in school. Talking with the pupils, I did not mention targets as such until we had discussed how they learned in school. I asked them to tell me about:

- what they were currently doing;
- what helps them learn;
- how they knew what was coming next in a lesson or unit of work;
- how they knew how well they were doing;
- what they were good at;
- what they were trying to get better at.

Only then did I ask the pupils whether they had targets and, if so, what these were and how they worked.

After each of my visits, I sent to the school a summary of my findings, such as appears below, together with a verbatim account of what the pupils had said. Those accounts appear in Appendix 1.

Main findings

The pupils I spoke to appeared to perceive targets as having a beneficial effect on their motivation and learning inasmuch as targets contributed to their sense of one or more of the following:

- what they were doing;
- why they were doing it;
- how they were setting about what they had to do;
- what they were good at;
- what they were trying to get better at.

Many of the pupils I spoke to indicated that their targets provided a focus for their efforts and a sense of progress and satisfaction. Pupils spoke well of targets when they also spoke well of other features of classroom and school life which helped them to feel safe and clear about what was expected of them and what to do when things did not go well.

Pupils who were generally well disposed towards school or the particular teacher did not find the use of targets problematical or objectionable. At worst they described them as making little difference to their performance in, and feelings about, school. Most pupils said targets were quite useful, and a minority was confident that targets positively added to their motivation, focus and success. Older primary school and middle school pupils were more positive and articulate about how they used targets. These pupils were also clearer than very young or secondary school pupils about how targets benefited their learning.

Many pupils said that targets did more than concentrate their own sense of motivation and satisfaction. They pointed to targets as helping them to work well with the teacher, with one another and with adults other than teachers in the classroom.

No pupil in any of the nine schools I visited indicated that using targets had transformed their school or classroom experience. The pupils seemed rather to take targets for granted as belonging to a range of in-school arrangements and behaviours whose function was to enable pupils to be aware of their purposes and achievements in learning. Pupils did not seem to think having targets guaranteed they were being well taught or that they would succeed in their tasks. Targets were no panacea.

Targets seemed to be just one of the factors contributing to the pupils' understanding and acceptance of tasks, rationales and procedures. Other contributing factors included the pupils' confidence in arrangements for breaktimes and playground security, trust in the teachers and non-teaching staff, and appreciation of specific teaching strategies, especially those that helped them grasp what was expected of them and how to get support when they needed it. Using targets was generally thought of as being in harmony with and representative of the teacher's and school's values and practices.

When pupils felt targets were being used merely because they were required to be used, they found little positive meaning in them.

Some pupils said that targets played a part in helping them understand what they were doing, why they were doing it and how they were setting about what they had to do. Lesson objectives also contributed to the pupils' being clear about those things. But lesson objectives did not ordinarily give pupils insight into what they were good at. Nor did lesson objectives reflect pupils' personal aspirations. Several pupils linked having targets with their confidence about their strengths and areas for improvement.

Talking with pupils about targets sometimes sparked comments about other aspects of school life and about life outside school. Talking about targets led to comments about what pupils felt most important about their experiences and activities, about the ways they were treated in school, and about their own aspirations and determinations. It also prompted pupils at times to reflect how they thought teachers saw them.

This kind of conversation humanises schooling. And it is not only visitors to school who can talk with pupils in this way. Teachers and school managers can make time to have these conversations whereby the pupils are drawn, implicitly or explicitly, into deciding how their school should work. Governors too can discuss such matters with pupils. Talking together in this way, everyone can try to make things work to everyone's best advantage.

Many of the issues raised here are explored further in the next two chapters – on teaching and formative assessment. Implications for whole-school development are pursued in Chapters 5, 6 and 7.

Findings school by school

January School – first, 4–8, town and surrounding area

Overall, in the seven classes spanning Reception, and Key Stages 1 and 2, I found that the younger the children were, the less aware they were of having targets as such for their learning. The younger they were, the more likely they were on occasion to follow their own agenda, rather than the teacher's, and the more likely they were to emphasise personal and social aspects of school life rather than the straightforwardly academic. Pupils throughout were able to mention areas in their learning where they were successful and areas where they were trying to make improvements. They showed they trusted their teachers and appreciated what the school was doing for them. The older pupils were more conscious of their targets, for example, in the context of the National Numeracy Strategy whose impact seemed positively clear, the children showing delightful enthusiasm about their learning of techniques and gains in understanding. Targets did not appear to be at all intrusive or even special. The pupils treated them as part of what happened in school, and so they were used to paying particular attention sometimes to targeted aspects of their work.

February School – primary, 4–11, town

The school had worked on the issue of target-setting, partly in response to LEA policy mediated by the link inspector. The teachers had devised targets in all subjects for their pupils, and recorded these in folders. There was no policy to communicate targets to the pupils. Pupils talked readily about what they were doing, about the successes they had had, and about things they were trying to improve. I could not tell whether these perceptions bore any relation to what the teachers had originally recorded as targets at the beginning of the year. The headteacher planned to revise policy with the staff, and it seemed likely that ways of discussing targets with the pupils would be developed.

March School – primary, 4–11, town

Pupils here mentioned targets when answering questions about what they found helpful. They also mentioned targets when they spoke about their future learning, and about what they were trying to improve on. This was more consistent and more widespread here than in other schools I visited. All of the pupils were able to say what their targets were. I was particularly impressed that, when I asked pupils to think about past targets, they were able to do so without difficulty, recalling successfully hit targets. And some pupils referred to past targets without being prompted.

It appeared that in this school a coherent strategy had been successfully implemented for the use of individual pupils' targets in literacy and numeracy. Key factors appeared to be the concentration on literacy and numeracy and the use of target cards enabling the pupils to have clear, frequent and easy access to their targets. These practices seemed to address what could otherwise create problems: the potential plethora of targets across the curriculum, and the adoption of loose or overlong time-scales. Interestingly, several of these pupils mentioned looking back over their work to see how they were doing or to check progress. This looking back might be an essential ingredient in the successful use of targets.

It seemed to me that it was the school's approach to personal and social education which supported the successful implementation of the policy for targets. The pupils I spoke to reflected that they felt secure and confident in their environment. They knew the school's procedures for conduct in lessons, for moving around the building, for behaviour in the playground, and for circle time. They knew what procedures to use when they had difficulties of any kind. The pupils understood there were differences between them regarding their academic abilities. They spoke in a relaxed and friendly way about the extra help which they or their classmates were getting.

April School – primary, 4–11, town

The pupils gave a strong impression of enjoying their schooling. They showed they trusted their teachers and were grateful for the help they, a student teacher and the classroom assistants provided. They understood the systems set up both to help them and to let them know about their progress. They knew what they were learning and what their targets were for further improvement in their work.

As happened in other schools I visited, pupils gave the impression of being confident and enthusiastic about their maths or numeracy and rather concerned to improve on their literacy, which they felt posed them more problems and challenges.

In at least one class the custom was to have two targets: a personal, self-chosen one, and a group or class one agreed by the teacher and the pupils. Interestingly, the teachers have found it makes a positive difference when the pupils themselves have an investment in the selection of targets. In Y1/2, in Y2, in Y3, and in Y5/6 at least one pupil referred to targets before I got to the final question explicitly mentioning the word targets. The teachers told me afterwards that the pupils reported their targets accurately, with the exception of some children who experience special educational needs. In the younger children the two seem to be associated: lack of academic success and weak recall of what was expected of them.

By Y3 the targets mentioned by pupils were very specific, showing their understanding of detailed techniques and skills. In the reception class the children used actual targets painted on the playground wall to practise their aim when kicking the football, and referred to this when answering my questions about having targets.

May School – middle, 9–14, town and surrounding area

A number of teachers here have introduced pupils' targets of their own volition and without any specifically agreed system. From the pupils' responses it seemed clear that the targets worked best when they were wrapped up in the teaching and learning activities, rather than being something artificially bolted on. These teachers drew the pupils' targets from key learning objectives for lessons and units of work. The targets were recorded in a special place in exercise books or on cards, so that the pupils knew where to find them and could regularly refer to them while they were working. Interestingly, some of these pupils were able to use their experience of targets to refer back as well as forward: they could plot the progress they had been making, as well as say what they were now aiming to achieve. The pupils seemed to understand that their targets gave a priority to some aspects of their learning, but that the targets by no means accounted for all that they were doing in school.

I drew together some provisional conclusions from my conversations with the pupils, and discussed these with the senior management team who made additional suggestions of their own. As a working statement towards a whole-school policy, we agreed that individual pupils' targets are likely to help learning if their targets:

- are close to the action, in time and space, i.e. arise from and feed back into classroom activity and are not a separate or artificial system;
- relate to key valued learning objectives or assessment criteria;
- from the teacher's point of view, evidently motivate the pupils;
- from the pupil's point of view, are felt to be helpful;
- are recorded in a specific place, so that the pupils know where to find them and have easy access to them;
- are referred to whenever that is helpful, and do not lie dormant;
- enable the pupils and teacher to refer back as well as forward, i.e. do not just tell the pupils what to aim for, but help them plot the progress they have been making;
- are manageable, in number and scope, for the pupil to accomplish and for the teacher to keep track of;
- are part of a developing practice, periodically reviewed and refined;
- leave room for other spontaneous, worthwhile pursuits and unanticipated outcomes, and do not take over everything you do.

June School – secondary, 12–16, suburban estates

The school has tried several approaches to using targets over recent years. Members of staff did not claim that policy and practice were consistent across the school, and a training need was acknowledged. A head of year planned to introduce a system whereby targets would be reviewed after six weeks. Currently feedback to pupils about progress in relation to their targets was delayed for a term and sometimes was not given at all. The relationship between targets set in subject lessons and targets set in tutorial time had not been explored. The picture here was of disparate practices, any number of which might be successful, but the best effects were not being identified and so could not be built on.

July School – secondary, 11–18, town outskirts and villages

Almost without exception, the pupils I spoke to either knew their targets or knew how to find them quickly, at least in the subjects and with the teachers I visited. Most valued having targets: a minority were enthusiastic and articulate about them; the majority were mildly positive; a second minority did not value, but also did not resent, having targets. The impression I gained was that pupils saw targets as part of proper teaching – showing that the teacher had a clear plan and focus for their learning, that the teacher cared about their learning and was good at helping them learn.

The pupils were clearer about the targets they had in their subject exercise books or folders, less clear about the targets that sometimes were recorded in their planners. The school system of the planner did not seem to be operating fully or efficiently, whereas the individual teachers' systems, however experimental, were having an impact on many pupils' attitudes and work in the classroom.

Could the majority of targets be made more specific and related to key assessment criteria? The teachers and pupils appeared to emphasise superficial or secretarial skills. I wondered whether the teachers would agree that was the case, and, if so, whether they were content with that. I suggested the teachers might like to repeat or extend the exercise I carried out, gathering a sample of targets and asking, 'Are those the kind of targets we want to see? If not, how could we shift the focus to more fruitful areas of learning and achievement?'

It seemed to me that there might be further benefits to the pupils if the teachers distinguished between targets, which were really lesson objectives for the class, and targets, which related to individual pupils. (See the table on this distinction in the Introduction, p. 7.) Every lesson might be expected to have lesson objectives; some lessons or units of work might profit from the pupils' having targets.

These considerations raise interesting questions. For example:

*   When might it be desirable and appropriate for the pupils to have individual targets?
*   What benefit is there in the pupils sometimes setting their own targets?
*   Can pupils benefit from working in pairs or partnerships to set and to assess progress against their targets?
*   Does it help the pupils, and the teachers, to use targets if, in addition to noting the target at the outset, there are specific routines for recording achievement by the end of the work or unit?

Careful task-setting for the class might come before individual target-setting. For example, in one of the lessons I joined, the class was working on a newscast. I was able to draw out of the pupils what it was they were aiming to achieve. I asked them, *What defines quality in this performance?* The pupils came up with the following: A good newscast is one which:

*   includes more than one point of view;
*   gives you correct information;
*   is interesting to watch, e.g. has emotive language;
*   keeps you updated.

Their answers could have been used as success criteria and as guidance for the task.

Is there an equivalent in science? For example, would it be desirable for the pupils to define what good quality work is, e.g. in carrying out an investigation? Would such a specification provide class objectives or personal targets?

August School – secondary, 13–18, rural and small towns

The leading religious studies teacher here had evolved a very successful approach to targets over a number of years. It was her practice for important assignments to award the pupil a realistic grade, that is the GCSE grade they would attain if their work were submitted now for accreditation. Alongside that she would give a target grade, and the pupils had the necessary assessment criteria information to see what they needed to do if they were to reach the target.

Observing this teacher, it seemed to me that the attitudes the pupils showed depended on her projecting certain fundamental messages about herself, her pupils, the subject, the course and the issues they were tackling. I summarised as follows the messages she seemed to convey to the pupils through her preparation, the physical layout of the room, and her behaviour and teaching:

- *This is what we've got to do.*
- *It is worthwhile, interesting, and relevant to our lives.*
- *I've prepared this course with you in mind: for example, you can build on your personal interests and experiences, or you can use tailor-made booklets to guide your thinking, record your efforts, and provide revision materials when you need them.*
- *Join in; do your best.*
- *I'll show you how to get better at every aspect of the course.*
- *Everyone counts; nobody gets left behind.*
- *I've done this before, and you can benefit from what previous learners have taught me on this course.*
- *Based on previous experience, I'd set you a target of grade X; but you can take that as a challenge and prove me wrong.*
- *So you've done this well so far; how can you improve on that?*

Towards the end of the lesson, I was able to talk to the class as a whole. I told them that I had noticed a number of things which were part of the teacher's way of working and which I thought were very helpful to the pupils' successful learning and achievement in the subject. I told them I wanted them to tell me what *they* found helpful.

What is it about how your teacher works that helps you? The Year 10 religious studies pupils answered:

- *Making sure we all understand.*
- *Quick tests – fifteen minutes most weeks, revising key points in past units.*
- *Lots of discussion; not just writing.*

- *Respect for our views.*
- *Referring back to past work all the time to keep it clear and fresh.*
- *Splitting the course into sections.*
- *She gives up her own time to help us, e.g. lunchtimes.*
- *Going through things again and again to make sure we've got it.*
- *She gives us a grade for what we've done now and then sets a target grade with information about how to achieve that.*
- *She is patient.*
- *She asks us what we think and then provides an answer for us to compare or learn from.*

Then I asked the pupils to use a three-point scale to rate one of the items they mentioned, namely targets: 'How do you rate the use of targets as a key to successful learning?' Their responses were:

Targets are absolutely essential	2 votes
Targets are quite important	15 votes
We could do without targets	0 votes

Using targets here seemed to belong to an extensive repertoire of strategies and techniques, all focused on achieving success for all of the pupils in terms of the examination syllabus they were following. Other qualities in the teacher's teaching that I noted were:

- Referring explicitly to the mark scheme or assessment criteria.
- Putting pupils on the spot through questioning – really challenging them to think.
- Giving time for the pupils to think.
- Making it OK for the pupils to be wrong, make mistakes, or not understand.
- Praising specific good work and contributions by feeding back precisely what was well done.
- Breaking tasks, objectives and study skills down into concrete, finite, manageable steps, e.g. revision is made up of these specific component actions . . .
- Providing topic materials for the pupils to use and keep.
- Not wasting any time; keeping a total focus on what is required.

Though individual teachers may be able to work in that way on their own, strength evidently comes from team effort. This teacher had over a number of years developed with her colleagues in the department a systematic and collective approach. They work as a team by asking these questions about each year's available performance data:

- *Are there trends emerging in our results?*
- *Do our pupils attain what their Key Stage 3/NFER-Nelson scores predict?*
- *How well are our high, mid and low attainers doing?*

- *How are our well-motivated and not so motivated pupils doing?*
- *What qualities do pupils have who achieve high grades?*
- *What conclusions do we draw about the effectiveness of our teaching styles?*
- *How well ought we to be doing? Are our expectations high enough?*
- *What needs to be done?*
- *What specific actions will we carry out now? Which pupils are affected?*

In the Year 10 science lesson I joined, the equivalent of the discussion work in the religious studies lesson was practical work. The pupils were busy deciding how to carry out the experiment, setting up equipment, sorting out roles and responsibilities, pouring, weighing, measuring, recording, checking . . . . Everything revolved around that purposeful activity. Each pupil's target was to do it as well as s/he could and to get the credit through writing it up according to explicit instructions or criteria.

In both lessons there was an overall social dynamic, underpinned by the teachers' personal communication with each of the pupils. Each class had common objectives and benefited from a common assessment process with explicit criteria. Targets were effectively a personalisation of the shared system.

September School – special, 3–18, town and surrounding area

I visited Year 5 to Year 9 classes towards the end of the summer term. In one class, the pupils came out of their lesson to talk to me in the library. Generally I joined them in the lesson and either spoke to them individually, briefly interrupting their work, or I put my questions to them as a class and those who offered gave their answers. I was not able to put my questions to the pupils in one Year 6 class, because their needs were such that my enquiries seemed irrelevant or inaccessible to them.

All of the pupils I managed to engage in conversation expressed positive attitudes towards their school, class, teachers and classroom support assistants. They took my questions seriously, responded courteously, and were entirely willing to reflect on achievements and aspects of their school experience. Quite often when I was talking to a pupil one to one, we would discuss issues at some length: they would give me considerable detail either spontaneously or when I asked supplementary questions. The pupils showed enthusiasm for and involvement in their experiences in school. In some classes, targets were part of the language of the lessons or part of the furniture, as it were. A chart, for example at the back of one room showed the pupils' names and the number of targets they had hit this year: when a certain number was reached, they had a reward.

I could see that the teachers used targets as one of a number of strategies designed to support learning. The challenge was to close the gap between what the teacher intended for the pupil and what the pupil found interesting. These teachers were skilful at closing that gap, and the pupils appreciated what was done for them.

Targets seemed useful when they helped the pupils be clear and content about what they had to do. Targets were also sometimes used by the teachers to help them monitor and plan for progress. It was clear to me that it would be possible to take an overview and see whether or not the whole-school targets, that I knew existed, were being met. (Examples of whole-school targets for this school are included in Chapter 6.)

My conclusions overall were very similar indeed to those of Keith Pugh, deputy headteacher in a middle school, who interviewed thirty-seven of the Year 8 girls and boys in his school. He reported to his staff in January 1999 as follows.

> One of the things I set myself to do in the role of assessment co-ordinator was to find out just what the pupils think of our attempts to get them target-setting. The good news is that almost all the comments were favourable, and individuals really see them as a great aid to making progress. As one person said, *They definitely help me because as soon as I see my target written down I want to achieve it.*
>
> The bad news is that the pupils themselves still need reminding of the system before they make their favourable comments, which I guess means they don't feel ownership of the system. This is partly because, as we have discussed as a staff, the system seems an add-on and is not yet part of everyday school life. Many of the pupils remarked that the system would be a lot better if the targets were in front of them daily. We have discussed this as a staff, and I am going to produce a prototype new Homework Diary for the end of this term, incorporating this idea.
>
> I would not claim the survey was extensive or exhaustive. I deliberately concentrated on Year 8 pupils as they have had most experience of the system and were likely to offer the most expansive commentary. I tried to get a balance of boys and girls across the ability range, and did the survey on a one-to-one, conversational basis. I talked to a little over one-third of the year group. I deliberately arranged the questioning to see if pupils themselves would see our target-setting as an aid to learning. Only two of the thirty-seven interviewed did so.

'What helps you learn?'

A high priority was given to a relaxed and friendly atmosphere being set by the teacher. Humour, being in good mood and teachers bothering to develop a relationship with the class all figured highly. One individual actually mentioned the improvement from a previous school because teachers here are not always shouting instructions at you. It was also very clear that the majority of pupils do feel able to ask for help when they need it, which is important to them.

Being involved came up several times and two people mentioned extension groups in maths and French. Many people also mentioned seating as being crucial – *by friends* but not *by disruptions* (e.g. *I can only work when I can concentrate*). Talking about work, looking at others' work, watching things, and listening were all seen as really helpful to learning. Only two of the pupils I asked volunteered information that target-setting helped them to learn. For the others I went on to the second question . . .

'*Do you think the target-setting we do with you in school helps you to learn? Why/Why not? Could it be improved?*'

I could tell from the pupils' reaction that this was something they did appreciate, and the response was almost unanimous: targets are really useful. They were seen as *setting a standard, giving me something to aim at.* One pupil wondered if targets had as much meaning as you got older, and another if it might be better to concentrate on only two at a time. Another pupil echoed this, saying *there are too many targets.*

The pupils liked targets as being individual, and many made reference to the fact that it is down to you and that targets are only successful if you stick at it. One remarked that they are not good when you are made to do them and went on to explain that you have got to have the motivation yourself.

All of this leads me to the conclusion that we have something that is making a difference. What we now need is to refine and improve procedures and practice.

We need to remember that under our system the actual target is in some sense secondary to many other things we are hoping to achieve. Targets are of importance in that they signify progress. They are reached if progress is made. Nor should we underestimate the powerful influence that verbalising a target, or desire, may have for many pupils, even if they fail to reach it. Having said this, staff must prevent the demotivation that can occur from failing to meet targets, by helping pupils set realistic and achievable targets and helping pupils to refine them as necessary.

This report illustrates how much can be gained from a senior manager's researching pupils' perceptions, and how monitoring and evaluation can lead to lively and incisive discussion and development work.

3   Ethos, teaching and targets

In this chapter I put forward seven features of good teaching, and describe the part that targets have to play in them. The seven features characterise subject teaching, but can also inform occasions when teacher and pupil take time out to discuss progress, difficulties and targets, as in one-to-one or tutorial time.

Other authorities, including Ofsted, the Teacher Training Agency and the consultancy firm Hay/McBer, have drawn up specifications for teaching competences, and these are discussed in Chapter 9. The seven features I propose inevitably reflect some aspects of those accounts. My version is distinctive, at least inasmuch as it refers to the role that using targets plays in school teaching and learning.

At the outset, I shall sketch the kinds of target that might be used to enhance individual pupils' learning. This will provide a reference point for what follows. I derived the target types from a study I was asked to carry out in several schools. I collected targets from a scrutiny of exercise-book marking in all subjects, coursework, records of achievement, student planners and annual reports to parents and carers.

A taxonomy of targets for individual pupils

- *symbolic* targets do not explain what the pupil has to do, but mention signs of improvement, such as get better marks, be promoted to a higher set, and gain more merits;
- *basic* targets refer to (pre-)conditions for learning; without these, little progress can be made; examples would be attendance, paying attention, listening to instructions, and putting in effort;
- *generic* targets are cross-curricular skills, such as reading comprehension, presentation of written work, note-taking, and working as a member of a team;
- *meta-cognitive* targets are reflective and refer to the manner, rather than to the content, of the pupils' learning; examples include thinking about what you want to achieve, thinking about the effort you are putting in, thinking about what affects your learning and achievement, and thinking about how you will know you have achieved what you set out to achieve; these are processes of expressing thoughts and feelings about learning, which help the

pupils plan, steer, monitor and evaluate their learning;

- *partial* targets are components of subject performance and specific units of work, such as paragraphing, use of tone, long division, and using variables; these overlap somewhat with the following;
- *definitive* targets are skills, qualities or understandings that lie at the heart of the subject, and help make up what it means to be a writer, a scientist, a historian, a musician, and so on; for example, audience awareness, hypothesising, empathy, and rhythm.

These kinds of target for individual pupils can be compared with the kinds of target that are used for whole-school improvement. (See Chapter 5, p. 71–2.)

Defining effectiveness in teaching is notoriously difficult. There are so many variables to contend with. What works on one day does not work on another. What works with one class or individual does not work with another. What one teacher finds successful fails to work for another. It is impossible to predict whether this or that particular piece of teaching will result in effective learning. If teaching is the cause, and learning the effect, it is virtually impossible to establish stable, predictable relationships between the two.

The problem is that teaching is an interaction. Its essence is what takes place between a teacher and one or more pupils.

Most of the seven features of effective teaching that I propose relate directly to the interaction between teacher and pupils. Taken as a whole, these features help define an ethos for educational settings. The pupils whose responses I discussed in Chapter 2 indicated that ethos was crucial. The particular strategy of using targets did not appear sufficient to make a lesson, course, subject, or teacher effective in enabling pupils to learn. What the pupils in my research reflected was that a range of routines, relationships, behaviours, attitudes and values determine the satisfactoriness of their experiences: in a word, ethos. Let us remember also that education is as much a matter of being as it is a matter of doing.

I suggest that the following seven features of teaching are likely to be conducive to learning that pupils will appreciate and benefit from. The seven features reflect my experience and research in education, and constitute a set of intentions for a teacher. The work a teacher has to do in order to develop in these ways touches being, feeling and outlook, as well as technique, skill and strategy.

Each of these features has a bearing on the use of individual pupils' targets. Classroom practice in relation to individual pupils' targets is a vital foundation for the approach that a whole school takes to cohorts' targets and improvement planning.

Features of successful teaching

1   The teacher expects everyone to learn about how to help one another and work together.
2   The teacher welcomes opportunities for the learners to make connections between their interests and curriculum objectives they are set.

3   The teacher sets the learners tasks in which they have the ability to succeed with some support.
4   Teacher and learner develop a language they can both use about learning.
5   The learners realise there are choices to be made about how to communicate ideas.
6   The teacher shows the learners how to turn negatives into positives.
7   The learners assess themselves and one another, set their own targets, track their own progress, and record their achievements for themselves.

A number of themes connect the seven features. The teacher's having high expectations, for example. Running through most of the seven features there is a positive challenge to the learner: *You can do this; you will grow to achieve it; there is belief in you and support for you; hard though it might sometimes seem, we feel you can succeed.* Similarly, co-operation is a keynote: learners working together and with their teachers. And the implication is that teachers do likewise. In effective education teachers support and learn from one another.

Effective teaching emphasises the positive, the constructive, the co-operative, the purposeful, and the engagement of the learner in explicitly meaningful activity. Because learning is as much about *being* as it is about *doing*, education has to be concerned with feeling as well as with thinking, with perceptions as much as with actions and behaviour. Significantly, the effective has to involve the affective. The articulation is a springboard to the meta-cognitive.

The teacher expects everyone to learn about how to help one another and work together

The first point to emphasise is the word *everyone*. It is vital that a teacher believe every pupil can achieve.

In his extensive review of the research literature, Albert Bandura lends significant weight to teachers' believing that success is not only desirable, but feasible also. This positive conviction motivates teachers' efforts to overcome difficulties inherent in school and community circumstances, as well as difficulties experienced by pupils and by teachers. Believing that every pupil can succeed keeps the teachers' focus firmly on constructive efforts to promote learning, and averts distraction or demoralisation.

Bandura identifies 'self-efficacy' as the crucial factor in educational success. This concept concerns the belief that you can influence events enough to increase your chances of success. Self-efficacy is defined as the ability to exert influence in spheres of your life where you have some control, so that you are better able to bring about the futures you want and forestall the futures you do not want. According to Bandura, the teachers' purpose is to increase pupils' self-efficacy. In an effective school, teachers who believe they can control important aspects of their work, and who strive to be effective through that control, are themselves seen as having self-efficacy:

Teachers with a high sense of instructional efficacy operate on the belief that difficult students are teachable through extra effort and appropriate techniques and that they can enlist family supports and overcome negating community influences through effective teaching . . .

Teachers who have a high sense of instructional efficacy devote more time to academic activities, provide students who encounter difficulties with the guidance they need to succeed, and praise their academic accomplishments. In contrast, teachers of low perceived efficacy spend more time on non-academic pastimes, readily give up on students if they do not get quick results, and criticise them for their failures . . .

Those who have a low sense of instructional efficacy favour a custodial orientation that takes a pessimistic view of students' motivation, emphasises control of classroom behaviour through strict regulations, and relies on extrinsic inducements and negative sanctions to get students to study . . .

(Bandura, 1997, pp. 240–1)

The second point to note is that teaching and learning in school are *social* and *interpersonal* activities. A pupil's learning in school is bound up with her/his relationship with the teacher and with other pupils.

That social and interpersonal factors determine maturation and the development of cognitive abilities was explored by Lev Vygotsky (1978) and, in specific experiments involving identical twins, by A.R. Luria and F.I. Yudovich (1959). Their work demonstrated how closely connected the two factors are: variation in the organisation of mental processes, i.e. maturation in the child, on the one hand, and changes in the child's conditions of life, including who s/he may interact with, on the other hand.

Luria and Yudovich state that: 'The essential moment which calls forth development of speech is undoubtedly the creation of an objective necessity for speech communication.' They continue with a point that will relate directly to our consideration below of the fourth, fifth and seventh features of effective teaching: 'Special speech training, which made speech an object of conscious perception, accelerated conscious application of speech and helped the child to acquire an extended grammatical structure of speech' (1959, p. 75).

That is to say, helping a child to think about what s/he does and how s/he does it enables her/him to develop capability. We will take the development of metacognition as a significant theme in our discussion of targets.

The quality of interaction, then, between the pupil and those s/he encounters in the classroom, has a significant bearing on how well the pupil manages life at school and on what s/he achieves there. Central to a teacher's concern, therefore, is helping the pupils to develop constructive relationships with one another, with the teacher, and with classroom assistants. The practical routines that a teacher sets out for a class, for example, entering and leaving the room, handling equipment, indicating a desire to speak, taking turns, resolving conflicts, defining problems and finding solutions, and so on, reflect respect for people and things, and help foster co-operation.

What stays with us more than *what* we have been taught is *how* we have been taught. Not so much what we have learned, more the manner of our learning. The ethos of the classroom and the school is profoundly significant, as my reporting of pupils' perceptions indicated in Chapter 2. It matters first and foremost that teachers expect to succeed, for, if they do not, it is all the harder for their pupils to believe they can succeed. It is next most important that teachers develop an ethos of mutual respect with their pupils, working together and helping one another. Pupils develop respect and co-operation when their teachers act as role models, when their teachers praise them for their demonstration of these qualities, and when they engage in the meta-cognitive activities of considering and working on the qualities.

This feature of successful teaching is a pre-condition for, as well as goal and outcome of, education. If it is not sufficiently established to allow learning to develop, or if it is under threat, or in decline, then it becomes a priority, a target for individual pupils, or the whole group, and the teacher. This, then, would be a target which does not relate directly to academic performance. It is an example of an area of learning which is not measured by subject assessments, and illustrates how vital non-academic targets can be. In terms of the taxonomy, given at the opening of this chapter, the kinds of target considered under this feature of effective teaching might be seen as basic (e.g. believing that being in school is potentially worthwhile and that success is possible, or getting on with other people) or generic (e.g. helping others with their work and being helped by others). But perhaps this kind of target is most usefully seen as meta-cognitive, for example, thinking about what helps you learn, thinking about how others learn, and thinking about how everyone might get along better.

Chapter 7 explores in greater detail targets for aspects of school life beyond curriculum subjects, and from time to time we will refer to these as *process* targets, designed to improve *how* the pupils learn, rather than *what* they learn.

The teacher seeks opportunities for the learners to make connections between their interests and curriculum objectives they are set

What a pupil finds interesting varies. It can be something playful and imaginative, or something factual and precise. It can be the familiar as well as the unfamiliar, the abstract as well as the concrete. It can be the way something is presented as much as the subject-matter itself. As they get older, pupils are likely to be interested in things they believe are relevant to the lives they will lead on leaving compulsory or formal education. And almost without exception, human beings are drawn to whatever reflects on themselves as individuals and members of cherished groups. Individuals and groups vary and change, so their interests do too. Pupils' sense of personal and social identity is a powerful force that education may strive to work with, especially during adolescence.

According to John Holt, children's 'curiosity grows by what it feeds on. Our task is to keep it well supplied with food' (Holt, 1971, p. 153). The pupils are entitled by the law, by the reasoned choice of the school, and by the teacher's conscience, to a curriculum that will promote their learning. It is the teacher's task to manage an accommodation between that curriculum and the pupils' interests. This appears as a cornerstone in Bandura's summary of international research:

> Activities can be creatively structured in ways that capture and heighten interest. This is achieved by building positive features into tasks that make them enjoyable, creating personal challenges through goal setting, adding variety to counteract boredom, encouraging personal responsibility for accomplishments, and providing feedback for progress.
>
> (Bandura, 1997, p. 222)

It may not always be straightforwardly possible. But engaging the pupils in discussion and choice is a step towards their developing commitment and achieving success. Some researchers, for example, Askew *et al.* (1997), have explored this under the term 'connectionist' teaching which involves the pupils' making of connections with:

- 'real' problems;
- their existing knowledge, skill and understanding;
- a learning community in dialogue.

Such teaching seeks to enable pupils to see how they might connect their school learning with situations outside the classroom. Links can be made in the pupils' imagination, by simulating actual contexts, or through real problem-solving.

Teaching can also, for example, incorporate 'mind mapping' exercises whereby the pupils express what they currently know about a given area of knowledge or skill. The pupils' expertise can then be extended, misconceptions can be benefited from, and gains in understanding and skill made clear in a changing picture of what they know and can do. Essential to such teaching and learning is dialogue between teacher and pupils. The essence is growth in mutual understanding and joint inquisitive activity in relation to objects of interest.

Crucial here is the notion that the pupils make their own sense of their experience, and that their learning depends on this. It is a characteristic of 'constructivist' psychology and pedagogy: that pupils do not merely receive their teaching; they rework the information they receive, and they represent it to themselves in the act of learning. (See, for example, von Glasersfeld, 1978.)

Using my taxonomy, targets in this respect might be termed basic (e.g. taking an interest) or, better perhaps, meta-cognitive (e.g. thinking about how aspects of a task or topic or unit of work might connect with what you find interesting). A class's target might be to give an interesting spin to a task or topic or unit of work, to tease out its relevance to their community or futures. It can also be a teacher's target, or 'objective' in a performance-management context, to work on engendering pupils' interest, as much as it can be a pupil's target. And teaching and care teams similarly can take on such targets.

One-to-one conversation is an obvious medium and ideal opportunity for a teacher's learning more about a pupil's interests and seeking ways of enabling her/him to incorporate these in targets and projects. Again, these are targets which do not map directly on to the content of the taught curriculum. In certain circumstances, it might be most productive for a teacher or staff to make a concerted effort to learn about the pupils' concerns and enthusiasms, so that these might find connections with the topics and opportunities their curriculum provides.

The teacher sets the learners tasks in which they have the ability to succeed with some support

We might say that there are three kinds of task that a pupil can be set in school. First, there are tasks which the pupil can carry out successfully, quickly, easily and independently. Second, there are tasks which the pupil has a good chance of performing with some assistance. Third, there are tasks which are too difficult and the pupil has no chance of completing. Too easy; well matched to the pupil's developmental needs; and too hard.

Tasks well matched to the pupil's developmental needs were thought by the Russian psychologist Lev Vygotsky to define a zone of proximal development, or zpd. Such an area of activity is closest to the limits of a person's capability, such that s/he might succeed in it if support is available to help overcome difficulties:

> The zone of proximal development defines those functions that have not yet matured but are in the process of maturation, functions that will mature tomorrow but are currently in an embryonic state. These functions could be termed the 'buds' or 'flowers' of development rather than the 'fruits' of development. The actual developmental level characterises mental development retrospectively, while the zone of proximal development characterises mental development prospectively . . . [D]evelopmental processes do not coincide with the learning processes. Rather, the developmental processes lag behind the learning processes; this sequence then results in zones of proximal development. Our analysis alters the traditional view that at the moment a child assimilates the meaning of a word, or masters an operation such as addition or written language, her development processes are basically completed. In fact, they have only just begun at that moment.
>
> (Vygotsky, 1978, pp. 86, 90)

Casual observation would seem to tell us that pupils are likely to be bored by tasks that are too easy, and demoralised by tasks that are too hard. It could be that tasks that are both feasible and stretching are intrinsically stimulating and engaging. This is perhaps the teacher's central challenge: to create tasks that are within the pupils' grasp, will stretch them, possibly require support, but in the end lead to fulfilment. Such tasks are ideal recipes for individual pupils' targets.

The concept of tasks which stretch a pupil may help illuminate what teachers mean when they talk about 'potential'. Some of us might argue that it is impossible ever to know what a person's potential truly is, but teachers are almost bound to have a working, if not scientifically valid, knowledge of potential. A teacher sets a task and observes the pupil's response, and this process is repeated over and over again. The response indicates something of the pupil's capability, and the gap between what s/he can apparently do now and what s/he might be able to achieve, given certain support and favourable conditions, can be taken as defining the pupil's potential.

Vygotsky's zone of proximal development is what many teachers, intuitively perhaps, understand to be what a pupil is capable of. In practice it is something fluid, dynamic and evolving, by means of which teachers adjust their choices of initiative, response and intervention. If teachers had no such concept, they would more often set tasks and make interventions that were mismatched to pupils' needs and capabilities. That teachers manage a match at all as often as they do means they must have a feel at least for what we can loosely term the pupils' potential. And without that concept the notion of target would collapse. A teacher's contribution to defining a pupil's target is informed precisely by her/his empirical and pragmatic sense of what can, with fairness and with an acceptable degree of challenge, be expected of the pupil's capability.

This also has a psychological function in the interaction between teacher and pupil. The teacher's sense of potential implies an act of faith on the teacher's part that the pupil can rise to the challenge. The effect can be to support the pupil's motivation. And I have argued that such messages conveyed both inadvertently and deliberately by the teacher to the pupil are crucial to the teaching's, hence the learning's, success.

In a one-to-one review and target-setting conversation, the teacher can explore with the pupil just what support s/he might need in order to achieve a target. The support might consist of certain conditions, such as time, space, quiet, resources, or help from a parent, carer, sibling, friend . . . Focusing on the means by which the pupil will hope and aim to achieve the target is probably the most significant part of the discussion. It entails visualising the achievement and steps along the way. It prompts the making of a provisional plan and foreseeing possible contingencies. It implies, and may make explicit, the effort the pupil will need to make. It ties effort, in terms of energy and attention, to the specifics of the undertaking, and can entail the elaboration of success criteria. If pupils are engaged in these ways, they are far less likely to say merely *I must try harder*. This kind of thinking about learning is characteristic of meta-cognitive targets.

This feature helps us define what makes a good target. This is something we shall explore further in Chapter 4, but for now we can see that a good target is one which challenges and stretches the learner. In Vygotsky's terms, it is developmental. Developing such teaching can, of course, be a teacher's objective in a performance management context, for example. It can be a teaching or care team's target. And it can be a whole-school improvement target that teaching strive for such a quality.

Teacher and learner develop a language they can both use about learning

As much as a teacher might teach, the object of the exercise is the pupils' learning. However good the teaching is, the learning has still to be achieved by the pupils.

The teaching's focus is the pupil's learning. The most important thing a teacher does is pay attention to what the pupil does and how the pupil seems to be. What the pupil does and how s/he seems to be are central to her/his learning.

Responsibility and initiative lie firstly with the teacher and her/his intentions or objectives for the pupil's learning. These relate to criteria for performances which the teacher intends the pupil will be enabled to learn and carry out. The criteria effectively translate into algorithms or specifications for action or ways of being. Ultimately an educator intends that the pupil take responsibility for and ownership of the prescription or guidance, incorporate the rules into her/his repertoire of performances, and apply them freely in the pursuit of her/his own projects and aspirations.

These, then, are the three most important things that a pupil does in a lesson and during a unit of study:

1   think about algorithms or recipes for action or a way of being, offered, for example by the teacher;
2   apply algorithms or recipes in practice;
3   account for what s/he intends to do, is doing, and has done, so that s/he can prepare to apply the algorithms or recipes again, perhaps in different contexts.

That is to say, it is most important for a pupil to:

1   think about how to do or be whatever is targeted by the lesson or unit of study;
2   practise doing or being whatever is targeted by the lesson or unit of study;
3   explain her/his action or being and know how to do or be that again.

In reality, the three rarely form a straightforward sequence. Learning involves going to and fro between considering a model to imitate or a specification to follow; practising, rehearsing, repeating; and planning, reviewing, analysing.

From the teacher's point of view, the objective is to bring those three into alignment. If this can also become the pupil's objective, teaching and learning will be mutually reinforcing. Then the pupil's agenda will coincide with the teacher's. The guarantee that the traffic is not all one way – that it is not merely a question of the pupil's accommodating to the teacher – is partly in the teacher's trying to build on the pupil's interests and aspirations. (See the second feature above.) We shall explore below, in the seventh feature of successful teaching, how response partners and the teacher's use of language can contribute to the kind of learning we are concerned with here.

All of this is far from easy to accomplish. Militating against teachers' capacity to talk with and listen to pupils, for example, is their sense of having so much to cover. The pressure is on to deliver results, and it can easily feel as though the safest policy is one-way communication. The more teachers feel obliged to dictate to the pupils, the less they feel allowed to be open to spontaneity and to what the pupils have to offer:

> teaching in today's primary schools at Key Stage 2 is very much a matter of teachers talking and children listening. Of this talk by far the largest amount consists of teachers making statements. When questions are asked of children, these questions require them either to recall facts or to solve a problem for which their teachers expect a correct answer. Open or speculative or challenging questions, where children are required to offer more than one answer are still comparatively rare ... As one teacher commented ... 'There just isn't time now to listen to the children.' While it is true that there is now more task-related activity in the primary classroom than 20 years ago, the introduction of the National Curriculum appears to have resulted in an increase in the traditional secondary style of teaching, creating a one-way communication system where, for most of the time, teachers talk and pupils sit and listen.
>
> (Galton *et al.*, 1999, pp. 33–4)

Jenny Mosley's 'circle time' (2001), for example, has clearly benefited many classrooms and enhanced teachers' and pupils' capacity to discuss and develop how they work, both as individuals and together. Getting better at talking about learning can, therefore, be an appropriate target for a pupil or group of pupils. It might also be an objective, for example, in a performance management context, for a teacher or for a team of teachers. (A team's targets are explored in Chapter 8, and individual staff members' performance management objectives are discussed in Chapter 9.) It involves a wide range of skills, knowledge and understanding.

Any opportunity the teacher and pupil have to discuss and plan progress can help develop mutual understanding and a shared language. This is another example of a target area which underpins, yet extends beyond, academic performance. It points to the processes that are essential to effective learning. The more pupils can learn about learning and about how to learn, the more satisfaction and success they are likely to have.

In terms of the taxonomy, given at the start of this chapter, such targets best fit the category of meta-cognitive target. And as the language that teacher and pupil develop becomes more sophisticated, for example referring to subject-specialist terminology and using academic discourse, the targets might become partial or definitive.

The learners realise there are choices to be made about how to communicate ideas

The first point to emphasise here is that much of what pupils engage in at school is the communication of ideas. In physical education it is the intention to incorporate notions of line, force and balance, or to capture territory, out-manoeu-vre opponents, and/or propel target objects into given spaces. Elsewhere in the curriculum the task is to communicate one's own and/or other people's imagina-tion, facts, concepts, propositions, and so on.

It is vital for pupils to realise that there is rarely a single valid way of commu-nicating ideas. How you present information can be as important as what you present. There may be conventions of expression, style and format that pupils can usefully be made aware of, but ultimately it has to be for them to decide how best to formulate their meanings and messages, if they are to be committed to the communication.

If pupils understand the purpose of their task in communicating, they can be helped to see the range of possibilities before them. They can be helped to choose. We shall explore this in greater detail in the next chapter through the work of Paul Black and Dylan Wiliam. For now it is enough to note that pupils who understand what a successful performance looks like can be enabled to make choices about how best to produce such a performance. When they do that, they engage in definitions of quality. In choosing how to achieve quality of perfor-mance, their learning is powerfully enhanced.

All of this is confirmed in Margaret Donaldson's wonderful book *Children's Minds*:

> . . . the normal child comes to school with well-established skills as a thinker. But his thinking is *directed outwards* on to the real, meaningful, shifting, dis-tracting world. What is going to be required for success in our educational system is that he should learn to turn language and thought in upon them-selves. He must become able to direct his own thought processes in a thoughtful manner. He must become able not just to talk but to choose what he will say, not just to interpret but to weigh possible interpretations. His con-ceptual system must expand in the direction of increasing ability to represent itself. He must become capable of manipulating symbols . . . awareness typi-cally develops when something gives us pause and when consequently, instead of just acting, we stop to consider the possibilities of acting which are before us. The claim is that we heighten our awareness of what is actual by considering what is possible. We are conscious of what we do to the extent that we are conscious also of what we do *not* do. The notion of *choice* is thus central.
>
> (Donaldson, 1978)

And for the child who does not come to school with well-established thinking skills it is a longer journey through the same territory. Black and Wiliam (1998) report that when pupils make the kinds of choices addressed by Donaldson their learning is significantly more successful. There is convincing evidence that pupils learn more effectively and are far more engaged in their tasks when they:

- understand what to do;
- understand what their tasks require;
- understand some of the different ways of carrying out the tasks and satisfying the requirements.

Individual pupils' targets which play a part in helping them realise there are choices to be made about how to communicate ideas are meta-cognitive targets. Examples of partial targets would be to become more proficient in talking, listening, reading or writing, or to extend one's range of communication styles, or to become more adept at choosing appropriate styles according to the demands of the given context, purpose or audience. And communication skills are often strong candidates for cross-curricular targets discussed in one-to-one tutorial sessions. For older pupils and students, this target area has clear relevance to key skills, a source of very many partial targets.

The teacher shows the learners how to turn negatives into positives

It is difficult to succeed if you believe you have little ability or little prospect of success. Whether you believe the problem lies within you or outside you, until you can see your way round the problem, your learning will stay stuck. Effective teachers try to find different ways of trying to dissolve learners' negative thinking.

A good teacher breaks down tasks into small steps: getting started can bring some success and unlock some optimism. A good teacher says *Look at what you have done well*, rather than overemphasising what has not gone well. S/he offers alternatives, and encourages the learner to do the same: *If we can't do it like that, let's try it another way instead.* S/he prompts the learner to identify what helps progress and to decide how best to get rid of obstacles. These are meta-cognitive strategies.

What a good teacher offers is a vision of things that are open to change. Learning is a process that can be tackled in many different ways. The task that the learner faces is not to be seen as something given, fixed, finite, unalterable. This characteristic of good teaching relies on understanding the subject content and on being flexible about how to approach it. A good teacher sees 'the big picture' and is prepared to take any route that will serve the overall intention. S/he must be able to 'scaffold' the learner's understanding and activity, that is to say, structure tasks so that they support learning. Lateral thinking, pragmatism and attention to the individual learner's responses and initiatives are essential. (See Mel Ainscow's 1999 research referred to in Chapter 7.)

This constructive approach informs the way a good teacher talks to the class and the way s/he talks to individual pupils. When it is appropriate to counsel a pupil, strategies contained in 'solution-focused practice' may help. This is an approach designed originally in the USA by Steve de Shazer and developed in the UK by Bill O'Connell, among others. It is illuminating to consider this kind of process, in part because use can be made of it when talking ordinarily to pupils.

Formal counselling situations are by no means always necessary, and may in any case rarely be possible.

This is an outline of a complete process, based on O'Connell (1998), from which selections of specific strategies may be made to suit the given situation.

1   Invite the pupil to say what is going wrong. Encourage the telling of anecdotes to show when, why and how the problem occurs. Then ask for one word or sentence to clarify the main issue. If the pupil cannot do that, offer your own summary and see whether the pupil feels you have understood well enough. After that, avoid getting stuck in the problem; transfer your attention to exceptional occasions when the problem does not arise, or is diminished.

2   Feed back and affirm all the areas in which the pupil has already done well whilst dealing with the problem. For example saying what the matter is, seeking help, keeping going despite the problem, maintaining friendships, still looking cheerful, talking to friends, coming in to school, keeping out of trouble, keeping up with work . . . Tell the pupil all the ways in which you can see that s/he is already succeeding in managing such a difficult problem: e.g. *I think it was really good that you said you had spoken to . . . about this* or *It is great that you have tried doing . . . to help make things better.*

3   Use a scaling question:
    *   *On a scale of 1 to 10, with 0 being no problem at all and 10 being a big prob-lem, how big would you say your problem is?*
    *   *On a scale of 1 to 10, how confident would you say you feel that you can tackle this problem?*
    If it would help the pupil, use something visual rather than numbers, e.g. bricks or counters. You can then go on to ask questions that begin to envis-age tackling the problem and finding solutions. For example *Can you imagine making the problem just a little bit smaller?* And you might remove one brick. *Can you suggest how you can be a little bit more confident about coping?* Explore how the pupil feels s/he might improve the situation.

4   If you think you will see the pupil again about the problem, any suggestion the pupil makes about how s/he might improve the scale rating becomes a task to work on. Whether or not the pupil can think of a way to ease the problem, give the pupil a task to work on. The task focuses on what you want the pupil to notice during the rest of the lesson or session, or over the coming days, when the problem is either not there, or is a little better. When you talk to the pupil next time, ask the pupil to tell you about any of these better times or situations, and what the pupil noticed about them.

5   Follow-up conversations can look at rescaling. Concentrate on what the pupil notices about times when the problem is smaller or absent. Ask the pupil to describe as much as s/he can, e.g. the time of day, who s/he is with, what is going on, etc. Scaling is useful for the teacher and for the pupil, showing whether the problem is increasing or decreasing. Solution-focused talk helps shift attention from the problem to whatever helps the pupil gain perspective on ways of making improvements.

6   After three or four such conversations, use the success that has been experienced as a basis for bringing this kind of contact to a close. Suggest that the pupil can continue the process on her/his own, or through any other supportive relationship. Focus on what has gone well, the reasons for things going well, and steps that might be tried to improve things further.

These practical strategies can be seen to relate strongly to Bandura's concept of self-efficacy, discussed above. In terms of my taxonomy, such a target area strongly suggests the meta-cognitive. A pupil's target, for example, may be to try a new positive approach, or to notice when things work best. This approach may be helpful in the context of one-to-one teacher–pupil reviewing and target-setting meetings.

The solution-focused strategy may also be used in the context of subject teaching, or more generally inform teachers' attitudes and responses towards pupils. Perhaps its chief value is that it provides a means of target-setting and reviewing, but it also supports efforts to achieve targets set in any context.

The learners assess themselves and one another, set their own targets, track their own progress, and record their achievements for themselves

The all-important premise here is that pupils understand what it is they are trying to achieve. They can use this as a guide when they set off on a task, at any time during the task, and finally when the task is over and they look back on what has been achieved. This feature highlights something that is arguably a natural, albeit sometimes latent, part of all deliberate learning. When we mean to learn something, we put ourselves in a position to judge the effect of the learning on our skill, knowledge and understanding, on our behaviour or being. And intentions can be expressed as targets.

When pupils set off to learn something, they must have a sense of their target. As they learn, they must be able to recognise how well they are doing. When the learning activity is over, they must notice how far they have come. Pupils may commit each of those self-conscious acts – making projections, taking stock, and reviewing – whenever they have sufficient reason or cause to do so. Deliberate learning necessarily involves all three meta-cognitive acts possible.

The problem is that it is also possible for pupils in school to have tasks which lack these characteristics of deliberateness, intent and self-consciousness. When pupils take up an activity merely because they have been told to, or because they believe it is what is expected of them and doing it will avoid trouble, targets have little genuine or constructive meaning for the pupils. The prospect of deriving a measure of self-satisfaction from a task is a pre-condition for using a target and benefiting from it. So where a teacher faces pupils who appear disaffected or unwilling to engage in activities, s/he has to think of ways of involving the pupils and enabling them to develop commitment. Merely setting targets will not do. We are driven back to some of the features of effective teaching which we discussed earlier: the first, second, fourth and sixth features in particular.

A further problem is what pupils think a target might be, and how it might function. Certain attitudes are enabling, and others are disabling. Carol Dweck, whose work is quoted by Harry Torrance and John Pryor (1998, pp. 88–9), distinguishes between **learning goals** and **performance goals**. Dweck sees the quality and effectiveness of pupils' motivation as being bound up with their choice of goals, the choice being between: 'learning goals in which individuals strive to increase their competence, to understand or master something new' and 'performance goals in which individuals strive either to document, or gain favourable judgements of, their competence or to avoid negative judgements of their competence'.

Dweck found that productive attitudes were associated with learning goals, and that inhibiting attitudes were associated with performance goals. Her research shows that pupils with **learning goals**:

- choose challenging tasks, regardless of whether they think they have high or low ability relative to other pupils;
- make the most of their chances of success;
- tend to think that they can develop their intelligence, and do not so readily subscribe to the view that people are born with a finite and unalterable amount of intelligence;
- go more directly to generating possible strategies for mastering a task;
- attribute difficulties to unstable factors, such as that they have not tried hard enough, even if they perceive themselves as having low ability;
- persist;
- remain relatively unaffected by failure in the sense that their self-esteem does not drop sharply.

In contrast, pupils who choose **performance goals** were found to:

- avoid challenge when they have doubts about their ability compared with others;
- tend to handicap themselves so that they will have an excuse for failure;
- tend to see ability as a stable entity;
- concentrate much of their task analysis on gauging the difficulty of the task and calculating their chances of gaining favourable judgements of their ability;
- attribute difficulty to their own low ability;
- give up in the face of difficulty;
- become upset when faced with difficulty or failure.

According to my taxonomy, both learning and performance goals might match any of the target types, and so be symbolic, basic, generic, meta-cognitive, partial or definitive. But moving from performance goals to learning goals, which is surely what Dweck would look for in a pupil's learning, would be well supported by meta-cognitive activity.

In Dweck's terms, learning goals reflect and contribute positively to pupils' sense of self-worth and self-direction. Having learning goals seems to equate with being intrinsically motivated, having performance goals with being extrinsically motivated. Having learning goals seems associated with perceiving the so-called locus of control as being to a considerable extent within oneself. Having performance goals seems associated with perceiving the locus of control for one's actions and destiny as lying outside oneself, within other people, circumstances or fate.

Having learning goals would seem to make a pupil more responsive to formative and diagnostic, criterion- and self-referenced assessment. Whereas having performance goals would seem to make a pupil responsive to normative and summative, norm-referenced assessment. (These terms and issues are fully described in Chapter 4.) The crucial distinction between the different kinds of goal centres, I believe, is the pupil's capacity to analyse and act on intentions, processes and outcomes. In the one approach to teaching, when pupils have learning goals, they have to know what they are trying to achieve and what counts as success, and they have to reflect on their progress as an indication of growing capability and control. In the other approach to teaching, when pupils have performance goals, they have to seek and compete for merit as defined by external authority.

One of the most effective ways of practising and developing the learning-goals approach is to provide each pupil with one or more response partners, that is, someone to work with them when setting targets, tracking progress and recognising achievement. We return therefore to the spirit of the first feature of effective teaching: the apparent paradox of individual development being dependent on social and interpersonal factors.

Shirley Clarke has described this very clearly from a pupil's point of view:

A response partner is someone who:

- talks to me about my work against the success criteria
- makes me feel good about my work because s/he points out what I have done well
- tells me how I could improve my work
- helps me with my work
- tells the truth about my work
- helps me to make my work better.

To do this I need the teacher to tell me the learning objectives and my success criteria.

(Clarke, 1998, pp. 78–9)

She also shows how the teacher can model the setting of targets by using the very language that a response partner might use in discussing the learning. For the purposes of shared professional planning and accountability, the teacher's objectives may well be expressed in language which is not readily understood by most pupils. The test of these intentions, though, is that they be grasped and discussed by the pupils. Clarke illustrates how a teacher might translate intentions from a professional context into terminology that will communicate effectively to pupils. So she expresses objectives first as they might appear in a teacher's short-, medium- or long-term planning, and then as the teacher might talk to the pupils. A learning intention here is the equivalent to a **target**, and the equivalent to a learning goal in Dweck's terms – for a group or class. The teacher's colloquial explanation gives the **task**. Here are just a few examples:

> Learning intentions and *words used by the teacher in class talking to the pupils:*
> To learn about repeated addition.
> *I want you to tell me an easier way of working out how many eyes you would need for five teddies. This will help you to add up the same number quickly.*
>
> To be aware of how Anne Fine develops character.
> *What I want to know is how you know what the chicken is like. The reason you are doing this is because it will help you to find interesting ways to describe characters in your stories.*
>
> To be able to use their knowledge of insulation in setting up a fair test.
> *What I'm looking for is how you have recorded the investigation, making every stage you went through very clear. This is to improve your investigation skills and to show me that you understand about insulation.*
>
> (Clarke, 1998, p. 51)

In terms of my taxonomy, these are all partial targets.

In some of those examples, the teacher's explanation included a rationale for the task. Clarke has promoted and researched the effectiveness of a number of strategies in this respect, and these have become popular in a growing number of schools, encouraged by her training sessions and books. For example, some teachers have taken to using acronym cues for the focus and rationale of pupils' activities:

- WILF = What I am looking for is . . .
- TIB = This is because . . .
- WALT = We are learning to . . .
- OLI = Our learning intention is . . .

In the excellent *Gillingham Partnership – Formative Assessment Project 2000–01* (Clarke, 2001b), Clarke and her colleagues report that WILF tends in some classrooms to become *What will you need to do to achieve this?* This shift signals decreased teacher domination, greater pupil ownership, and increased negotiation between the pupils and the teacher as the last stage before the activity starts, clarifying the means to the end, in the way that Black and Wiliam emphasise. Clarke's report also underlines the value of separating out the four components: topic, task, learning intention and success criteria.

The focus is firmly on the learning, and the pupils' activity has the function and status of being the means by which the learning should come about. Clarke discusses how explaining or exploring the rationale for activity in the classroom can be done in very flexible and spontaneous ways. She refers to this teaching strategy of reflecting on the reasons for the learning as an 'aside'. And Clarke demarcates both learning intentions and asides from success criteria. Success criteria complete this kind of sentence stem: *We will know we have achieved this when* . . . Here is an example from a Year 6 lesson:

> Learning intention: *To be able to name and design a mini project based on the theme 'World issues'.*
> How will I know?: *What I'm looking for is to see how you plan and organise your project and tell us about it through a two-minute speech.*
> Aside: *We're doing this so that you can become more responsible and involved in the project we'll be doing next term.*
>
> (Clarke, 2001a, p. 47)

An aside is akin to the area of meta-cognitive targeting, according to my taxonomy. It opens up understanding of the processes by which learning might be achieved through classroom activity. Clarke's learning intentions and success criteria might be generic, partial or definitive targets, in terms of my taxonomy. Her work in helping teachers to 'script' their instructions for, and interactions with, pupils lays a foundation for the pupils' learning how to set their own targets.

A further device that some teachers use, as a way of trying to meet the needs of different groups of pupils in a class, is to set out objectives according to an implicit hierarchy. The learning intentions are presented as being for all pupils, many pupils, and some pupils. For example, *You must* . . . applies to all of the pupils in the class. *You should* . . . applies to many pupils; and *You could* . . . applies to some or a few pupils. This highlights the value of giving a rationale for tasks.

The kinds of communication we have been considering belong to an ethos which has a number of instructive functions. It enables pupils to know what they are aiming for. It invites them to consider how they might proceed, and how they might register progress and achievement. It prepares them for a role as partners in a process of education, whether they are working in the classroom on solo or co-operative activities, whether they are working with a response partner, or whether they are engaged with their teacher in one-to-one review and target-setting discussion. As was shown by the evaluators of the 1980s records of achievement schemes (PRAISE, 1988), pupils, given the opportunity to reflect on and discuss what they achieve in subjects, in cross- and extra-curricular activities, and outside school, can validly and vividly represent their capabilities to other interested parties, with benefits to their own motivation and self-esteem.

Pupils may be helped to articulate their achievements, but a range of creative strategies is needed if dull routines are to be avoided. One of the problems that records of achievement initiatives, for example, have encountered is that pupils can fail to find relevance or interest in being asked flat questions about what they enjoyed and what went well. Clarke reports (2001b) how pupils, given experience of handling learning intentions, success criteria and asides, are enabled to be clear and confident about their purposes and achievements. And there are other approaches open to teachers.

Norman Schamroth, teacher and independent consultant, has developed a 'two-chair' technique which enables pupils to interview themselves and to act as their own one-to-one teachers. It is a variation on the drama technique of 'hot-seating'. The pupil speaks alternately as teacher and as learner. In an unpublished paper, this is Schamroth's account of an interesting instance: a Year 3 boy, 'Peter', interviewing himself about his writing.

Peter as teacher: So how do you feel your writing is going?
Peter as pupil: Oh it's going well.
Peter as teacher: In what way is it going well?
Peter as pupil: Well, my writing is neater and I'm using better words.

Schamroth thought the pupil was letting himself off lightly and so intervened, whispering into the pupil's ear in his role as teacher *Don't make it easy for him – ask him why he's hardly written anything.* Peter the teacher responded positively and challenged Peter the pupil to face up to his progress being not quite as good as he had claimed.

Peter as teacher: So how come you let Miss X (adult helper) write so much for you, and you haven't hardly written anything yourself?
Peter as pupil: Well, I just find it difficult to think of what to write.
Peter as teacher: You've got lots of ideas.
Peter as pupil: Well, y'know I just can't be bothered to do it.

Schamroth notes the following.

> This was going on while all the other pupils were busy 'conferencing' with themselves. I am aware that this is an odd thing to have done, but I knew Peter would go for the easy option (*It's going well*) and needed an opportunity to be more honest. Finally, he was. As a reluctant writer, who has a lot of good ideas and a reasonable degree of ability to write coherently and correctly, Peter is underachieving, probably knows he is underachieving, and is at a point where he may or may not do something about it. When he came to complete the questionnaire I gave the class after the writing project, he was reluctant, but gave way to persuasion. His answers to the questions were all bound up with neatness and size of handwriting. For the future, he set himself the target: *I must join up my handwriting and speed up my writing.*

Applying the language of my taxonomy, given at the start of this chapter, the pupils in Schamroth's class were using meta-cognitive skills to focus on whatever might benefit their learning. And Peter, in the end, chose a cross-curricular generic target or an English-based partial target, albeit in an evasive or shallow way.

Though Schamroth acknowledges this teaching strategy to be unusual, it does reflect his work as a teacher and as an adviser in curriculum and staff development. He commonly uses devices which are designed to enable pupils and teacher to act within a playful or imaginative analytic framework, and so to get outside concepts and skills in order to probe and manipulate them. The conventions of 'thought-tracking', 'multiple viewpoints' and 'forum theatre' are further examples of such disciplined approaches to using dramatic fictions as a way of examining ideas and feelings. (See Dorset County Council, 1988.)

What this illustrates is that pupils do not communicate a straightforward truth or reality. What they say or write depends on context, purpose and audience, on self-image and the image they wish to promote. When pupils speak and write about their targets, they may be aware of how they might appear to others. Some will probably want to please the teacher, others will perhaps want to keep a low profile and take a line of least resistance. Some have to cope with feeling that the topic, the learning, the subject in general, or school itself, is just not a priority for them. Here again, we return to the question of ethos. How teacher and pupil cope with short-lived or lasting disaffection depends on the quality of their relationship and interaction.

Asking pupils to use targets does not guarantee all will go well. Even asking pupils to interrogate themselves by playing the roles of teacher and learner does not have to bring out the 'truth' about their efforts, abilities, prospects and aspirations. What the teacher can do is work conscientiously with what the pupil is prepared to reveal, seeking to find appropriate levels of comfort and challenge that will enable her/him to grow in insight, endeavour and satisfaction. The more and the better experience pupils have of assessing themselves and one another, of setting their own targets, of tracking their own progress, and of recording their achievement, the more likely they are to feel motivated, and the more likely to succeed in fulfilling their own and their teachers' expectations. This is because teachers, who enable pupils to do those things, help create an ethos which affirms the pupils and seeks their fulfilment in autonomous endeavour.

Evaluating the pilot records of achievement projects of the 1980s in England and Wales, whose principles and aims were very much the same as those of using individual pupils' targets, the PRAISE team concluded:

> It would appear that the recognition of achievement in records and reports is a necessary, but not a sufficient condition for the realisation of the core principle of improving learning. For this latter aim to be fulfilled, process as well as product criteria must be met. If schools and teachers are not changed by records of achievement, pupil attitudes are also unlikely to be intrinsically changed.
>
> (PRAISE, 1988, p. 165)

We might say the same about any project to introduce or improve the use of individual pupils' targets. Pupils' use of targets may be a missing link in the development of meaningful records of achievement. When records of achievement were promoted in the 1980s, there was little emphasis on personalising the learning or on planning ahead. These issues were addressed in the subsequent DfEE-sponsored work which produced the Progress File (DfEE and Folio InfoBase, 1998), though this appears cumbersome and has failed to achieve anything like universal implementation in schools. It could be that if recording achievement and planning progress connected with the teachers' use of targets in formative assessment, and with the individual pupils' use of targets in the classroom, then the Record of Achievement and Progress File might rise above the apparently bureaucratic stalemate they have so far found.

This chapter has highlighted the significance of the personal and the interpersonal in pupils' experience, in their sense of purpose, progress and achievement. In order to bring about significant changes in school provision, pedagogy, and pupils' attitudes, we need to explore further the role of assessment as a way of promoting individual pupils' learning. (Definitions of teaching are also discussed in the context of performance management and lesson observation. See Chapter 9, pp. 94–9.)

4   Formative assessment and targets

Let **task** define what a pupil has to do. Let **target** define the learning that a task is designed to bring about, reinforce, or develop, in an individual pupil. Remember the distinction, made at the end of the Introduction, between **lesson objectives** and **targets for individual pupils' learning**. A lesson objective defines the learning that a task is designed to engender in a class of pupils. It is less personal than a pupil's target, and does not have a target's necessary connotations of personal meaning and ownership.

Learning in school is bound, then, to involve tasks. Since the introduction of a National Curriculum and Ofsted inspections, teachers have become more explicit about lesson objectives. Now school improvement and performance management are heightening interest in the setting of targets.

This chapter develops the final feature of effective teaching discussed in the last chapter – that effective teaching enables learners to assess themselves and their co-learners; to set their own targets; to track their own progress; and to record their own achievements for themselves. Here, we will explore, more extensively and in greater depth, the psychological and interpersonal processes that are involved in school teaching and learning. We will see that, for their learning to be effective, pupils need to grasp the learning objectives or targets that are inherent in their tasks.

In this chapter we will consider:

- implications of research findings for the use of pupils' targets in the classroom;
- different purposes and kinds of assessment, and the role that targets might play within them;
- how different assessment cultures can impinge on the quality of teaching and learning;
- what a teacher might have in mind when deciding on a target for a pupil;
- what might affect a pupil when s/he thinks about choosing a target;
- the difference between targets for individual pupils and targets for groups or classes;
- how targets can be broken down, and the component parts of the learning explained in detail;
- the values and functions of using targets in teaching and learning;

- a draft policy for the use of targets as a way of promoting pupils' learning;
- a checklist of points to keep in mind when communicating with pupils about targets.

Implications of research findings for the use of pupils' targets in the classroom

Paul Black and Dylan Wiliam (1998), at King's College, the University of London, drew on extensive international research to provide an illuminating account of formative assessment, that is, assessment designed to enable the pupil to take the next step in their learning. Black and Wiliam use the concept of a 'gap' articulated by Ramaprasad (1983) and Sadler (1989), and state that there is at the core of formative assessment this sequence of actions: first, the learner sees a gap between what s/he wants to achieve and her/his present ability to achieve that; second, the learner tries to close that gap in an effort to reach a desired goal.

It may be the pupil who sees what s/he will have to do if s/he is going to achieve what s/he wants. But it does not have to be the pupil. It may be another person, the teacher, for example, who perceives the gap between goal and capability, and the teacher might then enable the pupil to act on it. When it is the teacher's assessment that guides the pupil in the second action of developing skill, knowledge or understanding, it is important to realise that the pupil has to respond actively to the call to action.

Black and Wiliam believe there are complex links between:

- the way in which a pupil comes to see there is a gap between what s/he can currently achieve and what s/he might want to achieve;
- the way in which that perception motivates the pupil to choose from different courses of action that might be open to her/him;
- the action taken subsequently to close the gap between current capability and goal.

The action of trying to close a gap between current capability and goal might be framed as a target. Individual pupils' targets can provide a natural extension to formative assessment. Both formative assessment and targets rely on criteria being made explicit and on the pupil's deliberate involvement. A pupil's having a target converts formative assessment into a project to be acted on. The target is a message for the pupil about what to do to cover the distance between what s/he can do now and what s/he wants to achieve. Targets embody volition; if they do not, they mean little to the individual concerned.

Formative assessment cannot support effective learning if pupils carry out their tasks because they are asked to, or because they are in school and feel they have to conform merely. Formative assessment presumes pupils can exercise deliberate and reflective agency. Carrying out formative assessment may be the teacher, the pupils themselves, peer pupils, or other observers of the performance. The important point is that the pupils come to possess the information, and to see its relevance to what it is they intend to go on to achieve.

Different purposes and kinds of assessment, and the role that targets might play within them

In order to explore further the role of formative assessment in promoting learning, we need to distinguish more carefully between different purposes and kinds of assessment. Consider the following definitions:

- **formative** assessment is designed to enable a person to close the gap between what s/he can currently achieve and what s/he aims to achieve; it may be carried out by teachers, by pupils themselves, by peers, by adults other than teachers, or impersonally via tests or examinations;
- **normative** assessment is designed to set a standard, for example, establishing who can, and who cannot, use full stops in their own prose writing; but note that this term is not often used; it is a theoretical construct, indicating the knowledge, skills and understandings that are valued by the education system; it usually depends on the impersonal administration of tests and examinations;
- **summative** assessment summarises a person's capability in given respects at a certain stage or transition point in their life; this may take the form of teachers' reports to parents, transfer documentation or references; it might take the form of the pupils' own records of achievement, validated, for example, by governors and others;
- **diagnostic** assessment is designed to illuminate a person's learning style and/or difficulties, so that action can be taken to help her/him make the best possible progress; it usually takes the form of standardised testing or professional observation.

Discussion of these different forms of assessment has tended to make certain assumptions. It has usually been assumed, for example, that formative assessment is naturally characteristic of classroom interaction, that it is inextricably bound up with the processes of teaching and learning, and even helps define them. It seems generally to have been taken for granted that teachers cannot help but assess in a formative way, and that, if they did not, they could scarcely be said to be teaching. An implication of Black and Wiliam's work, however, appears to be that formative assessment need not be integral to teaching, because teachers can teach without inviting pupils to develop perceptions of their own ability, without enabling them to be aware of their own aspirations, and without expecting them to find ways of closing gaps between current capability and desired goals.

Before Black and Wiliam's work, a common definition of formative assessment was merely that it was designed to help pupils learn. In the TGAT report (DES, 1987), which was seminal in launching the GCSE and the National Curriculum, and to which Black contributed, the purpose of formative assessment was held to be 'that the positive achievements of a pupil may be recognised and discussed and the appropriate next steps may be planned' (para. 23). Just who recognises and discusses the pupil's achievements remained ambiguous in TGAT's definition; and who would be planning the next steps? But normative and summative assessments can also be used with the intention of recognising and discussing achievements, and of planning next steps. Formative assessment's unique feature was not made clear in those terms. Prior to Black and Wiliam, formative assessment's definition lacked the element of the pupils' being deliberate in their efforts to close gaps between what they currently achieve and what they want to achieve.

Public accountability tends to favour normative and summative assessments. Now that comparisons between pupils and schools are routinely made, for example, in PANDA reporting and Ofsted inspection, teachers are encouraged to think in their planning, teaching, assessments and evaluations about whether or not their pupils have attained certain standards. Are these high, mid, or low attainers, for example? How many have matched standard expectations? As a result, normative and summative assessments play a prominent role in managers' and teachers' evaluations and attempts to improve their school's performance.

In the past decade, normative and summative assessments' dominant share of the limelight has not been diminished. Ofsted inspections, governors' having to publish attainment results and targets, performance management and threshold assessments have all seen to that.

The normative serves the interests of accountability, while the formative serves the interest of the specific pupils' learning and of teachers' involvement in it. The summative might serve either normative or formative purposes. The diagnostic helps teachers analyse pupils' strengths and weaknesses, and might be put to formative use.

If those, then, are the possible purposes, on what kinds of reference or measure might assessment be based?

The simplest kind of assessment gives a positive score to the features judged correct or competent in a performance, and expresses the result as a straightforward total or percentage. More sophisticated than that, standardised assessments are based on results achieved by significant populations of people, and present the result in terms of a comparative measure, such that 100 is average, though there is usually a 10 to 20 point margin of error. Standardised assessments present a person's capability on a scale showing how close to or far from the norm, how far below or above 100, the person is calculated to be.

What a result might mean depends on what matters most to the person concerned. A person might be interested in comparing what s/he scored with what other people scored. Alternatively, a person might prefer to rate what s/he achieved against descriptions of differing qualities of performance. Or a person might feel a need to compare the latest result with what was scored on a previous occasion. Or a person might focus on comparing her/his result with what s/he aimed for. We can see these different options in the different forms of assessment: norm-, criterion-, and self-referenced assessment.

Norm-referencing is based on the view that it is useful to place people in rank order, and to divide up the population on a pre-determined scale. Classically, a bell curve or curve of normal distribution is drawn, giving 10 per cent of the population A, 20 per cent B, 40 per cent C, 20 per cent D, and 10 per cent E. In this kind of assessment everyone competes against one another.

Criterion-referencing awards grades on the basis of the quality of each person's performance, as explicitly defined, irrespective of how other people perform. Everyone might earn a *1* or a *6*, an *A* or an *E*: what matters is the quality of performance as the assessor matches it to the set of grade descriptions. Here, everyone competes against pre-determined standards.

Self-referencing, or ipsative assessment as it is sometimes called, recognises achievement in a person on the basis of comparison with what s/he has previously accomplished. If a person has made great progress in a given field of skill, knowledge or understanding, then the assessment will be highly positive. Conversely, though a person's starting point may be advanced, if little or no progress is made, the assessment will not be positive. It does not matter that many people out-perform you, nor that you outstrip everyone else. Competition is against yourself.

Norm-referencing has been characteristic of traditional examinations and was associated with the maintenance of standards, hence serving a normative purpose. You can interpret your norm-referenced assessment result as meaning you are better than so many people, or not so good as so many people. If you wanted to use norm-referenced assessment to improve your performance, you would strive to exceed other people's performances.

Criterion-referencing is characteristic of public assessments introduced or expanded in England and Wales from the late 1980s, chiefly through GCSE, vocational qualifications, and the National Curriculum. You can interpret your criterion-referenced assessment result as meaning you have this particular set of skills, knowledge and understandings. If you wanted to use criterion-referenced assessment to improve your performance, you would need to develop what is demanded by the next level of criteria.

Self-referencing suits anyone who attempts to improve on their previous best. It is characteristic of coaching and reflects contemporary psychology's notions of 'focus', 'zone', 'inner game', 'visualisation', and so on. If you wanted to use self-referenced assessment to improve your performance, you would need to make the most of your capability and achieve further personal best performances.

How different assessment cultures impinge on the quality of teaching and learning

Targets used within a norm-referencing context would tend to be expressed in terms of going up a level or of advancing to the next most successful group of pupils. Criterion-referenced targets would tend to be expressed in terms of the skills, knowledge and understanding that represent higher levels of achievement. Self-referenced targets would tend to be expressed in terms of a quality of performance beyond your current capability.

The culture of a school influences how pupils think and feel, and makes it more likely that they will conceive of their targets in one or other of the possible assessment modes – norm-, criterion-, or self-referenced. It is certainly interesting to note what pupils predominantly answer when they are asked *What are your targets?* When they answer *I want to get better marks*, or *I'm aiming to go up a set*, it suggests the pupils are used to a norm-referenced culture. When they answer *My target is to learn how to use the decimal point* or *paragraphs*, it suggests the pupils have been taught in a criterion-referenced culture. When they answer *I am trying to swim further* or *I want to improve how I use texture in my art work*, it suggests the pupils have experienced a self-referenced culture.

Formative and diagnostic assessments can have immediate and significant effects on teaching and learning processes. Normative and summative assessments provide a cooler look at performance; their messages need to be translated into spurs or plans for action. Self-referencing gives you a sense of your own trajectory in an area of skill, knowledge or understanding. Whether or not it is explicitly conscious in the pupil or shared with teachers, self-referenced assessment is probably an essential ingredient in learning. Criterion-referencing is a prerequisite of learning, allowing a person to reflect on performance and apply it in different circumstances. Norm-referencing may be beneficial to those who respond to information about how well they perform compared with other people.

Targets used by the individual learner can be the nexus of the formative and diagnostic, self- and criterion-referencing in assessment. Whole-school targets are more likely to reflect and use normative, summative, and norm-referenced assessments, though this does not have to be the case. It is possible for pupils to provide summative assessments by recording their achievements. And whole-school targets can be made to correspond with the emphases that individual pupils' formative assessments and targets have, and so take on a more criterion-referenced character.

The conclusion about my research into pupils' perceptions, reported in Chapter 2, suggested that individual pupils' targets have the potential to contribute positively to effective teaching and learning, but that using targets might not alone determine the quality of pupils' experience and schools' performance. The same conclusion was reached by the records of achievement evaluation team about the power of that initiative to improve pupils' lives in school.

> There would appear to be agreement that all young people should be provided with a learning environment which allows them to make maximum use of their potential and with a record of their achievement which gives them the best possible chance of being happy and satisfied in their future lives. The key to the realisation of both these goals appears to be the incorporation of processes into the life of the school which have the power to transform the negative messages that many pupils have experienced in the past. The provision of records and reports by itself cannot achieve this. Rather it is clear that such documentation is the catalyst which can bring about a more fundamental change in understanding on the part of both pupils and teachers

about the ingredients necessary for all pupils to experience pleasure and fulfilment in their learning.

(PRAISE, 1988, pp. 165–6)

The PRAISE team pointed to issues of 'ownership' and 'penetration' as being
essential to effective educational change. 'Ownership' needed to be felt by the
pupils – of the processes and documentation which served to record their achievements in, across and beyond the curriculum – and by the teachers – of the strategies
and systems that were developed in the school to facilitate the shifts in values and
control that the initiative required. New and better procedures needed to 'pene-
trate', and then permeate, the culture and ethos of the school, if they were to be
truly successful. It was not enough for teachers and pupils merely to follow the fash-
ion and pay lip-service to laudable principles. The same must apply with the
development of individual pupils' targets. Merely mechanical or superficially con-
formist routines will not bring significant benefits to motivation and self-esteem.
Both records of achievement and individual pupils' targets have this potential to
shift the pupils' sense of who is in control of their education, to increase their sense
of purpose and satisfaction. Both take us back to principles of effective teaching,
such as we explored in Chapter 3, and both take us forward into questions of
whole-school strategy, such as we will explore in Chapters 5, 6 and 7.

What a teacher might have in mind when deciding on a target for a pupil

Context is all important. Within instituted education, the ethos and pattern of
interaction between teacher and learner crucially influence a pupil's perception,
motivation and action. Remember how significant ethos appeared to be in my
research, reported in Chapter 2. For a target to be meaningful, the learner must
feel its value in taking her/him in the desired direction. In the dynamic of the
classroom, the teacher can play a part through many different kinds of initiative
and intervention: prompting or carrying out assessment; setting, guiding or supporting task performance, and so on. What the teacher brings to her/his thinking
about what might be an appropriate target includes her/his:

1 general knowledge of the pupil;
2 awareness of particular circumstances which are likely to affect the pupil's
   motivation and performance;
3 awareness of objectives and challenges the pupil might already have, deriving
   from other contexts in the school, such as Special Educational Needs, other
   areas of the curriculum, or extra-curricular activities;
4 perception of the pupil's recent progress;
5 recent assessment, formal or otherwise, of the pupil's attainment;
6 perception of the pupil's progress and achievement in comparison with other
   pupils, perhaps involving a grouping as, for example, high, mid, or low attaining pupils;

7 predictions of the pupil's expected eventual performance, derived from results in earlier given tests (e.g. NFER-Nelson CATs or NC end-of-key-stage tests), for example using chances charts;

8 awareness of targets the school or subject leader has;

9 awareness of objectives the teacher her/himself has relating to her/his own performance management or membership of a management, teaching or care team;

10 awareness of the kind of support the pupil might receive, for example from other pupils, the teacher, classroom assistance and home;

11 awareness of the practicalities of setting and trying to hit a target for the pupil, in terms of how long the target is to last, where it is to be kept, how progress and outcome will be recorded, and how the pupil will get feedback.

These awarenesses derive from extensive familiarity with individual pupils and the school's culture and systems, as well as from sophisticated combinations of assessment styles and results. A teacher has to choose a balance between the formative, normative, summative, diagnostic, norm-referenced, criterion-referenced, self-referenced, with an emphasis, I would recommend, on the formative, diagnostic, criterion- and self-referenced.

What might affect a pupil when s/he thinks about choosing a target

It can be useful to speculate about what affects a pupil's use of targets. What the pupil brings to her/his thinking about possible targets includes:

1 current mood and feelings;

2 general attitude towards school and/or the teacher concerned;

3 other pupils' choices of targets;

4 what the pupil believes the teacher and/or other pupils and/or her/his parents (will) think of her/him;

5 what the pupil thinks s/he is capable of achieving;

6 previous experience of setting targets;

7 desire to achieve within the subject, in school, and/or beyond school;

8 judgement about how best to try to maintain her/his current performance and image, if that is what s/he wants to do; or judgement about how best to try to change her/his current performance and image, if change is what s/he wants.

Considering a target raises, implicitly at least if not explicitly, questions about any or all of those matters. How targets are used depends on the nature of the relationships that have been developed in the classroom and school, and on the interactions that take place daily and from minute to minute. We see again the importance of context, ethos and culture.

The difference between targets for individual pupils and targets for groups or classes

One of the most important, and perhaps neglected, dimensions of using targets is whether pupils perceive what they have to do in the classroom and in the school as being common to every pupil, or as being in some way unique to themselves as individuals. Much of what happens in lessons and in school is the result of **social** arrangements, but every pupil experiences their teaching and the culture of the school **personally**.

We have already acknowledged that pupils tend to find their tasks acceptable, meaningful, or purposeful when they appreciate:

- what they are doing;
- why they are doing it;
- how they may set about what they have to do;
- what they are good at;
- what they are trying to get better at.

They do not always have to be explicitly conscious of such considerations. It appears sufficient that they take enough of those considerations for granted as present and positive. Or to put the converse case, when pupils are not content with the tasks they face, or the reasons or procedures for their activities, when they are uncertain about how well they are doing, or have no clue about how they are developing their skills or knowledge, they soon enough stop trying. And pupils are sensitised to these things as a result of both **social** arrangements and **personal** communications.

Pupils find purpose and satisfaction in lessons and at school insofar as they feel properly treated as a member of the class, or year group, or school, and insofar as someone on behalf of the school addresses them individually. Much research testifies to pupils' appreciation of teachers who talk to them one to one, and of systems which provide individual attention, for example, by way of special educational needs teaching, or tutor time, or pastoral care time and space. (See, for example, Keys and Fernandes, 1993.)

Another way in which pupils may feel personally addressed by teachers is through marking. This conventionally takes the form of written comment in exercise books or folders, but it includes whatever the teacher says to the pupil by way of praise, correction or guidance as part of their ongoing interaction within lessons and units of work. Indeed, that is a significant value of marking or responding to pupils' work: it confirms to the pupil that the teacher is concerned for the pupil's progress and success, that s/he appreciates what the pupil has done well, and that s/he wishes to guide the pupil's further learning. Marking is an obvious vehicle for formative assessment and a way of communicating about personal targets. (Appendix 2 contains guidance on marking policy.)

Marking can reinforce a pupil's sense of being treated as an individual. Targets can have that effect too. The more individualised a pupil feels her/his treatment and tasks to be, the more likely s/he is to feel that school has personal meaning. Pupils whose experience of school is merely social or impersonal are more likely to feel disaffected or alienated.

How targets can be broken down, and the component parts of the learning explained in detail

Let us turn to the level of detail that is necessary in the framing of targets. Just how specific does a target have to be?

In the early days of developing the use of targets in school, it was an easy criticism made by outsiders that targets appeared vague. My own experience has now led me to be cautious about judging whether a given target is specific enough. I suggest rather that the parties to the target agree periodically to ask themselves, *Are we being specific enough?*

The test of a target is whether or not the pupil is helped to understand what s/he needs to do, and by when. If s/he is clear about what s/he is aiming for, and knows enough to proceed, the target is well framed. If s/he can use the target as s/he sets about the task as a guide to checking or adjusting her/his effort, it is a well enough defined target. If s/he can look back on what s/he has done and gauge the success, the target has done its job well enough. And if the pupil understands what s/he has to do in terms of learning, rather than merely in terms of doing, the learning will be more significant.

Any worthwhile process of learning is likely to entail a number of skills, qualities, knowledge and understandings. A target is unlikely to express them all. Behind the target we can expect to find strategies and steps that will support the effort to succeed. A target selects one or two aspects of learning for special attention. Successful performance will depend on many more aspects of capability than can be referred to by a target.

Here are some examples of how targets may be broken down and supported by specific steps. This is commonly done for pupils who have special educational needs, but clearly applies to all pupils. What we see here us that there is much more to a target than its surface specification.

> *Target:* for S to focus more on his tasks.
> *Activities to be used in support:*
> * S will be given for each task a number of specific steps to take, e.g. complete three sums.
> * S will be expected to take the necessary steps without drawing undue attention to herself from the teacher.
> * S's success will be rewarded by being able to choose a favourite activity, such as listening to a story tape, doing a puzzle, using the computer.
> * Moves S makes towards his task completion will be praised with specific feedback.
> * Consideration will be given to ways of individualising aspects of S's timetable.

Target: for P to build positive relationships with her peers.

Activities to be used in support:

- P will continue to join a weekly social skills group which focuses on turn-taking.
- Consideration will be given to the formation of a hand skills group.
- P will receive a daily certificate which commends her kind acts towards peers.
- P will have regular, timetabled opportunities to practise being a supportive friend to a younger pupil.

There are limits to how much detail can be made explicit in a target. The target needs to provide a sufficient platform for the teaching and sufficient impetus and direction for the learning.

It is by means of such personalising and particularising that targets can be made to confirm and enhance an ethos which values individuals' welfare, progress and achievement. Whenever a target is set, teacher and pupil need to understand how the task or project will be carried through. Their respective responsibilities need to be clear. In the context of one-to-one discussion about progress and prospects, this spelling out of how to proceed is especially important.

The values and functions of using targets in teaching and learning

To summarise the discussion so far, and to refer again to my research reported in Chapter 2, using targets can be seen to have particular functions and values in teaching and learning. These are distinct from the functions and values of using targets for whole-school improvement, which we will examine in the next three chapters. The evidence I took from my conversations with pupils in the nine schools I visited led me to conclude that targets can be effective both as metaphor and psychological process because they:

- allow the pupils to play a part in determining their current capability;
- enable the pupils to express what it is they want to learn or achieve;
- focus pupils' attention on the gap between what they can currently achieve and what they want to learn and achieve;
- complement any approach which scaffolds the stages the pupils will need to go through to get where they want to be;
- lead the pupils to see the teacher as someone working with them and helping them attain their goals;
- enable the pupils to decide what steps to take in order to achieve their goal;
- enable the pupils to influence how they are taught;
- increase the likelihood that the pupils will feel motivated and committed to their tasks;
- help the pupils derive personal satisfaction from their achievements.

We might say that using targets effectively to achieve those things would inevitably bring about school improvement. However true that may be, there remain areas of decision and activity beyond the reach of individual pupils' tasks and targets. These areas of decision and activity are the basis for efforts to improve a school's performance, and are the focus of Chapters 5, 6 and 7. For now, though, we will stay close to the pupils' experience, and recognise it as the cornerstone of all the different forms of targeting that are used in school.

Using targets to help pupils learn – guidelines

To help us now draw together many of the issues we have discussed in this chapter, let us consider two checklists of key propositions. Do they describe your school? Are there statements here that you would reject? Can you improve the lists by amending or adding items that are relevant to the needs of your pupils and your vision for your school?

One way of using these suggestions is as a stimulus to discussion when you are drawing up or revising your policy. The first checklist deals with principles, systems, and arrangements. The second deals with aspects of relationships and communication.

- The school's philosophy is that pupils learn most effectively when they know what they are aiming to learn. Targets are one of the ways in which the pupils are helped to have a sense of purpose and direction.
- The school's calendar makes clear the various activities designed to help the pupils set and review their targets for learning. These include staff training days, staff meetings, teacher–pupil one-to-one sessions, and parents' consultation evenings.
- The school tries to work towards achieving the performance targets indicated by DfES statistics and negotiated with the LEA consultant, but tries never to lose sight of the fact that school performance is most likely to be enhanced by working closely with the pupils and helping them to achieve the best they can.
- Subject teams have agreed ways of helping the pupils use targets. Common to such strategies is a focus on:
  - the progress made since the last review;
  - ways in which the pupil can evaluate progress;
  - what the pupil is good at;
  - what the pupil is aiming to improve;
  - suggestions as to what the pupil might have to do in order to improve.
- Subject and year teams review and refine their strategies for using targets, trying to maintain a balance between being systematic and consistent, on the one hand, and being flexible and responsive, on the other hand. We try to keep an eye on the manageability of procedures, for example, avoiding duplication of documentation.
- We recognise that personal and social targets may need to be prioritised by some pupils.

- Targets are worded so that it is possible for the pupil to say after a period of time *yes* or *no* to the question, *Have I hit that target?*
- We have agreed ways of recording the targets that the pupils set and review. Such recording serves, and does not constrain, the varied approaches used by different subject teachers in their day-to-day work with the pupils, classroom assistants, and colleagues.
- The pupils collect examples of their work, comments on their work, and testimonials in a portfolio that represents their achievement, including targets they have successfully worked on.
- Reports include at least one target for the future.
- When teacher and pupil discuss targets, they look at their record of progress. Target reviews always include some successes, as well as the setting of new targets.
- The way targets are used is not so rigid as to squeeze out room for the pupils to talk personally about things that happen in their lives and that matter very much to them.
- Monitoring and evaluation activities check the correspondence between individual pupils' targets and targets used in other contexts, for example, in whole-school-improvement planning, teams' development and performance management.

A checklist of points to keep in mind when communicating with pupils about targets

Policy might also focus specifically on pupils' interactions with their teachers and assistants. Here is an example taken from a special school where communication is seen as the key to using targets. The teaching and care staff of this independent residential special school for boys with emotional and behavioural difficulties together devised the following checklist of points to keep in mind when communicating with pupils about targets.

October School – special, 4–11 boys, wide catchment

- We keep the targets clear and achievable.
- We make the targets understandable to the child.
- We emphasise the positive, i.e. the obstacles are seen as 'out there' for us to work on.
- We think about depersonalising the problems, by identifying the behaviour rather than the person.
- We make sure the child values the target and effort.
- We make the targets promoting and encouraging, rather than demanding.
- We make sure the child knows what s/he has achieved already.
- We think about how targets can be valuable for others, as well as for the child her/himself.
- We try to be consistent and fair as a staff and community.

- We involve the child as much as possible in the setting and reviewing of targets, e.g. s/he may have practical suggestions to offer about what to aim for and how to go about it.
- We negotiate with the child but keep our eye on 'stretching' the child, showing we have faith that s/he can do it.
- We try to use an appropriate time-scale, bearing in mind when the target will be reviewed.
- We make the targets specific.
- We avoid connotations of blame.
- We emphasise that we are all here to help.
- We show the child how to get support.
- We think about the links between different skills, e.g. motor skills in handwriting, eating . . .
- We think about our body language when we are discussing targets with the pupils.

The cornerstone of all work relating to targets and objectives is individual pupils' experience, and their perceptions are essential to every effort to bring integrity to whole-school improvement targets and all other forms of targeting.

In many ways, this exemplifies what we have been considering throughout this and the previous chapter. These two policy statements combine and define clear values, systems and provision, and so set out a principled, practical and challenging agenda for teaching, assessment and the use of individual pupils' targets. We can now take up questions of whole-school policy and development in the next chapter.

5 Whole-school targets and improvement

In the previous chapter we considered the use of individual pupils' targets as a means of advancing pupils' learning. This chapter is the first of three which focus on the use of whole-school targets as a way of improving schools' performance. This chapter concentrates on subject attainment and progress. The next chapter is devoted to special schools' use of whole-school targets. Chapter 7 deals with aspects of school life beyond the academic and concentrates on inclusion.

At the end of this chapter there is a list of all the different kinds of whole-school target mentioned in this and the next two chapters.

Several appendices take further some of the issues raised in this chapter. Appendix 3 deals with consistency in teachers' assessments, because teachers' use of targets is only as good as the accuracy and validity of their assessments. Appendices 5 and 6 illustrate how schools' development can be pursued, presenting case studies of a primary and secondary school, respectively. Appendix 7 contains an example of a calendar for school self-review and target-setting activities and occasions. Appendix 8 presents a complete draft policy, serving as a means of checking all aspects of assessment practice, including the use of targets.

The targets we will be discussing in this chapter either relate to particular groups or cohorts of pupils in the school, or they relate to all of the pupils in the school. These targets define what relatively large populations of pupils should gain from their education over a given period of time. They also indicate how a school intends to improve its provision so that pupils might benefit more. As with individual pupils' targets, the focus is ultimately on learning. But whole-school targets concern many pupils' learning in the context of innovation or modification to the way the school works.

Setting a target brings with it a responsibility to improve the school's resources, systems or culture in some way. It makes no sense to set a whole-school target and then proceed as you always have done in the past. A whole-school target is not a prediction or an expression of mere hope; it forms part of a plan to bring about something that has not yet been achieved. It is a matter of setting out to scale new heights.

In this chapter we will explore:

- some possible drawbacks in using whole-school targets;
- what to take account of when setting whole-school targets;
- why using whole-school targets is not a matter of moving through a simple plan-do-review cycle;
- how whole-school improvement targets vary;
- different ways of comparing pupils' achievement, hence different ways of targeting improvements to a school's performance;
- how using targets at a whole-school level can connect with using individual pupils' targets, teaching and care teams' targets, and objectives in performance management;
- how to check whether or not your whole-school targets are challenging.

We will not lose sight of the kinds of target and data that have public prominence. These include the targets to be set for Key Stages 2, 3 and 4, referred to in Chapter 1 (pp. 10–11). But we will take a broader view of targets and data than that.

Some possible drawbacks in using whole-school targets

It is essential to realise that end-of-key-stage test results and much of the data that are used for judging schools' effectiveness should be treated with a very great deal of caution. There are, for example, serious questions to be asked about the reliability and the use of test results to make comparisons. Different years see different assessment instruments being used, with the result that there is no common yardstick. But the political imperative that accountability be measured means that this is sometimes overlooked. (See Goldstein, 2001.)

When you do use targets for end-of-key stage results, it is preferable to use average levels or grades to be achieved by your cohort of pupils. This is much more informative than using mere thresholds such as level 4+ or A* to C grades. Ian Schagen (2000), in his excellent *Statistics for School Managers*, counsels:

> Performance indicators based on percentages achieving a certain threshold are inherently unstable and can have a distorting effect on educational practice. Those based on average levels or grades take account of and are sensitive to the performance of all in the cohort, and are to be preferred. However, any single performance indicator is likely to give a misleading picture, and a range of different indicators is to be preferred.
>
> (Schagen, 2000, p. 61)

We should also bear in mind potential ill-effects of using whole-school targets. One possible negative consequence is that teaching can be narrowed and made shallow because pupils are led to concentrate on meeting the selective demands of tests. Their learning is kept at a superficial level, and their ability to consolidate and apply their learning in new contexts is neglected. Another danger is that areas of teaching and learning that are not targeted are distorted or sidelined by the focus on statutory tests. Literacy and numeracy can be privileged at the expense of the arts and humanities, for example. There is a damaging implication that pupils who do not fall within targeted groups matter less than those who receive targeted attention. Focusing unequal resources, time and effort on pupils at the borderline of key levels or grades, such as level 4 and GCSE grade C, for example, may be something teachers and managers feel obliged to do. It is also possible that, by highlighting test success, standards of achievement are artificially raised at the end of a key stage, leaving the teachers in the next key stage to bring the pupils, and parents and carers, down to earth and then pick up the pieces of morale. And it can be very tempting to misrepresent the school's performance in an attempt to maintain or improve the school's reputation.

We will try to remember that education is not a simple matter of cause and effect, of having good intentions which translate necessarily into good results. We will try not to let statistics and targets beguile us. We will try to heed Michael Fullan's warning about

> the problem of brute sanity identified by George Bernard Shaw when he observed that 'reformers have the idea that change can be achieved by brute sanity' . . . Brute sanity is the tendency to overlook the complexity and detailed processes and procedures required, in favour of the more obvious matters of stressing goals, the importance of the problem and the grand plan. Brute sanity overpromises, overrationalises and consequently results in unful-filled dreams and frustrations which discourage people from sustaining their efforts and from taking on future change projects.
>
> (Fullan, 1988, p. 16)

What to take account of when setting whole-school targets

Having targets can help, but targets do not get things done. Most of the time teachers and managers attend to matters and concerns that are felt to be more immediate and less abstract than targets as such. Using targets belongs to a kind of time out, when you pause, reflect, get your bearings, and refocus your efforts. Minute by minute, day by day, when you are engaged in the business of caring for and teaching the pupils, or managing the school, your target commitments might run through what you actually do, but they cannot often be at the forefront of your consciousness. Urgent tasks mean some things have to be taken for granted.

Targets in the form that they appear now only became a focus of attention in the very late 1990s. They tend not to cause radical policy overhauls in school, but they can lead to changes in routines and strategies. If you want to rethink your vision or mission for your school, you will need to go further back than targets.

It is essential that setting a target should entail careful consideration of how you plan to bring about the desired result. Setting a target has necessary implications for how you shoot. The preparation helps to determine whether or not you will be successful. Teachers and managers need to be clear and confident about any changes or additions to their structures, strategies, methods or resources. If they are not, their work towards achieving the target will be flawed.

The contribution that using targets can make is significant. If you are clear about what you are aiming to achieve, and you have prepared your resources and plans of action, you can benefit from the impetus that a target gives you and feel secure in your purpose and your method, at least for as long as there is reasonable progress. Setting and reviewing targets need, then, to be built into schools' structures and systems so that these can make their contribution.

In using targets for whole-school improvement, you have to recognise that targets are being used elsewhere: pupils' use of targets; the use of targets by teaching, pastoral, and management teams; and the use of targets ('objectives') by managers and teachers in their performance management.

A target gives direction to endeavour and allows a judgement to be made about how successful the endeavour is turning out to be or has been. In setting a target, you have to take the following into account:

- who the pupils are;
- what they have achieved in the past and what they can currently achieve;
- calculated probabilities of what they might achieve in the future – using, for example, chances charts available in the Autumn Package;
- understanding what it will take for the pupils to close the gap between what they can do now and what can be expected of them;
- how long is allowed for the target to be hit;
- the teachers' and resources' capacity to support the envisaged trajectory of the pupils' learning;
- the sustainability of everyone's efforts: pupils', teachers', support staff's, parents' and carers', other agencies';
- the correspondence between specific whole-school targets and other target fields: individual pupils' targets; targets being used by teaching, pastoral and management teams; targets ('objectives') being used by individual managers and teachers in their performance management.

Going for a target depends on dynamic and ongoing analyses, decisions and actions, relating to:

- the teaching and support provided, in order to enable the pupils to achieve at least their predicted potential;
- circumstances, foreseen and unforeseen, which impinge on events as they unfold;
- as time passes, provision of feedback information to all concerned about progress;
- the quality of experience, as felt by everyone concerned;
- whether or not those concerned learn from their experience;
- awareness of other kinds of target being used in the school, including performance management.

Why using whole-school targets is not a matter of moving through a simple plan-do-review cycle

Going for a school target is not a one-off event. The effort to achieve the target will be spread over many months and many different contexts. The contexts include subject lessons, personal and social curriculum activities, pastoral arrangements, and the ethos and culture of the school.

Targets feed on a wide range of performance data, and then become part of those data. Schools are sent plenty of data, including, from central government, the annual PANDA report and the Autumn Package. These are partial, so schools also gather data for themselves in order to highlight areas that might otherwise be overlooked. Schools' self-evaluation is becoming in government's eyes the focus of efforts to enhance the quality of education, and the use of data and targets are the staple of such work. Many professionals welcome this increasing emphasis on taking responsibility for their own analysis of performance and improvement. Data are best seen as prompting you to find useful answers to questions that will help the teachers teach effectively and the pupils learn successfully.

Data can illuminate the life and work of a school. Data lead to questions. Answers lead to hypotheses. Hypotheses help formulate priorities for development, and these are given impetus and direction by targets. Critically informed priorities and targets are couched in action plans. Action plans generate action. Action produces data, and the data include information about whether or not targets were hit. The cycle might be said to begin again.

Except that it is not that simple. It is when targets are treated simplistically that their negative effects, referred to earlier, can be felt. The diagrams you sometimes see on overhead projector screens, or powerpoint displays, or on paper, showing a progression around a circle – first plan, then do, then monitor, then review – need to be three-dimensional and interactive if anything like the complex reality of teaching and school management is to be captured. The work of a school is infinitely more dynamic than moving from prospect to action, then to retrospect, and round to prospect again.

A school does not have a single cycle of planning and development. Managing the budget alone necessitates frequent checks and adjustments. The reality of education is that there are many interconnected cycles of planning, targeting, action and reviewing. Targets have lots of different time-scales and lots of different ways of being attended to. (Appendix 7 uses the framework of the calendar to look at activities and occasions for school self-review and target-setting.) Working on whole-school targets involves from time to time looking elsewhere at the other fields of targeting activity in order to see how well the different kinds of target and objective correspond with one another.

How whole-school improvement targets vary

There is further complexity in the plethora of choices in using targets. You may want to target all the pupils' progress or attainment, or you may want to focus on certain groups: boys or girls, for example, or a specific ability group. You may want to prioritise a particular subject, English and mathematics, or all three core subjects; you may want to target achievement across all subjects. You may have non-academic aspects of school life in mind. (These are addressed in Chapter 7, while in this chapter we concentrate on academic or subject performance.)

Your targets may be expressed in terms of levels or grades, or in terms of average pupil point scores, or in the language of success criteria. You may use a single marker – level 4, grade C, or an average pupil point score, 21, for example. You may alternatively use a range – level 4+, grade A* to C, or a spread of average pupil point scores, 21 to 27, for example. Your targets may denote attainment at a point in time, or they may represent progress measures of pupils' gains between two assessments. You may be content to use government-supplied or commercial tests, or you may highlight teachers' assessments or observers' testimony to pupils' learning achievement. You may focus on one year's results or the trend over several years.

Whole-school targets vary, then, according to:

- the period of time allowed between setting the target and measuring the result;
- the nominated pupil group;
- area of the curriculum or aspect of school life;
- whether levels, grades, points, or words are used;
- whether a single marker or a band is used;
- whether attainment or progress is at issue;
- the assessment instrument that is used;
- whether a single year's outcome is the focus, or trend over a number of years.

(See the taxonomy at the end of this chapter for a fairly comprehensive list of possible whole-school target types.)

Different ways of comparing pupils' achievement, hence different ways of targeting improvements to a school's performance

There is a further complication in the definition and use of whole-school targets. You may aim straightforwardly for one particular outcome, without making any kind of comparison, and so prefer to use an absolute target. Alternatively, you may aim to beat previous years' performance in your school, or you may aim to out-perform other schools.

An example of an **absolute** target would be for every pupil to gain an athletics award; or for 90 per cent of pupils to show they can illustrate differences between another area of Britain they have visited and the area where they themselves live. The pupils' performance you are aiming for does not depend on any comparison with other pupils or with the pupils' previous performance.

When you say you are committed to raising standards of pupils' achievement, what do you want your standards to be higher than precisely? The choice begs the question about the basis of comparison.

You might aim during the coming year to raise the progress made by a given cohort of pupils above:

- last year's equivalent cohort's performance in your school;
- the average of all previous cohorts' performance in your school over recent years;
- the highest ever performance by a cohort of that age in your school.

In terms borrowed from the previous chapter, those are self-referenced targets for the school. But they are not self-referenced for the cohort of pupils concerned, and they could be called **school-self-referenced** targets. If you prefer **pupil-self-referenced** targeting, you might choose a target of raising a cohort's progress above:

- the cohort's own progress in the previous year;
- the cohort's best ever progress in previous years;
- the average of the cohort's progress over all their years in school.

School-self-referenced and pupil-self-referenced targets can be called **improvement** targets. They involve making comparisons with at least one aspect of the school's known performance and seeking to improve on that.

If you favour norm-referenced targeting, you might aim to raise a given cohort of pupils' progress above:

- the average measure of progress made in recent years by that age cohort in your LEA;
- the average measure of progress made nationally by that age cohort in recent years;
- a certain county or national percentile, e.g. to rise above the lowest quartile, to get above the median, or to enter the top 10 per cent.

These we might call **competitive** targets. They involve making comparisons with the other schools and seeking to outperform them.

It is important to realise you have some choice about bases for comparison. Between 1998 and 2001, that is, in the first years of the statutory requirement to publish whole-school targets, data such as the PANDA report and Autumn Package used the percentage of pupils taking free school meals as a way of allocating schools to bands, so that comparisons could be made about their effectiveness. This was contentious because many different factors were known to affect whether or not a family took up its free school meal entitlement, factors such as personal pride and the availability of school meals as such. With the introduction of unique pupil numbers (UPNs), allowing the anonymous collection of assessment data for every pupil in the country, and the creation of historical databases, you can now expect to have data that are better suited to your school improvement needs. The development has been from a socio-economic comparison to a prior attainment benchmark, and this seems to be welcomed by school teachers and managers as being fairer and more illuminating.

How using targets at a whole-school level can connect with using individual pupils' targets, teaching and care teams' targets, and objectives in performance management

It is possible to make connections between teams' targets, whole-school targets and targets for individual pupils. You need to be able to 'see' the individual pupils' targets in your whole-school targets. Unless you are aware of, plan for, and have the capacity to promote progress towards your individual pupils' targets, your whole-school targets will fail to connect with the all-important day-to-day activities of the classroom.

The closer you get to the pupils and their learning, the more **closely defined** your targets will be. When you deal with the performance of cohorts or populations, the more **coarsely defined** your targets will be.

Coarsely defined targets are expressed in terms that relate to statutory, publishable targets. Such a target would be for:

- 80 per cent of pupils who attained level 4+ in their KS2 tests to achieve 5 A* to C grades at GCSE, or their equivalent vocational qualification
- 75 per cent of Y6 pupils who attained level 1 at KS1 to attain level 4 in English tests and Teacher Assessments next summer.

More closely defined targets can be worked out from the components of the National Curriculum Level Descriptions or GCSE grade criteria, setting out prerequisite or underlying competences. Such a target would be:

- in English, in writing, for 95 per cent of Y6 pupils to describe events clearly by:
  - sequencing events in chronological order
  - highlighting significant events
  - referring to context or setting and chief protagonists
  - exploring feelings of characters in narrative . . .

- in English, in reading, for all Y10 and Y11 pupils to be able to:
  - detect bias in discursive texts
  - comment on writers' choices of vocabulary, style . . .

Two qualities are essential to teachers' and managers' being able to move to and fro along this spectrum, from the coarsely to the closely defined, and back again. First, sufficient subject knowledge and understanding are required. Second, assessments have to be accurate and consistent. Everything depends on the validity and reliability of the assessment data, whether they be the teachers' own or external and standardised. (Consistency in teacher assessment is fully explored in Appendix 3.)

You can make use of software packages, which facilitate the storage, manipulation and interpretation of teachers' assessments alongside data derived from formal or externally marked testing. You can scan pupils' progress, and make projections for their progress, on the basis of their past performance and their statistical chances of reaching notionally expected levels. You can think about the correspondence between these data, whole-school targets, performance management objectives, and targets that management, pastoral and subject teams have.

The most sophisticated use of assessment data in schools involves intelligent analysis at both extremes of the spectrum: at the micro-level of the classroom and individual pupils' learning; and at the macro-level of whole-school management and strategic decision-making. This is the key to the effective use of targets for whole-school improvement. (See the case studies in Appendices 5 and 6 for illustrations of this.)

How to check whether or not your whole-school targets are challenging

Those who look in from the outside on a school's performance are prone to ask whether the targets set are sufficiently challenging. And in school too you might want to assure yourself that your targets, while being realistic, succeed in stretching everyone to achieve their potential. With hindsight you can tell how challenging a target was. But how do you know before the event whether or not a target is challenging?

The concept of challenge hinges on expectation. Targets that do not match what a school can be expected to achieve are soft targets. Targets that represent achievement beyond what can reasonably be expected are very challenging targets.

The best basis currently available for your predictions about cohorts of pupils' performance is a statistical projection using their previously assessed attainments, moderated by teachers' experience and knowledge of the pupils. The hard data consist of Baseline Assessment, Key Stage 1, 2 or 3 National Curriculum tests, or GCSE results, and reputable standardised assessments, such as NFER-Nelson Cognitive Ability Tests. Given the measure of a year group's past attainments, a forecast can be made about the percentages of pupils that should attain targeted levels and grades. (See Appendix 4 for an explanation of essential statistical techniques.) While statistical projections are a very important source of information, they are not conclusive. All of the teachers' day-to-day experiences and knowledge of individuals should be used to moderate your decision-making about what can be expected of your pupils.

The teachers have available to them chances graphs which show what individual pupils can be expected to achieve, given their track record. They draw on much more than this, though, when considering what might be a reasonable target for each individual pupil. They tap their knowledge of how the pupil has responded in a wide variety of situations. They may also be aware of particular circumstances which are likely to affect the pupil's motivation and performance.

They can bear in mind any recent assessment, formal or otherwise, as well as how the pupil's progress compares with that of other pupils. The teachers consider the kind of support the pupil might receive, for example, from other pupils, teachers, classroom assistance, and home. And they can be aware of the practicalities of a pupil's trying to hit a target, in terms of how long the target is to last, where it is to be recorded and kept, how progress and outcome will be recorded, and how the pupil will get feedback.

So the school's senior managers, at times working with governors and LEA officers, need to take account of the teachers' perceptions. And the most advanced schools in this respect have developed ICT systems and databases, regularly updated, to track, monitor and make projections about pupils' performance. These include teachers' own assessments, which are closer to the action and more frequent than end-of-key-stage or even annual test results.

We will explore the role of school governance in using whole-school targets more fully in Chapter 10. For now we can note that the governing body should be a party to strategic decision-making about whole-school targets. There are two main moments in the school year when this can occur. The first is when the managers and teachers take stock of a year group's achievement, usually at the end of the school year or in September. The second is when managers and teachers define their expectations and set targets, usually in the autumn term. This can be given public formality by the visit of an LEA consultant and statutorily involves the underwriting of the whole-school targets by the governing body.

The operational key is for the school's managers and teaching staff to translate their expectations, expressed as levels, grades or points, first, into what the pupils will have to know, understand and be able to do if the expectations are to be fulfilled, and, second, into the teaching plan and provision that will deliver those expectations. This is the very stuff of teaching and learning, and the governors gain insight into it through the professionals' reports to them and through their own monitoring activities.

These, then, are tests for whether or not your targets are challenging:

- Are occasions for discussing whole-school targets and performance built into the school calendar?
- Are governors involved in those discussions?
- Does your local authority or diocese contribute to your discussions?
- Do expectations of your pupils' performance draw on both statistical probabilities derived from previous assessments of their attainment and the teachers' ongoing experience and assessments?
- Do you check the correspondence between targets that individual pupils are using, targets that management, teaching and care teams have, and the targets that appear in school-improvement planning, monitoring and evaluation?
- Do you link your personal performance management objectives to your whole-school targets?

- In your use of data and targets, do you try to find out more about what affects pupils' performance, about how teaching might better stimulate and support pupils' performance, and about patterns in pupils' talents, interests, needs and difficulties?

If your answers to all of those questions are positive, you can confidently claim that you are setting challenging targets. The guarantee is in the rigour of the processes, rather than in consideration of any given set of statistics.

By way of summary, these are the kinds of whole-school target identified in this and the next two chapters:

Taxonomy of targets for whole-school improvement
- **Attainment** targets define what pupils should achieve, as assessed on a given occasion such as end-of-key-stage tests or examinations.
- **Progress** targets define how much more pupils should achieve since they were last assessed.
- **Absolute** targets involve no comparisons: desired outcomes are expressed, not in terms of rising above others, nor in terms of improving on past performance, but in terms of achieving whatever is a feasible challenge for the school's own pupils.
- **Competitive** targets involve comparison with other schools; desired outcomes are expressed in terms of out-performing others.
- **Improvement** targets involve comparison with at least one aspect of the school's past performance, the intention being to improve on that.
- **School-self-referenced** targets should lead to the school performing as well as, or better than, could be expected, given the school's track record.
- **Pupil-self-referenced** targets should lead to groups of pupils performing as well as, or better than, could be expected, given those particular pupils' track record.
- **Process** targets concentrate on what the school provides for the pupils: these do not make the pupils' progress or achievement the defining factor for a target; they refer to the teaching, or classroom support, or resources and opportunities, or the school's ethos; these may have a particular value in a school for pupils who experience severe, profound or multiple learning difficulties; process targets focus on improvements to *how* pupils learn, as opposed to *what* they learn.
- **Outcome** targets define the results that pupils should achieve on a given occasion; these may be in general terms of levels or grades or points, or in specific terms of the skills, qualities, knowledge or understandings that pupils are to develop; outcome targets focus on *what* pupils are to learn, rather than on *how* they will learn.
- **Successive** targets apply lessons learned from the experience of one year's pupils to the subsequent teaching and learning of a following year's pupils; a next generation of pupils benefits from one of its predecessors.

- **Progressive** targets apply lessons learned from the experience of one year's pupils to the subsequent teaching and learning of the same pupils; the pupils who prompted the changes to teaching and provision should themselves benefit.
- **Coarsely defined** targets express a school's aspiration for pupils in terms of the levels or grades or points that a percentage of a year group should attain or progress by.
- **Closely defined** targets express in detail what the pupils should come to know, understand, be able to do or be.
- **Direct-benefit** targets define what certain pupils should gain as a result of new or increased access or opportunity; for example, pupils with hearing and speech impairment will gain in personal and social experience and communication skills from being integrated in mainstream classes.
- **Indirect-benefit** targets define what some pupils should gain as a result of other pupils' acquiring new or increased access or opportunity; for example, pupils in a mainstream class will benefit from having pupils who have hearing and speech impairment to work and play with them.

6 Using targets in special schools

There are three parts to this chapter. The first comprises a statement which colleagues in a number of special schools helped me prepare about using targets in their schools. The schools are Mountjoy and Wyvern Schools in Dorset and Linwood and Bicknell Schools in Bournemouth. The second part sets out steps that can be taken to make your use of targets relevant and helpful to your efforts to raise standards of achievement. In the third part I offer questions, based on work by Tim Kent and Brahm Norwich, which enable colleagues in special schools to evaluate their use of targets.

Some problems and their solutions

When whole-school target-setting was introduced in 1998, the initial concern in many special schools was that government policy appeared to have taken little account of special schools' particular circumstances. The policy's purpose was, and remains, to provide answers to questions about schools' effectiveness based on benchmarking. Schools are expected to use nationally and locally supplied comparative data in setting targets for improved performance. Agents in fulfilling the policy are school governors, for it is the responsibility of the governing body of every school with Year 6, Year 9, or Year 11 pupils to publish in its annual report targets at Key Stages 2, 3 and 4. (See Chapter 1, pp. 10–11, for details.)

All schools are required to participate in this policy. Where the number of pupils in a year group falls below eleven, exemption is allowed. Many special schools have ten or fewer pupils in a year group and so are not required to publish their targets for that reason. And reading the small print reveals a second possible reason for exemption. The legislation on using targets in schools refers to pupils who are taking the end-of-key-stage tests and GCSE public examinations. In other words, pupils not entered for National Curriculum assessment or public examination do not have to be included in the calculation and publication of targets.

At the outset and in practice then, teachers, managers and governors in special schools might have felt they were not specifically addressed by the statutory requirements for using targets. Many colleagues in special schools wanted to participate in the development of using targets to focus whole-school development. What they needed were valid and productive forms of target.

To assist in the making of comparisons between schools and their performance, the DfES publishes benchmarking statistics. These present the performance of bands of mainstream schools in end-of-key-stage assessments. The bands are determined by free school meal take-up (e.g. 0–8 per cent, 9–22 per cent, 23-50 per cent, 50 per cent+ of pupils taking free school meals), and by prior attainment, which is thought to be a fairer basis for benchmarking. Ofsted also has developed a special schools PANDA report, presenting bands of schools according to pupil numbers and the conventional categories of moderate learning difficulties, emotional and behavioural difficulties, and so on.

There are several problems here, but schools have been finding solutions.

It is important to be cautious about the use of targets, particularly in respect of schools for pupils with special needs. This caution stems in part from the frail validity and unreliability of assessments which are inevitably context-specific. A pupil may show her/himself capable or not capable of something on one day, and perform quite differently on another day. Pupils cannot necessarily be relied on to transfer skill and understanding from one time and place to another. This may be especially true of pupils with emotional and behavioural difficulties. And pupils with degenerative conditions challenge any assumption that capability demonstrated here and now will necessarily endure or even grow.

The statutory use of targets is based on an assumption of comparability, but in the field of special education it is often impossible to find pupils sufficiently alike in age, need and capability to warrant meaningful comparison. The labels used to categorise learning difficulty are notoriously inadequate. 'Emotional and behavioural difficulty' (EBD), for example, covers an enormous range. Ofsted reports in its *Principles into Practice* document (1999, p. 5):

> Some of these pupils may have temporary needs, perhaps provoked by sudden traumas in the family, or a long history of disturbed or delinquent behaviour of a serious kind, but alongside them may be children with conditions such as Tourette's Syndrome, Asperger's syndrome, or other psychiatric disorders. Additionally, a growing number of admissions are casualties of child protection cases. Most EBD schools are also required to admit pupils who in times past would have been placed in a Community Home with Education on the premises, or a psychiatric hospital.

Targets for special schools' performance cannot sensibly be derived from supposed norms. They must reflect the targets set for and used by individual pupils. Whole-school targets have to spur the work of management, teaching and care teams, and be sensitive to the perceptions of pupils and staff. The individual pupils' targets have, in turn, to show some correspondence with the targets that the school uses for improvement planning and activity.

If one major weakness in the current system is the inappropriateness and inutility of some of the categories for learning difficulty, a second lies in the scales that are used to rate pupils' attainments, hence schools' performance. The conventional scales are the National Curriculum and the General Certificate of Secondary Education or their vocational equivalents. These fail to identify with sufficient clarity, detail, and relevance the skills, knowledge and understandings which pupils with learning difficulties, or with emotional and behavioural difficulties, actually have, and which they need to go on to develop.

Commercial schemes are available for curriculum and assessment variations, including these three reputable examples: for pupils at Key Stage 4, *Accreditation for Living and Learning Skills (ALL)* (1995); the Royal Society of Arts' *National Skills Profile: Assessment Kit* (1998); and *ASDAN*, particularly the *Transition Challenge* and *Towards Independence* units. These may help schools to use approaches that are more appropriately matched to the pupils' capabilities and needs. It may also be possible to adapt the new early-learning goals, previously called desirable learning outcomes, for use in special schools at stages other than reception.

The government's department for education has acknowledged some of the difficulties. In 1998 the Qualifications and Curriculum Authority (QCA) distributed to special schools a curriculum and assessment scale deemed appropriate for pupils with SLD and PMLD. It consists of a set of three eight-point scales – one for Numeracy, one for Language and Literacy, and one for Personal and Social Development – leading to National Curriculum level 1 in mathematics and English. Some teachers are finding these pre-National Curriculum ('P') scales relevant to their pupils. Teachers might find it useful to refer to such scales when reporting to parents or conducting annual reviews. The scales can also serve to inform each school's own monitoring of its curriculum performance and, in addition, may give sensible progress and value-added measures where there is sufficient match between the scales and the school's own curriculum and individual planning.

As experience has developed, these P-scales have grown in status. In the first instance, the new P-scales were only offered by QCA as an optional extra, but from September 2001 special schools have to use P-scales in their whole-school target-setting.

Many special schools have experience of using targets other than National Curriculum or P-scales as a focus for development activities. Because cohort targets, expressed as percentages attaining levels, lack relevance to many special schools' development needs, they have used targets which highlight aspects of curriculum learning and achievement relevant to their pupils and circumstances. Year groups other than the statutorily targeted 11- 14- and 16-year-old can be focused on, for example.

Many special schools have found a rational response to the situation they find themselves in. They are using targets for whole-school improvement in as constructive a way as they can. We will look now at some examples in practice.

A cohort or school target, which informs and is informed by individual pupils' targets, might refer to:

- the achievement of a certain level or grade or standard, as defined in a reputable scheme or programme, by a specified number or proportion of pupils at a given age;
- a reduced number of permanent and temporary exclusions to be made in a year;
- improved percentages of half days' attendance and absence;
- a development which the school believes every pupil would benefit from experiencing: e.g. using directional signs around the school;
- a common element which the teachers see running through the learning objectives for a group of pupils; e.g. communicating requests, intentions, preferences and appreciation;
- the achievement of the learning objectives prioritised by the pupils' individual education plans;
- a scale of capability adopted by the school for this purpose: e.g. the QCA eight-point P-scale, or the *ALL* scheme . . .

Accordingly, whole-school development can be planned with focuses such as these:

- developing signing throughout the school;
- raising the proportion of pupils' achieving their IEP targets;
- developing the use of P-scales throughout the school;
- enhancing pupils' capabilities in interpersonal and social communication;
- enhancing pupils' capabilities in ICT;
- enhancing pupils' capabilities in mathematics;
- enhancing the breadth and quality of pupils' records of achievement;
- increasing the integration of our pupils in mainstream school activities;
- increasing our older pupils' residential and outdoor pursuits experience;
- increasing our oldest pupils' qualifications portfolio.

Such areas of development can give rise to specific performance targets. Here are some examples, taken from actual schools:

- most pupils to show they have begun to use a specific signing system;
- all pupils to have achieved the learning objectives recorded in their IEPs;
- all pupils to have reached the points on the QCA P-scale which were set as their individual targets;
- 66.6 per cent (i.e. 4 pupils) of present Nursery 2 and Reception pupils to demonstrate improvement over the next two years in personal competences against the P-scale: 4 additional points within Language and Literacy; 2 additional points within Numeracy; 4 additional points within Personal and Social Development;
- the present Y1 pupils to demonstrate improvement in ICT from 1.22 (mean unprompted score) to 2.00 (cf present Y3 1.80);
- most pupils at the end of Y2 to communicate requests, intentions, preferences and appreciation;

- 70 per cent of present Y5 pupils to demonstrate the ability to recognise numbers up to 100;
- six out of the eight Y9 pupils to attain level 3 by Teacher Assessment in English;
- 80 per cent of the present Y10 pupils with MLD to achieve bronze or above in the OCR Certificate of Achievement;
- by the end of Key Stage 1 all pupils to have worked with pupils in a mainstream school;
- by the end of Key Stage 2 all pupils to have taken part in a cultural visit;
- by the end of Key Stage 3 all pupils to have worked with pupils in a mainstream secondary school;
- by the end of Key Stage 4 all pupils to have taken part in a residential school visit;
- 100 per cent of post-16 (Y13) students to achieve at least one certificate at either introductory or first level;
- 31 per cent of post-16 (Y13) students to achieve at least three certificates at either introductory or first level.

But all is still not plain sailing. A criticism made by some Ofsted and local authority inspectors is that targets sometimes set out experiences, rather than achievements or outcomes, to be aimed for. Targets should function as targets for the pupils' learning and achievement wherever possible. They might be supported by explicit strategies, that is, the means by which they are to be achieved. In such instances, it maybe difficult to distinguish between target and strategy. For example, here is an amplification of two of the targets given above, so that the areas of learning implied by the targeted experiences is brought out:

- Work with pupils in a mainstream primary school will challenge a particular boy's communication and personal skills, for example, stretching him to express pleasure, preference, appreciation and thanks – areas already prioritised in his IEP.
- A cultural visit will challenge a particular girl to adapt to an unfamiliar environment and to communicate with unfamiliar adults – areas prioritised by her transition review.

Sometimes we might not be sure what a child is trying to communicate, and so the assumption that targets can be set to predict and assess the pupil's exact responses could be unrealistic. Sometimes we might need to concentrate purely and simply on aspects of provision, rather than making the pupils' progress and achievement the defining factor for a target. On occasion, then, experiences or aspects of curricular provision, rather than attainment levels, may need to appear as school targets, because it can be extremely difficult to gauge the exact responses to situations by some pupils with SLD or PMLD. These we may call **process** targets, as opposed to **outcome** targets. (See Kent and Norwich, below, and the taxonomy of whole-school targets at the end of Chapter 5.)

By way of conclusion, we might say that, where individual pupils' targets do not match standard targets, such as NC level 4 in English, or five or more GCSE A* to C grades, the exception should be allowed. In such cases, the school can be expected to set out its performance targets in a manner that is appropriate to the integrity of the pupils' actual needs, curriculum, and individual targets. This has been illustrated in the examples provided above. And as experience develops, we can expect targets to make more use of progress and value-added measures.

Schools face the challenge of adopting or adapting systems of performance calibration, so that they can not only track individual pupils' learning and achievement, but also evaluate, plan for, realise and record their collective performance and development. Cohort performance targets are educationally meaningful when they are underpinned by a carefully considered overview of individual pupils' targets. Aggregation is likely to be difficult and misleading, when the numbers of pupils are small, and when their special needs are widely divergent. A school's development and improved performance depend on there being a proper relationship between the teachers' assessment of the pupils, their targets, the targets used by teaching, care and management teams, individual staff members' performance objectives and whole-school targets.

Whole-school targets may encompass features of provision and other aspects of school life, as well as pupils' academic attainment. These process targets might include, for example, increasing integration with mainstream, improving facilities and equipment, or developing ways of recording and accrediting pupils' achievements. (See the next chapter for further discussion of this.) Comparative performance data may provide an informative backdrop to such targets, but it is not sensible for those kinds of statistics to determine the choice of whole-school targets. Whole-school targets make sense if they reflect individual pupils' targets and the needs of the school in providing for the pupils' welfare, achievement and self-realisation.

Steps towards relevant and productive targets

Here are suggested steps in developing targets as a means of raising achievement:

- Prepare to assert your beliefs about what is possible and right in the pupils' educational interests.
- Make sure that your whole-school targets are clearly related to your school-improvement plan. See that your school-improvement plan and your whole-school targets reflect individual teachers' performance management objectives and teams' targets.
- Involve the governing body in strategic discussion about whole-school targets. Involve governors as far as possible in:
    - gathering information about the school's performance
    - decision-making about whole-school targets
    - monitoring and evaluating the school's performance against its targets

- presenting aspects of the school's performance to wider audiences and authorities.
- Consider how the statutory requirement to use targets for Y6, Y9 and Y11 might benefit your whole-school development planning and implementation.
- Look at measures of progress from the point of arrival, and year on year. Concentrate on gains for pupils over the year compared with their previous performance. Take only a subsidiary interest in comparing one year group's performance with other year groups'.
- See if there are any patterns or trends in achievements.
- Consider which groups might benefit from a concerted effort in one or more given areas of the curriculum or personal and social development.
- Collect assessments of individual pupils' progress for each year group, and, as far as possible, formulate an overview of each year group's targets.
- Agree a definition of one or more whole-school targets. Be clear and concrete about how evidence will be gathered to show success against the targets. Think through the implications for any changes in staffing or resources.
- Agree the strategies that will have to be used if the targets are to be reached.
- Agree the time-scales. Agree how progress will be monitored, and how outcomes will be evaluated and learned from.
- Arrange, well in advance, a meeting for all staff to discuss how the process of using targets has contributed to the effectiveness and improvement of care and teaching, and how the process might be developed further.
- Check the correspondence between whole-school targets, teams' targets, teachers' performance management objectives, and individual pupils' targets.

Evaluating your use of targets

In a very helpful paper, Tim Kent and Brahm Norwich (2000) report their development research project and provide guidance about how targets might work for individuals and schools where there are special educational needs. When Kent and Norwich researched how special schools in the southeast of England were currently using targets, they found that most special schools in the study were using processes of identifying areas for development and monitoring procedures. Most schools in the study were using both qualitative and quantitative indicators in their evaluations of development work. The consensus of professional opinion was in favour of using whole-school targets based on pupils' and groups' previous attainment and progress rather than comparisons with other schools. Some schools were targeting provision, rather than attainment, as a focus for improvement. These findings accord with what I have proposed throughout this chapter.

The questions below are based on Kent's and Norwich's work and might serve to help you audit your use of targets.

- How do you check that your summary assessments of pupils present as full and valid a picture of their strengths, progress, attainments, and areas for further learning as possible? How might you improve the roundedness and validity of the summaries you make?

- How do you check that different members of staff make consistent and equiv-alent assessments of pupils? How might consistency and equivalence in assessments be improved? (See Appendix 3.)

- How do you make comparisons between your pupils' attainments and the attainments of other pupils? Do you compare the attainments of a given group of your pupils with:
    - the attainments of pupils in similar schools?
    - the attainments of similar pupils in other schools?
    - the attainments of similar previous groups or cohorts of pupils in your school?
    - the attainments of that group in previous years?

In what way might comparison help to raise standards in your school?

The next chapter continues this theme.

7 Targets for inclusion and other aspects of education

Targets can be used in order to improve aspects of school performance beyond the academic. Rather than making the pupils' progress or achievement in subjects the defining factor, aspects of provision and ethos can be targeted. In Chapter 5 we called these process targets.

Now that the National Curriculum and its assessment arrangements are in place, now that the National Literacy and Numeracy strategies have been implemented, now that Ofsted inspections are established, now that PANDA reports and the availability of comparative performance data are familiar, and now that performance management has been introduced, time and attention may be turned to other aspects of school life and learning. Perhaps the most significant of these is inclusion.

In this chapter we will address these questions:

- What is inclusion, and why work on inclusion?
- How can you expect inclusion to feature in Ofsted inspections?
- What type of target might you use for inclusion?
- How might you manage the tension between wanting to achieve 'good results' and wanting to be inclusive?
- How might you make your school more inclusive?
- What other aspects of school life might you aim to improve by using targets?

What is inclusion? And why work on inclusion?

A statutory context for policy on inclusion is to be found in the government circular 10/99 (1999). Comprehensive guidance is provided by the Centre for Studies on Inclusive Education via its *Index for inclusion* (2000). The National Curriculum Handbook for Teachers (DfEE and QCA, 1999) devotes eight densely packed pages to the topic of inclusion; one page only is given to literacy with plenty of margin space, and one page to ICT likewise. There is a message in that. Inclusion was high on the government's agenda for the new millennium.

The inclusion agenda builds on and reaches beyond policy and practice for special education needs and equal opportunities. The essence of inclusion is that obstacles to learning are to be looked for in the school rather than in the person.

So rather than being satisfied with seeing how a person differs from others in ability or need, look at how the school adapts to the person. Look critically at how the school provides access, opportunity, stimulus and support for individuals. According to the inclusion agenda, being supportive and inclusive means increasing the school's capacity to respond to the full range of young people in the community. It means taking responsibility for what you can be responsible for, namely how you think and what you do.

By working on inclusion, you will be testing and raising the quality of all aspects of educational ethos, provision, and outcomes in your school. The effects of working to make your school inclusive should be a healthier school, a school well focused on learning, and a school that meets the needs of more young people than might have been thought possible some years ago.

How can you expect inclusion to feature in Ofsted inspections?

The government is committed to promoting inclusive education. All Ofsted inspectors have to be given training in what to look for regarding inclusion. According to that training, these are questions which inspectors may ask managers, teachers, non-teaching staff, governors, parents and pupils, in order to inform their judgements about a school's inclusivity:

- Are all the pupils achieving as much as they can? Do all pupils derive the maximum benefit from their education according to their individual needs? How are needs established? How are achievements measured and presented?
- Are any pupils, or groups of pupils, not achieving as much as they might?
- What do you do to inform yourself about possible differences in pupils' experiences and achievements? If there are differences between groups of pupils' achievements, access to curriculum opportunities and experiences in your school, how do you explain these?
- What have you done to address any such differences? Have local or national initiatives been used, for example, in relation to: literacy, numeracy or ICT skills; behaviour; attendance; reducing exclusions; access; out-of-school learning; in-class support; mentoring; study support; a specific key stage; flexible work-related curriculum arrangements; continuity between the phases of education; parental involvement; family learning; using funding or emphases arising from the school's status as a centre of excellence, investor in people, charter mark school, specialist or beacon school?
- What have you done, and what do you plan to do, to promote racial harmony, to prepare the pupils for living in a diverse and increasingly interdependent society, to prevent and challenge racism, sexism and other forms of anti-social discrimination?
- How do you monitor and evaluate your efforts to make what the school provides more just and more effective?

- How just and how effective is the experience you provide for all the pupils in your school?

What type of target might you use for inclusion?

Your choice of target can be made to reflect your choice between different kinds of success. Do you want academic success, as represented by the newspaper league tables? Do you want success in areas of school life that concern attitudes and behaviour, ethos and relationships? Do you want success in spiritual, cultural, moral and social respects, as well as in academic respects?

Applying the taxonomy at the end of Chapter 5, a number of options are clear. You might use absolute targets, involving no comparisons, in which case you would aim simply to broaden the intake to the school in certain ways, or aim to provide specific teaching or support or resources for pupils with particular needs or learning difficulties. You might use competitive targets, in which case you would aim to be more inclusive in certain respects than other schools with whom you want to be compared. You might use improvement targets, involving comparison with at least one aspect of the school's past performance, in which case you might, for example, aim to reduce exclusions or increase integration time for certain pupils currently taught apart from the mainstream.

Such targets might be school-self-referenced, relating to the school as a whole, or alternatively pupil-self-referenced targets, leading to individual or groups of pupils having opportunities that were previously unavailable to them.

You might use outcome targets which specify understandings, attitudes or qualities that you aim certain pupils to develop and show. The pupils concerned might be those intended to benefit directly in terms of gaining new access to opportunities. Alternatively, the pupils who should benefit might be those whose experience is intended to be extended as a result of their having greater contact with pupils previously not admitted to the school or some of its provisions.

You might use successive targets, and so apply lessons learned from the experience of one year's pupils to the subsequent teaching and learning of a following year's pupils. Or you might use progressive targets, in which case you would apply lessons learned from the experience of one year's pupils to the subsequent teaching and learning of those same pupils.

These are possible areas for targets you might consider in relation to inclusion:

- increasing opportunities for special and mainstream school pupils and teachers to work together, to learn together and from one another;
- deploying classroom assistants to work with pupils who might be at risk of receiving less support than you would wish;
- developing pupil mentoring or buddy arrangements, with training opportunities for the pupils in these roles;
- developing parents' and carers' involvement in curricular and extra-curricular activities;

- developing teachers' observation of one another as a way of exploring class-room interaction and intervention: seeking answers to the questions, *What helps pupils participate? What hinders pupils' participation? What can we do to remove barriers to participation?*
- developing a portfolio of examples of how barriers to pupils' participation can be overcome, and how participation can be increased and enriched.

How might you manage the tension between wanting to achieve 'good results' and wanting to be inclusive?

Change and development have to be seen as complex processes. It is possible for a school to become a victim of its own success. If its recent results are good, its targets will be set high. But if a current year group has a higher proportion of pupils with personal, social and educational needs, and if the school has a positive policy of inclusion, that is, welcoming into the school pupils who experience learning difficulties, the school may well face 'failure' inasmuch as it might fall short of achieving good results as measured by tests and norms. It might appear that the more a school accepts the pressure to get 'good results' in tests, the more it will have to penalise existing or prospective pupils with special educational needs; the more a school accepts the pressure to include pupils with special educational needs, the less likely it will be to meet high academic targets. This, at least, is how it can feel to head-teachers and staff, aware of the media and some expressions of public opinion.

Faced with conflicting demands, one option is to address the contradictions head on. A school's policies for inclusion and for performance targets can take account of one another, and be placed in the context of an overarching statement of intent for the school: to care for and raise achievement for all pupils. Allowance can explicitly be made for the fact that some pupils' achievements are not most appropriately gauged by means of norm-related test results. The appropriate measure for some pupils will be analysis of their progress. And pupils' Individual Education Plans offer a way of tracking progress.

You will be able to make connections between activities relating to individual pupils' needs, progress and attainments, and activities relating to improving cohorts' results. *Raising standards* has to be translated into *promoting the best possible welfare and success of every pupil*, for which both test results and individually focused considerations are appropriate. The micro-picture has to inform the macro-picture.

How might you make your school more inclusive?

Trying to make a school inclusive involves making systematic efforts to remove barriers that stand in the way of everyone's participation in education. It is likely to involve challenging and changing attitudes.

If you have not done so recently, you will want to audit your school's policy and practice. Your audit will inform your plan for development. These are questions you will need to ask yourself:

- Do people in your school work together and help one another?
- Are bullying and negative discrimination addressed and learned from so that their frequency drops?
- Is classroom discipline based on mutual respect?
- Do lessons develop the pupils' understanding of how people differ?
- Are all pupils equally valued?
- Are there high expectations for all pupils?

You will want to seek a complete range of views, and refer to results and statistical performance data, as well as to the evidence of people's perceptions. You will want to build a picture of how inclusive your school is, and then plan to work on areas which might be improved by means of targeted activity.

Given the intention to develop inclusive practices, and given structures to support monitoring and evaluation, what strategies might bring the benefits you want? Mel Ainscow, in his book *Understanding the Development of Inclusive Schools* (1999), presents valuable research which directs our attention to fundamental principles and processes of professional, interpersonal and social change. He outlines a number of ways in which you can seek to promote conditions such that every member of the school community is encouraged to learn. These strategies have been found to be associated with successful inclusion in particular, and with effective teaching and learning in general.

A key strategy involves making the best possible use of available resources to support learning. Chief amongst these resources are, of course, people. When assistants, parents, and the pupils themselves, play more of an active part in helping everyone learn, the more the school opens up. Improved pupil-to-pupil co-operation, in particular, is shown by strong research evidence to contribute to the development of inclusivity and to be associated with better learning conditions for everyone. Development can grow out of giving expression to the instinct to help, to enquire and solve problems together. (This parallels the first feature of effective teaching, discussed in Chapter 3.) Whenever I have seen older pupils helping younger pupils to learn, the work has had a positive quality and there have been benefits to both sets of pupils.

Perhaps the most obvious strategy involves starting with what you already know and do. Plan jointly, visit one another's classrooms, share outcomes, discuss details of provision and teaching interventions, with a view to fostering better communication and co-operation between teachers and pupils. Using what is familiar and current, rather than requiring change at the outset, development can grow out of your increasing shared experience, mutual trust and analysis.

As an extension of this, you can strive as a staff and management team to develop a shared language for your reflections on your work and its effectiveness. The more time you can spend together, learning about how one another think, feel and act, the stronger your basis for beneficial change. Discussing video-recordings of lessons, for example, has been found to be a very powerful stimulus to analysis and experimentation. This is not a new finding and resonates, for example, with the classic action research work of the Schools Council, reported by Ashton *et al.* (1980). Colleagues there were committed to making time and space at least once a week during a lesson to make a note of: what the pupils were doing; what the pupils were learning; what the pupils would do next; what they as teachers had been doing; what they were learning; and what they would do next. They would then meet every four weeks or so to report and debate issues emerging. Development can grow out of your making a community of people who think and talk about learning and teaching.

At the heart of developing more inclusive practices is a way of looking at people and the world. Inclusion means seeing differences between people as opportunities for learning. When you meet something you have not seen before in a pupil, it is a challenge. Do you try to fit the pupil to preconceived patterns; or do you pay attention, enquire, try a fresh approach, and learn? The second option relies on your feeling confident and supported enough to improvise when you meet pupils who appear not to fit in with what is expected and prepared. As an English teacher, I have learned more, for example, about reading and discussion work from pupils who have found these difficult than I did by any other means. The difficulties which individuals confront have caused me to probe more deeply into what I have taken for granted. Development can grow out of your learning how to use the surprise a pupil causes you as a spur to adapt and extend your teaching repertoire.

As well as treating difference as potentially instructive, you need to look out for blocks to pupils' participation. Be ready to focus on how pupils are put off from learning by physical features in the environment, by 'normal' ways of working, by expectations and attitudes they pick up on in teachers, assistants, peers and others. You can learn a great deal about this from how pupils respond and how they say they feel about how they are treated. Development can grow out of your increased awareness of barriers to learning and your willingness to overcome them with the pupils' and colleagues' support.

Crucially you need to create and maintain conditions that encourage experimentation. There is perhaps no greater challenge for teachers and managers than this. Risks have to be taken if teachers are to open up to fellow professionals and others. During the 1990s, it seems, visits to the classroom took on a monitorial or inspectorial character. What is needed is trust, respect and mutuality of endeavour. A culture and ethos of shared purpose, communication and willingness to innovate and try the unusual are demanding, but they are necessary if a school is to meet the challenge of including those who might ordinarily be excluded. Development can grow out of your feeling secure that new ways can be found to meet the new demands you face.

What other aspects of school life might you aim to improve by using targets?

Other ways in which aspects of school life might be targeted include:

- increasing pupils' participation in specific extra-curricular activities;
- developing indicators of spiritual, cultural, moral and social learning, and pro-moting activities accordingly;
- developing the use pupils make of breaktimes and recreational areas;
- improving the quality of pupils' experience at the beginning of the school day before the first lesson and at the end of scheduled lesson time;
- improving the quality of what pupils eat and drink during the school day;
- increasing pupils' opportunities to discuss and tackle personal problems.

You might go back to your school's mission statement or to the vision contained in your school-improvement plan. Which aspirations are being fulfilled, and which less so? A valuable source of information is provided by discussions with the pupils. Questionnaires and surveys of pupils' and parents' perceptions of the school are vital ingredients in the processes of enquiry, planning and development.

Ian Schagen (2000) offers valuable advice about how pupils', staff's and parents' opinions can be collected, measured and quantified, to help give as clear a picture as possible of a school's performance. He reminds us that 'Schools are multifaceted organisms whose features cannot be captured by any single indicator' (p. 56). The list of possible indicators which Schagen gives provides us in turn with an enriched view of the targets which a school might consider setting. So we might add to the list above:

- levels of unauthorised absence or lateness;
- types of destination chosen or achieved by pupils on leaving the school;
- money spent on books per pupil or on other resources;
- parents' attendance at meetings;
- staff turnover;
- levels of supply cover required for staff absence;
- percentage of pupils for whom the school is first choice;
- extent of over- or under-subscription.

All of this has to do with trying to make a school a better place for everyone to learn in. The choice of target depends on the school, its needs and potential, and the views of its members and community.

8   Subject teams and targets

In this chapter we shall consider how colleagues responsible for subjects and curriculum areas can monitor and develop their teams' effectiveness. I will refer to a number of ways in which this book might help you check and enhance your policy and practice, and to some research into the 'missing link' in school-improvement theory and practice – the work of subject teams. I believe the material I offer is relevant to year, key stage and subject teams in primary schools, as well as to departments in secondary schools, sixth form and further education colleges. Finally I will present statements for you to use in self-review. I believe also that the material presented here can be adapted to help care teams review and develop their work.

You can use the taxonomy of individual pupils' targets, at the start of Chapter 3, as a means of guiding, monitoring or evaluating practice. You can use the taxonomy of whole-school targets, given at the end of Chapter 4, as a means of guiding, monitoring and evaluating your subject team's use of cohort targets. You can refer to Appendices 2 and 3, respectively, as ways of checking or revising your marking policy and arrangements for consistency in assessment. Appendix 8 provides an overall policy statement which you can use to audit and develop the work of your team using assessments and targets.

My experience and instincts tell me that the work of teams is vital to the development of pupils' learning opportunities and schools' provision and effectiveness. We find this also in some research, though the territory is less well covered in the literature than we might expect. We saw testimony to the significance of teachers' and managers' teamwork in several contexts through Chapter 3, and Ainscow's research, referred to in the chapter before this one, bore it out quite emphatically. I want now refer to Alma Harris's findings, based on empirical evidence from her two evaluative studies of secondary school departments (2001) which offers strong and clear indications of the central role that teams play in curriculum and staff development.

Harris establishes that 'a positive "climate for change" is an important prerequisite of departmental effectiveness' (Harris *et al.*, 1995). She goes on to illustrate how:

> leadership, collaboration, communication, a focus on teaching and learning, enquiry and reflection were all shown to be important processes in fostering and sustaining departmental improvement. Those departments that had

improved and were contributing to school improvement had successfully built their internal capability to change and develop by working specifically upon these processes.

(Harris, 2001, p. 484)

The qualities of effective leadership were found to be the subject leader's having a clear vision and an ability to communicate it to colleagues. Subject leaders who were too authoritarian or laissez-faire were less successful and, in their cases, improvement proved very difficult to achieve. And more than that:

> Successive research studies have shown that within the most effective schools, leadership extends beyond the headteacher to encompass other levels within the school organisation (Harris, 1999; Busher and Harris, 2000). Indeed, the-orists are calling for a new perspective on leadership, one which involves a decentralised, devolved and shared approach to leadership within the school (Lambert, 1998). Within the improving departments, the evidence showed that heads of department had adopted a devolved approach to leadership that gave priority to the leadership of others within the department.
>
> (Harris, 2001, pp. 482–3)

Both school-effectiveness and school-improvement research underline the central importance of teachers' and managers' focusing on teaching and learning (Harris *et al.*, 1995). It was found that:

> those departments that were improving recognised that without a central focus on teaching and learning, their improvement efforts would become marginalised and the possibility of sustaining improvement would be sub-stantially reduced . . . . They had also engaged in enquiry and had involved students by consulting them about the quality of teaching and learning processes within the department.
>
> (Harris, 2001, pp. 483–4)

As we saw in my report on the Religious Studies department in August School (Chapter 2, pp. 21–3), a team's collection and scrutiny of pupils' performance data were essential to analysis of strengths and weaknesses, and to the definition of possible areas for development:

> The analysis of student-level data was shown to offer an important means of self-review within the departments. In addition, it provided the opportunity to set departmental targets closely related to teaching and learning.
>
> (Harris, 2001, p. 484)

Much of the work of Carol Fitzgibbon at the universities of Newcastle and Durham has been to provide teachers and managers with means to handle, interrogate and interpret performance data. Some LEAs also provide such services.

It may be that practitioners recognise the significance of developmental work at team level more readily than researchers. This would be an interesting area for further research. In the meantime, it is the core argument of this book that the four dimensions of activity relating to targets need to take notice of one another. Correspondences need to be confirmed between:

1   individual pupils' targets;
2   teams' targets;
3   managers' and teachers' performance management objectives;
4   whole-school targets and improvement.

To help you audit and develop the work of your team, here are some checklists. I suggest you decide whether your practice matches the statements. If it does not, are there good reasons, or do you have better ways of working?

As a subject team:

- We have a progressive scheme of work, addressing programmes of study and attainment targets.
- Our long-term planning sets objectives for key stages and year groups.
- Our medium-term planning sets objectives for units of work.
- Our short-term planning sets lesson objectives.
- Our planning addresses the needs of high-, mid-, and low-attaining pupils.
- Our planning addresses the needs of pupils who experience SEN.
- We use individual pupils' targets, and we monitor, evaluate and develop the part they play in helping pupils learn.
- We follow an agreed marking policy.
- We have a consistent approach to the assessment of work both within units and across the school year.
- We standardise our formal assessments.
- We transfer information about the pupils' progress and attainment at the end of each year.
- We have a consistent approach to annual reporting to parents and carers of the pupils' progress and attainment.
- We take account of whole-school targets and improvement planning, and of our own professional development, through performance management.

Our annual subject review informs senior management and governing body of:

- year groups' progress and attainment;
- targets for year groups in the coming year;
- strategies to support the pursuit of those targets;
- staff-training needs and action;
- extra-curricular successes and plans;
- other needs and developments;

- our team's contributions to whole-school improvement and targets.

Our subject file contains illustrations of:

- our scheme of work and planning;
- pupils' tasks;
- pupils' work and assessments;
- pupils' targets;
- records and reports of pupils' achievements;
- exemplars of work, assessed and standardised at given levels.

Our subject leader conducts an annual self-review, referring to progress and attainment indicated by the following:

- pupils' individual needs and goals;
- expectations for pupils of that age;
- expectations for pupils whose prior or predicted performance is at given levels
- National Curriculum (or P-Scale) levels or relevant qualification criteria;
- progress in our subject's performance related to whole-school improvement and targets.

9 Performance management and objectives

This chapter concerns the targets that professionals in school use as a means of developing their performance. Because the language of performance management calls these 'objectives', we shall follow suit.

In this chapter we shall consider:

- how using targets and objectives might illustrate and enhance your capability as a teacher;
- performance management legislation;
- relating performance-management objectives to whole-school improvement;
- defining effective teaching;
- lesson observation: purposes, consequences and methods;
- critical friendship, and how to use objectives to improve your performance;
- how to check changes you make to your ways of working.

How using targets and objectives might illustrate and enhance your capability as a teacher

Your use of targets and objectives might provide valuable evidence of capability in every aspect of your work. The judgements an observer or inspector makes about your capability may be informed by the way you:

- set appropriate targets with and for pupils;
- monitor and promote pupils' progress towards their targets;
- assess, record and report pupils' achievement measured against their targets;
- work towards your own performance management objectives;
- help to achieve your subject or year team's targets;
- help to achieve the school's targets.

By focusing on one or more of these, you may seek to improve your pupils' learning, your own performance, the performance of your team, and the performance of the school as a whole.

Performance-management legislation

It is not a recent invention that school managers and teachers think about their strengths and achievements, and try to identify ways in which they might improve their effectiveness for the benefit of pupils' welfare and learning. Affecting such concerns now, though, are the performance management arrangements introduced in the autumn of 2000 (DfEE, 2000c). These oblige every headteacher and teacher to have an annual appraisal meeting in order to review performance and set new objectives.

Headteachers are joined for this purpose by two or three appointed governors, whose responsibilities are discussed further in the next chapter, and by an external adviser, accredited and contracted by Cambridge Education Associates (CEA) on behalf of the DfES. Each teacher's performance management is facilitated by a Team Leader, who may be the headteacher or a colleague delegated by the headteacher, often a deputy, senior teacher, subject leader, head of year, or key-stage co-ordinator.

Both headteachers and teachers have to set at least one objective relating to pupils' performance. Headteachers have to set at least one objective relating to leadership and management, and teachers may do likewise if that is appropriate to their role in the school. Teachers are expected to set one or more objectives relating to their own continuing professional development, and headteachers have that as an option too. Objectives are expected to be clear, precise and challenging.

The governing body of every school has a salary committee, which should consider information deriving from the performance management process. In other words, the prime focus of performance management is enhancing the school's effectiveness and promoting the continuing professional development of its employees, but it may be called on to contribute to decisions about salary.

Performance management is also the context in which we should view threshold assessment. For teachers, who have appropriate qualifications and experience, and who are not in a school's leadership team, there are eight standards which define qualification for threshold status and its additional payment. Headteachers make the initial judgement about teachers' applications for threshold, and this is checked by threshold assessors appointed by CEA on behalf of the DfES.

Performance management, threshold assessment and initial teacher training have combined to make maintaining a professional development portfolio a virtually essential practice for every teacher. This records evidence of and testimony to: knowledge and understanding; planning; teaching; use of assessment, recording and reporting; pupils' progress; continuing professional development; contribution to the school's wider aspirations; and professional characteristics.

Relating performance-management objectives to whole-school improvement

Performance management is perhaps the last piece in a jigsaw. It brings closer to realisation the prospect of making coherent connections between whole-school development, teachers' professional development, and pupils' learning.

The fulcrum of development and the source of coherence are arguably provided by the work of teams. Senior management teams, subject teams, year teams and key-stage teams need to review and plan the further development of their work together, feeding into the performance management process experienced by each teacher. This provides a crucial link between the whole-school dimension and the particularity of pupils' learning.

When a headteacher reviews her/his performance and sets new objectives, it makes sense for her/him to take into account the achievements and needs of the institution as a whole, in other words, the whole-school improvement plan and agenda. The headteacher's performance has to be set in the context of the whole school's performance. The same can be said of every teacher's performance. When headteachers and teachers have their annual performance management meetings, they should address issues that are personal to them, as well as issues relating to their team and institutional issues reflecting the interests of the school as a whole.

The objectives that headteacher and staff set for the year should collectively inform, and be informed by, their team's and the school's improvement plan. Contradictions and tensions between individuals' priorities and team or school imperatives should be discussed and ironed out in the performance-management meetings. Team and whole-school targets need to be supported by the efforts that everyone is making. The work of every individual should be supported by the team's and the institution's resources, structures and systems, and by the measures taken to raise standards.

Defining effective teaching

It is far from easy or simple to judge whether or not a particular piece of teaching has been successful. The quality of the learning might only become apparent a very long time after a pupil has left the classroom and the school. Over the course of a year or a key stage, teaching effectiveness might be judged on the basis of outcomes, but attainment measures, as we currently have them, exclude a wide range of personal, social, attitudinal, physical and practical information about pupils' experiences, achievements and capabilities. The narrowness of conventional examination qualifications was a major reason for the development in the 1980s of records of achievement in England and Wales (see Burgess and Adams, 1980, and DES, 1984). Records of achievement are not widely used, though, to inform authoritative judgements about the quality of teachers' or schools' effectiveness.

The validity of judgements about the quality of teaching is greatly enhanced when pupils' perceptions are taken into account. It is impossible for any observer of mere behaviour to know what a pupil is thinking and feeling. One cannot know what a pupil is really doing when s/he appears to be on or off task, for example. Gazing out of the window may be productive contemplation, or time-wasting. Sitting bent over a text may, or may not, be reading. Who is to know? Having the benefit of the pupil's own account seems essential, but is in itself no guarantee of the 'truth'.

Research has not been able to establish the essential and necessary ingredients of successful teaching. For a variety of practical purposes, though, working accounts are required. Accounts of what it means to teach and to teach well are important, not least because teachers' performance is now scrutinised for several different reasons. It has become a feature of life in schools that teachers are observed or monitored several times a year. How what is being looked for is defined has had to evolve in response to the monitoring and evaluating that have necessarily taken place with or without policy and guidance.

Imperfect though they must be, checklists of competences are inevitably used to inform decisions across a range of contexts. Inspectors need to know what to look for, or they could not pretend to discriminate between 'outstanding', 'very good', 'good', 'satisfactory', 'unsatisfactory', or 'poor' lessons. As best they can, teacher educators and trainers have to articulate what it takes to teach and to teach well. Headteachers and assessors, whose task is to identify teachers sufficiently competent to 'cross the threshold', depend on explicit standards to make their judgements. Schools' performance-management policies, adopted during the autumn term 2000, usually contain lesson observation schedules and protocols.

Observation for the purposes of teacher education and performance management is perhaps less coolly judgemental than observation during Ofsted inspection. Any observation can now have a bearing on how well the teacher may be said to teach. We live in times which set some store by mechanisms of evaluation and accountability.

According to the Ofsted handbook for inspection, for example,

> In determining their judgements, inspectors should consider the extent to which teachers:
>
> - show good subject knowledge and understanding in the way they present and discuss their subject
> - are technically competent in basic teaching skills
> - plan effectively, setting clear objectives that pupils understand
> - challenge and inspire pupils, expecting the most of them, so as to deepen their knowledge and understanding
> - use methods which enable all pupils to learn effectively
> - manage pupils well and insist on high standards of behaviour
> - use time, support staff and other resources, especially information and communications technology, effectively
> - assess pupils' work thoroughly and use assessments to help and encourage pupils to overcome difficulties
> - use homework effectively to reinforce and/or extend what is learned in school
>
> and the extent to which pupils and students:

- acquire new knowledge and skills, develop ideas and increase their understanding
- apply intellectual, physical or creative effort in their work
- are productive and work at a good pace
- show interest in their work, are able to sustain concentration and think and learn for themselves
- understand what they are doing, how well they have done and how they can improve.

(Ofsted, 2000a)

Lesson observation: purposes, consequences and methods

Before 1990 few teachers were often observed teaching, and there was little consensus about how teaching performance should be evaluated. Times have changed. Now the identities of the observers, the reasons for observation, and the consequences, are many. Here are some of the possibilities:

Observer	*Consequence*	*Reason*
• senior manager;	• constructive feedback;	• to offer the teacher being observed feedback;
• subject leader/curriculum co-ordinator;	• planning and action to improve personal performance;	• to enable the observer to learn from the teacher being observed;
• colleague with no greater status;	• stages in capability procedures;	
• school governor;	• recording of evidence to support threshold assessment application;	• to make a judgement about the teacher's competence;
• trainee teacher;		
• classroom assistants;		• to promote public understanding of education;
• parents and carers;		
• LEA inspector/consultant;	• planning/reviewing the curriculum;	• to prepare support and advice for the teacher;
• Ofsted inspector;		
• HMI;	• commendation;	• to inform research;
• trainee/returning teacher;	• thanks and appreciation;	• to qualify the teacher for NQT status or for more advanced competence status.
• trainee teacher's mentor/ tutor;	• revised subject/school development planning;	
• colleague from elsewhere looking at good practice;	• recording of performance management evidence;	
• QCA/NLS/NNS monitor;	• award of certificate;	
• researcher;	• judgement of competence logged by headteacher;	
• IiP/charter mark assessor;		
• visitor, e.g. politician, civil servant, royalty, overseas guest.	• publication of research findings.	

Quality in teaching is defined differently for different purposes by different authorities. For example, the Teacher Training Agency's publication of standards (TTA, 1998) contains extensive lists of the knowledge, skills, understanding and qualities thought necessary for the job, and these may be referred to on many different kinds of occasion, including initial teacher training, mentoring, and assessment for qualified teacher status. The consultancy company Hay/McBer (2000) was commissioned by the DfEE at a cost of three million pounds sterling to provide a definition of teacher effectiveness, which served to determine the threshold standards, and whose claim to scientific rigour has been seriously contested by the British Educational Research Association (BERA, 2001). And Ofsted, in its handbook for school inspection (2000a) quoted above, sets out its criteria for judging teaching quality, and these have come to be used in many schools to inform internal monitoring of teaching by senior and middle managers.

It was the Hay/McBer work which informed the DfEE's guidance on lesson observation, given in its *Model Performance Management Policy* (2000b). There are other lesson observation schedules available to schools. Headteacher and staff are probably best advised to adapt any they think appropriate to their own circumstances. The framework offered here is simpler than many, including the Hay/McBer model.

The recording of weaknesses and areas for improvement is a sensitive issue. My suggestion is that the observer should note what pupils, teachers, and classroom assistants do, according to five key aspects of teaching. Concentrate on what the pupils do, and what they appear to learn, and use what you observe to illuminate:

- lesson planning, content and structure, and how well these are matched to the pupils' interests, prior learning and learning needs;
- the teacher's presentation of information, expectations, explanations and instructions;
- the teacher's responses to and interventions in the pupils' activities;
- the teacher's assessments and reflections with the pupils on their learning;
- how the teacher uses the time, space, assistants and resources available.

Notes can be made using the format below, and these would provide the basis for discussion afterwards between the teacher and the observer. The aim would be, through discussion, to reach agreement about what might be recorded, highlighting successes, any weaknesses and possible areas for development. Any record might later be used as part of the performance management process, as part of the teacher's continuing professional development portfolio, or for other purposes, with the teacher's permission.

I suggest that the observer's notes, against each of those aspects, should be placed under one of three headings. The observer should comment according to whether s/he:

- considers what s/he sees and hears to be successful teaching;
- is unsure about the success or otherwise of what s/he sees and hears;
- considers what s/he sees and hears to indicate something unsatisfactory about the lesson.

Afterwards, when the observer and the teacher come to discuss the lesson and the observer's notes, the convention should be that the teacher has the opportunity to give her/his own impression of the lesson and comment on what the observer noted. The discussion might cause the observer to change her/his view of what appeared successful, what s/he was ambivalent about, or what appeared unsatisfactory. The purpose of the discussion is for the observer and the teacher to agree what should be recorded, and what action, if any, is to follow.

The teacher might agree to let others see the record, and so has to approve its content. Very many different kinds of action might follow the observation and the discussion. Both the observer and the teacher have to be clear, and in agreement, with the record and about what is to happen next.

Observation Notes

	Successful	To think about	Unsatisfactory
Planning and matching			
Conveying expectations and information			
Enabling			
Assessing, reviewing and using targets			
Using time, space, staff, and resources			

Record of Observation and Discussion

Teacher: . . . .   Observer: . . . .

Date: . . . .   Lesson: . . . .

Strengths:

Weaknesses and action to be taken:

Areas for development and action to be taken:

Critical friendship, and how to use objectives to improve your performance

If we ask how teachers might develop the capabilities itemised by Ofsted, or by any other authority, a range of answers is possible. A range of steps is possible following any observation of teaching. No single prescription can be expected to guarantee a teacher's proficiency in all situations on all occasions. Essential though it might seem to be that the teacher respect the pupils, important though it might be that s/he plan conscientiously, sensible as it might seem that s/he share lesson objectives with the pupils, no single attitude or approach is powerful enough to solve what is a multifaceted problem. And using targets likewise can be no panacea for teaching capability.

As Ofsted's list implies, and as the Teacher Training Agency's standards (TTA, 1998) demonstrate, and as experience of lesson observation usually shows, teaching is complex and extremely wide-ranging in the demands in makes. Teaching is as much a matter of being as it is of doing. Who you are, as well as what you imply about yourself and others, as much as what you deliberately do, determines how pupils respond to you. And working with others, in a team and in partnership with individual colleagues who challenge yet support you, is an essential ingredient of continuing professional development. We have seen repeatedly throughout this book how significant ethos and teamwork are.

An early step in making good use of objectives to improve your teaching is to create a picture of your teaching strengths, any weaknesses, and potential areas for development, informed by:

- measures of your pupils' progress;
- your own reflections;
- pupils' perceptions;
- colleagues' perceptions and monitoring;
- parents' and carers' perceptions;
- observations made by welfare and classroom assistants, therapists, social workers and other staff who work in or for the school;
- governors' visit reports;
- Ofsted and LEA or diocesan inspection visit reports.

You increase the chances of benefiting from performance management, if you keep the number of objectives to a minimum, and at the outset arrange for your progress to be monitored and for evidence of your progress to be collected. It helps if your school has an agreed policy on how performance management objectives should be framed. I suggest good objectives:

- give a rationale for their being a priority;
- state what you aim to do differently or better;
- are supported by an account of what steps you will take;
- make explicit how you and others will know whether they have been achieved;
- are critically and constructively monitored and evaluated;
- help you and others learn about teaching, learning, educational provision, and pupils' experience.

Examples of objectives are given in the DfEE's *Performance Management Framework* (2000c), together with contextual information about each of the scenarios presented, and suggestions about how the teacher in each case might set about achieving the objective set.

A key to continuing professional development is commitment to reflection in the company of one or more critical friends. Being a friend means sharing common cause or interest. The cause or interest that colleagues share one with another, and with governors, is the school's well-being and improvement, the pupils' welfare and learning. Being critical means being explicitly aware that yours is just one point of view, dependent on your position and interest, implying that there are always alternative points of view, and that your own view can be enriched by being placed alongside others. Sometimes a visitor to the classroom is able to develop critical friendship with the teacher. At other times, as in inspection, the visitor has to take a judgemental stance, allowing the teacher no real scope to share her/his perceptions or agree an evaluation. Critical friendship grows through dialogue, and offers the possibility that the partners might resolve their individual views in consensus. This was what I set out to encourage in the lesson observation protocol outlined above.

How to check changes you make to your ways of working

Improving your pupils' performance means trying to work more effectively. This means changing what you do: stopping doing some things, starting doing other things, doing some things more and other things less. Performance management means little if it does not entail such change.

All of this implies and requires some means of taking stock, some means of gauging present energy output in order to prepare greater effectiveness, some means of representing to yourself, and perhaps to others to whom you are accountable, just what you have been doing and what you will be doing differently. Unrealistic assumptions could jeopardise innovative projects and wreck good intentions. To help in this respect, I offer a checklist of teachers' activities and a checklist of headteachers or senior managers' activities.

These checklists are simpler than many you will find elsewhere, simpler than the TTA's and Ofsted's accounts already referred to in this chapter. Neither checklist below claims to describe quality in teaching or in management. What each does is list the kinds of activity that teachers and senior managers respectively carry out, so that quantitative analyses can be made to support changes in the detail, scope and balance of their work. The checklists can be used to log the number of hours and proportions of time spent on different types of activity. This kind of itemisation serves not only to illustrate where new pressures may fall and so how change may be managed; it serves also to reveal the variety and extent of teachers' and managers' workloads for the information of, for example, governors and authorities, who need to understand educational professionals' commitments, both current and projected. Full and deliberate account has to be taken of the fact that there are only so many hours in the day, and a person's health can only tolerate so many demands of so many different kinds.

The teachers' checklist can be adapted according to the individual teacher's role and responsibilities.

> *Per week: total hours for each category*

1.0 *Teaching*
   i.e. promoting pupils' learning, individually or in classes.
1.1 Timetabled time:
   Plus number of classes, number of pupils, number of subjects.
1.2 Non-timetabled time
   arising directly from lessons, e.g. in breaks, lunchtimes, after school.

2.0 *Preparation*
   directly for lessons, carried out outside lesson time –
2.1 Planning, thinking, researching, reading, meeting.
2.2 Preparing materials, resources, hardware.
2.3 Writing up notes, before and after lessons.

3.0 *Responding to pupils' work and assessment*
   directly relating to pupils' work, carried out outside lesson time –

3.1   Marking pupils' work.

3.2   Making formal assessments, e.g. NC Teacher Assessments, coursework, practicals, orals.

3.3   Reporting to people outside school, including parents and carers.

4.0   *Pupils' welfare*
      directly involving the pupils in person –

4.1   As classteacher or pastoral tutor.

4.2   Supervising, e.g. on duty during breaks, bus duty, etc.

4.3   Formally or informally as counsellor or nurse.

5.0   *Co-operation and liaison*
      with colleagues in school and elsewhere, including parents and carers, social service, welfare and medical agencies, the police, probation officers, and so on –

5.1   Colleagues in school.

5.2   Parents and carers.

5.3   Other agencies.

6.0   *Extra-curricular work*
      with and for pupils –

6.1   Performance, display, publishing of pupils' work.

6.2   Organising or participating in pupils' excursions, competitions, activities, e.g. sport, drama, clubs.

7.0   *Continuing professional development*
      of self and others –

7.1   Attending courses, looking at other colleagues' practice.

7.2   Professional reading.

7.3   Training colleagues for initial and in-service training agencies.

7.4   Other activities, e.g. travel on school business, not to and from work.

8.0   *Special responsibilities*
      nowhere else referred to –

8.1   Formally provided for, e.g. as subject leader.

8.2   Informally undertaken, e.g. voluntarily, fundraising, promoting understanding of the school . . .

The equivalent for a headteacher or member of the senior management team (SMT) is closely based on the TTA's National Standards for Headteachers (1998).

1.0   *Providing strategic direction for and leading the development of the school*
      working with –

1.1   SMT.

1.2   Other members of staff.

1.3   Governors.

1.4   Other responsible agencies such as the LEA, diocese, trusts, or public finance partners.

2.0   *Securing and sustaining effective teaching and learning*
       relating to –
2.1   The environment, code of behaviour, and ethos of the school.
2.2   The curriculum and its assessment.
2.3   The quality of teaching.
2.4   The quality of care provided for pupils.
2.5   The use of individual pupils' targets, performance management objectives, and whole-school improvement targets.
2.6   Partnership with parents and carers, to support and improve pupils' learning and achievement.
2.7   The community, including business and industry, to extend and enrich the curriculum and other aspects of school provision.

3.0   *Leading and managing staff*
       e.g. by planning, teaching, meeting, monitoring, evaluating, and through performance management; working with –
3.1   SMT.
3.2   Members of staff with specific responsibilities, e.g. SENCo, subject leaders, co-ordinators.
3.3   Other members of the teaching staff.
3.4   Members of the non-teaching staff.

4.0   *Efficient and effective deployment of staff and resources*
4.1   Recruiting staff.
4.2   Deploying staff.
4.3   Developing staff.
4.4   Managing and organising accommodation.
4.5   Managing, monitoring, reviewing and improving the use of all available resources.

5.0   *Accountability*
5.1   Creating and developing an organisation in which all members of staff recognise they are accountable for the school's performance and reputation.
5.2   Providing information for and communicating with the governors of the school.
5.3   Providing information for and communicating with partners such as the LEA, diocese, trusts and private finance partners.
5.4   Providing information for and communicating with parents and carers.

The overall effect should be to enhance the quality of what each teacher and headteacher does under the headings in that job description.

10 Governance, school improvement and targets

In this chapter we will address governors' responsibility for performance management and governors' role in the school's use of targets. Many of the questions we will tackle have been raised by governors in training sessions I have run. We will consider:

- the purpose, process and priorities of school-improvement planning;
- why the governing body is involved in performance management (PM), and what the governing body's role is;
- how the governing body carries out its role in PM;
- a case study of a school's principles, and possible areas for the headteacher's objectives;
- the governors' responsibilities in relation to the use of targets and benchmarking;
- information available to help governors gain a view of their school's performance;
- questions you should be asking about your school's performance data;
- how statutory target-setting might be carried out;
- the pupils' role in the target-setting process;
- what happens if the targets you have set appear after a while to be too easy to achieve, or impossible to reach;
- how you avoid losing breadth in education and avoid teaching to the tests;
- whether you are just aiming for the average when you use targets indicated by the government's statistics;
- whether governors should have their own targets;
- the essential ingredients in your work with performance data and targets.

The purpose, process and priorities of school-improvement planning

In order to tackle school-improvement planning you need to be aware of your school's strengths and weaknesses. It is vital to recognise and celebrate the strengths the school has. But however well the school is doing, there will be ways in which the pupils might be helped to achieve even higher standards. This is the function of school improvement. School improvement involves making provision better, enhancing pupils' experiences and raising standards.

Provision refers to what the school offers its pupils. This comprises the accommodation, the resources, the staffing, the curriculum and its assessment, and the teaching. Provision also encompasses such elements as care of pupils and ethos. Any of these might be improved. The buildings might be extended or modernised. The resources might be increased or better targeted. Staffing improvements might focus on professional developments or recruitment. The curriculum might be better planned and the assessment better used to inform planning. Teaching and care might be better focused on pupils' individual needs.

What the pupils experience depends on what the school provides. Their experience is made up of the school's environment, the resources they are given, the level and quality of teaching and support staff, curriculum opportunities and lessons and an ethos of respect, care and encouragement.

The quality of pupils' experiences determines the standard of their learning and achievement. The word 'standards' refers to what the pupils achieve. Standards include pupils' attainment and progress in subjects as well as in their personal and social learning and growing maturity. It covers their attitudes, and evidence of this can be found in their responses to their peers and others in the community, in their confidence and in their levels of responsibility. Raising standards means pupils achieving better outcomes: academically, personally and socially.

Standards are what the pupils achieve. You cannot raise standards directly. What you can do is improve provision in order to enhance pupils' experiences, which in turn, should enable them to achieve higher standards. This is best done by staff and governors working together.

Your planning needs first to identify strengths and weaknesses in standards achieved. It is helpful to use two categories: high standards of achievement, and standards of achievement which are not high enough. Remember that standards of achievement are academic, personal and social, not just progress and attainment in subjects but attitudes and behaviour too.

Your planning needs next to take account of appropriate evidence. How will you know whether standards in any given area are high enough? How will you know whether the things you set out to improve by your current improvement plan are indeed being achieved? You need to refer to three sources of evidence, namely:

- performance data, particularly comparing your results with schools like yours;
- people's observations, e.g. through internal monitoring by staff and governors;
- judgements by inspectors and consultants.

Overall then, you draw on information created within the school and information provided by agencies outside the school. Some of the information is quantitative and some is qualitative. You use these sources of information to build a picture of your school's strengths and weaknesses.

Staff and governors should now have two lists. One list shows where standards of achievement are high and where improvements have been brought about by current school improvement. The other list shows where standards of achievement are not high enough or where school-improvement planning has yet to bear fruit. The successes need to be celebrated and this prepares the way to looking at the areas requiring improvement.

One way of deciding priorities is through the work of a school-improvement group, for example, comprising the head, deputy, chair and vice-chair, plus key personnel according to the given focus. But there is a variety of alternatives. Whatever method you choose, you need to draw on information from a range of people and agencies. The important thing is for staff and governors to agree an initial list of priorities for school improvement. These might include areas as diverse as, for example, ICT, geography, pupils' creativity, and behaviour in the playground.

When deciding priorities for school improvement, consideration is given to:

- the views of head and staff;
- outcomes from the previous school-improvement plan;
- performance data for each year group;
- expected attainment for each year group;
- performance against recent and relevant targets;
- a summary of curriculum strengths and weaknesses;
- the perceptions of pupils, parents and governors;
- resources, including people's time, and finance, i.e. the delegated budget, Standards Fund and other income;
- progress on the key points for action following Ofsted inspection;
- pyramid and/or cluster priorities;
- the school-improvement consultant's views, through the conclusions of her/his annual report to governors;
- the LEA's education development plan priorities;
- national policies and initiatives.

Of all considerations the most important is likely to be the views of head and staff. Their thoughts will be borne out by other sources of information. For example, it is always illuminating to find out what pupils think of their school experience. The school-improvement plan will have a number of sections dealing with different types of priority. These conventionally include:

- curriculum and assessment
- policies
- staffing, staff and professional development
- finance, premises and resources
- communication with parents and community links.

The section on the curriculum may well be the longest, but any of policies, personnel, finance, and communication could be vital to moving the school forward.

Although a group may suggest priorities to the governing body, the governing body needs to own the school-improvement plan. The way to do that is for the governors to discuss which of the suggested priorities they want the school to focus on. Using the head's steer, the governing body then sets down the direction for taking the school forward.

Once priorities are agreed, the head decides how each of the priorities will be addressed. The head takes responsibility for formulating an action plan, detailing:

- specific tasks
- responsibilities
- time-scale
- cost implications, including time and resources
- success criteria
- monitoring arrangements.

The governing body needs to feel a sense of ownership of the priorities in the plan, and the head and senior management team must be able to engage wholeheartedly with the content and implications of the plan. It is at this point that the governing body stands aside while the details are worked out and relevant staff are consulted. It is especially important that everyone who has a part to play in the plan's implementation knows how their contribution will be supported, monitored and evaluated.

Once the detailed plan has been drawn up the head gives copies to members of the governing body and explains the details to them. The governing body needs to feel that the plan has every chance of success, making sure that the priorities have been properly resourced and that clear evidence of progress and success will be made available. Once the governing body has confidence in the plan, it can approve it.

It may be helpful to delegate the deputy head to produce a summary of the plan to be distributed to all the staff and governors. Parents, too, may welcome a single sheet digest of the plan.

The areas that will concern the governing body's committees are likely to be those of policies, finance, premises, and communication with parents. The first time the committees meet, following the approval of the plan they will need to agree a schedule addressing the parts of the plan relevant to their committee.

It would be very helpful to the governing body if a school-improvement group received a detailed termly report from the head on progress with the plan. The group could then, in turn, provide a brief summary to the governing body. Progress reports might include: development activities; possible impact on pupils' performance; considerations of amendment to the plan. The first term's report could concentrate on initiatives that have begun. The second term might bring in signs of whether the activities are progressing as anticipated. There might, for example, be a need for more resources or a need to extend the time-scale. The third term's report could pick up on the possible impact on pupils' performance.

The governing body might receive and considers an annual report from a school-improvement group on the plan's outcomes at the end of the period of the plan.

As thoughts turn to making a new improvement plan, judgements have to be made as to how successful the current plan has been made. Decisions have to be made as to whether activities have been successfully completed or need to be taken forward. By the end of the second term it should be becoming clear which priorities are really working well and which, if any, will require a longer period or extra support to bring them to fruition. The formal report on the success of the plan will have to reach the governing body after the new plan has been agreed and begun to be acted on.

It is important for the governing body to congratulate staff on their success in implementing the plan. Useful ways of doing this include writing a letter to staff, minuting congratulations, and publishing a brief statement in the annual report to parents.

Why the governing body is involved in performance management (PM), and what the governing body's role is

The governing body is required by statute to oversee the school's PM policy. This enables governors to play a role that gives an active focus to their overall responsibilities, which are to give strategic direction, to provide critical friendship, and to be accountable to government and the community.

There are two parts to the governors' role in PM. Senior management, staff and governing body have to agree and review policy for performance management in the school. And two or three governors represent the governing body in carrying out an annual review and objectives setting exercise with the headteacher.

How the governing body carries out its role in PM

As far as the school's PM policy is concerned, your role as governors is to receive reports about how the policy is working in practice and to support its smooth running through questioning and discussion of issues arising.

In order to carry out the headteacher's performance management, the governing body is required to appoint a lead governor and one or two others for the purpose. These are called appointed governors and should begin their task towards the end of the school year, so that they can recommend the selection of an external adviser and make contact with that person. The team of appointed governors contacts Cambridge Education Associates (CEA: the contracted operating agency), agrees with the headteacher what information should go to the external adviser, and sets up the performance management review visit, perhaps in the summer term, but usually in the autumn term.

The main focus of the meeting is a review of the headteacher's performance over the preceding year and the setting of new objectives. In practice, governors and/or headteacher may raise any issue that is felt relevant to performance. There should be at least two objectives. They should be reflected in the school-improvement plan. At least one objective must relate to pupils' progress and attainment, and one to leadership and management. The headteacher can choose also to set at least one objective for her/his continuing professional development. One of the team of appointed governors makes a brief statement, summarising the discussion at the meeting, and providing a sound basis for future objectives and reviewing. Within ten days of the meeting this statement has to be sent to the headteacher and chair of governors. The headteacher has ten days to add written comments, if s/he wishes.

Further advice is provided by the DfEE in its *Performance Management: Guidance for Governors* (2000a), together with examples of headteachers' objectives.

A case study of a school's principles, and possible areas for the headteacher's objectives

November School – first, 4–8, rural

Statement of principles for the use of performance management objectives in our school. An objective:

- depends on the governors' and teachers' having time to reflect and discuss;
- helps us get where we want to go;
- is not a measure of teachers' performance or efficiency, because there are many variables beyond their control in the outcomes of the teachers' work;
- helps us all share our perceptions, strategies, reflections, values and beliefs;
- is like a manifesto for our school;
- can help us trace how a group of pupils develops and performs;
- relates to the school year, while our school development plan has the function of plotting expenditure against development activities for LEA audit purposes;
- may run over two years.

Possible areas for the headteacher's objectives:

- progress and attainment (e.g. expressed in terms of percentages of pupils attaining given levels);
- attendance;
- staff retention;
- budget;
- parental response and involvement (e.g. how many visit);
- pupils' response, attitudes and behaviour;
- prioritised items from the job description.

Next we turn to the governing body's responsibility for whole-school targets and the use of targets generally. In providing an overview, I will draw on several writers' contributions to a very useful magazine, *The Dorset Governor*, between spring 1998 and autumn 1999. In addition to myself, the contributors were: Les Cowling, Adviser for Assessment, Dorset School Effectiveness Service; Nigel Gann, Consultant, Trainer and Writer; June Nisbet, Team Leader on the School Government Team at the DfEE; David Rees, Dorset Governor Services Co-ordinator; Mike Young, Head of the Dorset School Effectiveness Service.

What the governors' responsibilities are in relation to the use of targets and benchmarking

It does no harm to remind ourselves that the governors' key tasks are to:

* help raise standards of achievement;
* provide a strategic view;
* ensure accountability;
* act as critical friend.

Having a bearing on each of those tasks are the analysis of performance data and the use of targets to guide and review pupils' progress and achievement. Governors need to make themselves familiar with:

* the school's results over at least the past three years;
* teachers' forecasts of predicted results;
* the LEA's, or equivalent agency's, analyses of test, exam, and assessment data for schools in the locality or similar schools;
* QCA's national benchmarking information which allows comparisons to be made between similar schools;
* the Ofsted PANDA report, published annually.

The governors' busy calendar now includes in the autumn, first, studying recent results, hence the school's performance against previously published targets, and, second, setting targets for the next cohort of pupils to be published in the annual report to parents, along with the last cohort's results. The challenge facing the governors and the school is to bring different kinds of target into meaningful relationship: individual pupils' targets for learning; management, teaching and care teams' targets; the school's targets for specific cohorts' attainment; the LEA's proposed targets for its locality as published in its education development plan; and the national targets set by the DfES.

LEAs generally have taken measures to support these requirements. For example, school-improvement consultants visit schools to discuss whole-school targets. Consultations tend to use a version of a five-stage cycle of enquiry and action:

1   How well are you doing?
2   How well should you be doing?

3   What more can you aim to achieve?
4   What must you do to make it happen?
5   Making it happen.

At the core of the responsibilities borne by schools and the LEA are the two concepts of **targets** and **benchmarking**.

While a school may set all kinds of targets for its own purposes, certain targets have to be set statutorily. These are for the percentage of 11-year-olds to attain level 4+ in English and mathematics; the percentage of 14-year-olds to attain level 5+ in English, mathematics and science; the percentage of 16-year-olds to gain five or more GCSEs at A* to C, five or more GCSEs at A* to G, and the average pupil point score for the 16-year-old cohort.

The dictionary defines a benchmark as 'a criterion against which to measure something; a reference point'. The Schools Curriculum and Assessment Authority (now QCA) wrote in 1997 that 'benchmarking is the term given to the process of measuring standards of actual performance against those achieved by others with broadly similar characteristics, identifying best practice and learning from it in order to improve'.

Benchmarking and using targets are not ends in themselves: they have always to serve the development of teaching and learning in the school. Prerequisite are describing and questioning both what you want your pupils to learn, and how you support and manage the teaching of your pupils. Given a culture of reviewing performance, you can explore further:

- How well are your pupils doing?
- Are some groups of pupils doing better than others?
- How does your pupils' performance compare with that of other pupils, in your locality, in the country as a whole, and in similar schools?
- How can you use targets to help your pupils do their best?

All of this presumes a basic understanding of how the national curriculum is constructed in key stages with attainment levels and then grades, and of how benchmarked comparisons lead to categorisations of how a school is doing.

Information available to help governors gain a view of their school's performance

When a 5-year old child moves out of the reception class into Year 1, s/he has begun Key Stage 1. This first key stage lasts for two years and ends, as do all key stages, with tests and assessments. Key Stage 2 runs from Year 3 to the end of Year 6, when the child is 11. Key Stage 3 runs from Year 7 to Year 9, when the child is 14. Key Stage 4 covers the Years 10 and 11 to the end of statutory schooling at 16.

National Curriculum subjects are assessed on a scale of eight levels of attainment. When a child is 7 years old, it is generally expected that s/he will attain level 2 in English, mathematics, and science. By the end of Key Stage 2, at 11, the expectation is that s/he will attain at least level 4. By the end of Key Stage 3, at 14, it is expected s/he will attain level 5 or level 6. At Key Stage 4, just to complicate things, GCSE (General Certificate of Secondary Education) switches to letter grades A* to G, and vocational qualifications have pass, merit and distinction grades which can be aligned to GCSE grades. It is expected that most pupils will attain the equivalent of five GCSE grades A* to C.

The governors' first and foremost source of information is the school itself. The headteacher, senior management team and staff can be expected to provide data on pupils' progress and attainment. But a great deal of information also comes to the school from external agencies. The challenge to most governors is how to make the wealth of facts and figures somehow digestible.

The government's benchmarking information rank-orders schools according to their test results and categorises schools according to certain percentage boundaries. If your school is in the bottom 10 per cent, it is in the lowest decile. In the top 10 per cent, you are in the highest decile. In the top 25 per cent, you are in the top quartile. In the bottom 25 per cent, you are in the lowest quartile. Schools are encouraged to set targets which will raise their performance and place them in a higher percentile for their benchmark group when the following year's tables are published.

To complement information about pupils' attainment, many LEAs provide schools and consultants with financial and contextual data. Early versions of such data included information allowing colleagues in school and consultants to make comparisons about performance in terms of the number of pupils on the special educational needs register, in terms of the number of pupils taking a daily free school meal, and in terms of the allocation of ancillary welfare assistance. Figures may also be given for categories and items of school income and expenditure, presented both as a sum per pupil and as a percentage of expenditure. Again comparisons are prompted, inviting managers, governors, and consultants to ask questions about the school. The intention is for this kind of financial benchmarking to assist schools in planning and using targets. The figures should be treated as a starting point or reference for discussion. A school may, for example, have staff costs well above or below the average for its size and type. The implication is not that strategy or management must be at fault. Rather, governors and managers should be led to explore the situation's origin and reasons, and consider appropriate courses of action for the future.

Questions you should be asking about your school's performance data

Comparing your school with similar ones can disturb complacency or confirm high relative attainment. Information on pupils' performance in a school with a privileged catchment area might show that, although they achieve results well above the county or borough and national averages, they actually should be doing much better, given their abilities on entry. Or they might be shown to be doing even better than expected. Whereas a school with a less advantaged catchment, well down the raw results league table, might be shown to be very successful in promoting progress beyond expectation.

Ofsted inspection may probe your school's use of targets. Here, for example, are key Ofsted questions, taken from the handbook (2000), linked with questions I suggest are relevant to the use of targets:

Ofsted inspection question	*Question about the use of targets*
How high are standards?	How well are targets used to help
a The school's results and pupils' achievements	raise standards, and to promote pupils' all-round education?
b Pupils' attitudes, values and personal development	
How well are pupils taught?	How well are targets used to help the teachers teach, and to help the pupils learn?
How good are the curricular and other opportunities offered to pupils or students?	How well are targets used to inform curriculum planning and other provision?
How well does the school care for its pupils or students?	How well are targets used in guiding and counselling the pupils?
How well does the school work in partnership with parents?	How well are parents and carers involved in the use of targets for individual pupils?
How well is the school led and managed?	How well are targets used to focus leadership and management?
What should the school do to improve further?	How appropriate, and how challenging, are the targets the school currently has?

How statutory target-setting might be carried out in school

Here is a model which you may use as a guide:

- The headteacher and relevant teachers meet to consider evidence of the past, current, and predicted performance of each pupil in Year 5, Year 8 or Year 10, and in other years too if that is thought desirable.
- A factor of challenge is added to the prediction for each pupil, based on the planned-for impact of in-house and government-sponsored developments.
- The pupils are involved in this process, at least to the extent that they are drawn into discussions about what is expected of them and about what they themselves aspire to.

- The pupils' individual targets are aggregated to yield percentage figures for the year group or cohort.
- The LEA consultant visits the school to discuss evidence of performance and proposed targets, initially often with the headteacher and relevant staff. The governing body is represented, for example, by the governor members of the school-improvement group at a subsequent meeting, which works towards finalising whole-school targets to be set for the future.
- A group of governors, perhaps comprising the curriculum committee, perhaps involving a school-improvement group, prepares a brief paper summarising:
  - the recommended targets;
  - how the targets were arrived at;
  - how the targets represent realistic yet challenging expectations;
  - what needs to be done for the targets be achieved;
  - the recommendation that the targets be adopted by the whole governing body.
- The governing body considers the proposal and, following explanation, discussion, and perhaps amendment, adopts the targets and returns its targets proforma to the LEA.

The governing body and the headteacher need to agree how progress will be checked. There should be a regular item on the agenda of both the curriculum committee or a school-improvement group and whole governing body meetings, checking milestones as progress is made towards achieving the targets.

The pupils' role in the target-setting process

It does not make sense for pupils to be involved in deciding the percentage of the year group to attain a certain level or number of qualifications. But whole-school targets only make sense if they bear some relation to the aggregate of all the individual pupils' targets. We know from research that it helps pupils to know what it is they are aiming for and to play a part in shaping the activities leading to learning and achievement. The pupils can therefore help in setting targets and reviewing performance by being aware of their own challenges, efforts and results. They do this by talking about their targets for individual education plans, by looking at how teachers have marked their work, by taking initiative in expressing and pursuing their own aspirations, by getting the best out of their teaching and making the most of their learning.

What happens if the targets you have set appear after a while to be too easy, or impossible to reach

One of the things that has to be realised is that targets go out of date. Circumstances change and new information becomes available about your school's pupils, their teaching, their performance. Pupils can surge ahead in their understanding, or hit unforeseen obstacles. New pupils can arrive, and some existing pupils leave, with learning difficulties or with outstanding capabilities. Teachers can develop new strategies or acquire new resources. The teaching staff can change and alter the balance of skill across the team for a crucial year group, for better or for worse. New assessments can reveal areas of strength or weakness in the pupils' learning. In other words, the picture changes, making a target look more or less formidable or accessible than was originally calculated.

Something else can cause a target to appear 'wrong' or out of date. As new information becomes available to the government and to the LEA, either of those authorities can decide to modify its expectations. Many LEAs use an analysis of results over a three- or five-year period to produce an indicative range for each school's targets. Initial aggregates of all schools' targets in a locality are part of the calculation of whether an LEA is within reach of its target set by the DfES. LEAs can use this kind of calculation to determine what each school should aim to achieve, and so enable the LEA to hit its target. If the targets actually set by a school fall outside the indicated range, the LEA consultant may prompt a review.

Whatever the reason for wanting to change a target, a review can be carried out. In such circumstances, three main sources of information should be considered:

1   recent evidence of the pupils' progress and attainments; for example, teacher assessments, test results and observations by classroom assistants, parents, carers and others;
2   changes in curriculum provision; for example, better or worse accommodation, resources, organisation or management and enhanced or diminished teaching skills and strategies;
3   changes in the pupil cohort, with higher or lower previous attainment.

A review leads to confirming or amending a target, and, though the published target cannot be altered, at least all involved parties can be informed of any adjustment. This will help in the final evaluation of performance, when the results are known and the school takes stock of the whole targeting process.

Central to any revision of targets are the teachers' perceptions. Having the greatest bearing on judgements about whether or not a cohort of pupils is on course to achieve a target are the teachers' views of curriculum planning, assessment arrangements, the deployment of staff and resources, and of the teaching and learning. The teachers' views may be challenged by their managers or other observers, including LEA consultants. But again and again we have to return to the teachers and how they see their pupils' provision, performance and progress. For it is they who choose whether or not to act on whatever information there is, they who are responsible for guiding, supporting, and extending the pupils' learning.

If there is a gap between what one group of people thinks a cohort will achieve and what another group indicates, the issue has to be discussed in the context of a review which draws on the teachers' perceptions. Moving the targets has an impact on the teachers and their work. The teachers have the closest view of the pupils and their targets, and they themselves may want to move a target.

Whatever happens, targets should not be disconnected from the pupils and their teaching. The numbers are not abstract or theoretical entities. The numbers concern the achievements of individual pupils.

How you avoid losing breadth in education and avoid teaching to the tests

You can choose to highlight aspirations and achievements in areas of the curriculum beyond the core, for example, in the arts, humanities, physical, religious, personal and social education. Although teachers do well to prepare pupils for the tests and examinations they will face, they do not help the pupils by neglecting areas of learning which form the basis for capabilities beyond literacy and numeracy, and which run across school subjects.

If teaching to the tests means ignoring or undermining the pupils' confidence and attitude towards learning, the effort will be counter-productive. If study skills are not seen as part and parcel of covering the syllabus content, the pupils will not be able to access and make use of their knowledge. If creativity, imagination and lateral thinking are sidelined in favour of rote learning and test practice, pupils are likely to lack the wit to perform under pressure in response to challenging tasks. (Chapter 7 deals with inclusion and other aspects of school life.)

Whether you are just aiming for the average when you use targets indicated by the government's statistics

Your aim is for all pupils to be as capable, confident and successful as they can be.

There is a danger of concentrating efforts in school on bringing the majority of pupils up to the government's minimum targets. You should strive to 'stretch' all of the pupils and not be satisfied with achieving the average. Targets for individual pupils' achievements are best set in the context of your best assessment of their past learning, their needs, talents and potential.

It may help to consider targets for pupils to attain standards above the average, for example: the proportion of pupils to attain level 3 at the end of Key Stage 1; or the proportion of pupils to attain level 5 and/or 6 at the end of Key Stage 2; or the proportion of pupils to attain four or more A* and A grades at the end of Year 11; or the average point score at A-level. Your LEA and Ofsted will almost certainly encourage you to raise your sights as far as possible.

Whether governors should have their own targets

Using targets is just one way of trying to focus your efforts to develop what you do. So yes, governors can have targets of their own to help them plan and work on providing improved support.

The governing body can, and some would say should, have its own development plan. Perhaps some governors will enrol on certain training courses. Perhaps a modified committee structure will help the efficient working of the governing body. Is it time, for example, to introduce a school-improvement group, consisting, say, of the headteacher, deputy, chair, vice-chair, and key personnel, depending on focuses of attention at any given time? Or you might decide, for example, that all your governors should meet once a year with their designated subject leaders. This might be something to aim for, and at the end of the year you can see how well you did.

What the essential ingredients in your work with performance data and targets should be

- If it is not yet the case that your senior management team, staff, governors and LEA consultant work together to set performance targets, make plans to bring that situation about.
- Arrange for the governing body to be represented at meetings when the LEA consultant visits to discuss and negotiate targets.
- Take a cautious view of any single set of statistical data on performance. Remember that results from one year or from a small cohort can be untypical. Look for the trend over at least three years, and be sensitive to the individual stories behind small numbers of pupils.
- When setting your statutory targets, make sure they clearly specify the cohort of pupils, the time-scale for the attainment, and the measure of the attainment in terms of levels, grades, or average point scores.
- When setting statutory targets, consider a range of relevant data, including aggregations of individual pupils' targets. Try to gain a sense from the school's managers and teachers of how the targets you publish can be translated back into steps to be taken in classrooms on behalf of and with the pupils.
- In addition to statutory targets, consider how targets other than statutory ones might be set to help the school develop the quality of its teaching and enhance the pupils' achievements.
- Make sure your use of performance targets forms part of your school development plan.
- Understand that the statutory, published targets cannot be changed, although expectations of performance are likely to change and need to be reviewed. Be prepared to explain why and how your targets go out of date, and where your school has currently advanced to.
- Discuss with senior managers and staff the information they give you about progress that is made towards targets.
- Consider how best to ensure that your staff receives recognition for their successes.
- Develop a strategy, agreed with staff and senior managers, for publishing your response to outcomes measured against targets.
- Remember to keep your sense of proportion and your sense of humour.
- Try to keep your collective eye on the question: *how will this help our pupils?*

Governors of special schools might also check the advice given in Chapter 6.

11 Monitoring and evaluation

Monitoring involves checking progress. Evaluation involves deciding how successful efforts to learn and improve have been. Both are essential to the productive use of targets for individual pupils, for management and staff teams, and for whole-school improvement.

This chapter does not by any means cover every aspect of monitoring and evaluation. What we will focus on is the monitoring and evaluation of the school's use of targets. The argument made by this book is that this is a key to effective education.

In this chapter we shall consider:

- how you can gauge what stage you have reached as a school in developing the use of targets;
- why monitoring and evaluation are vital;
- what makes a good target;
- evidence you might look for as an indication of how, and how well, targets are being used to promote individual pupils' learning;
- evidence you might look for as an indication of how, and how well, targets are being used to promote the effectiveness of teaching and care teams and of the school as a whole;
- key questions concerning the use of targets in school self-evaluation.

How you might gauge what stage you have reached as a school in developing the use of targets

The research I carried out in the summer 2000 (reported in Chapter 2) showed that there were considerable variations in the ways targets were being used at classroom level. I found few schools with a complete system operating for all staff across all year groups and subjects. At that time, most of the headteachers were being opportunistic rather than proactive, and encouraged teachers who had the interest and capability to experiment and forge ahead. The headteachers' intention seemed to be to build on the good practice that was being piloted in the classroom as and when the need or opportunity arose. Practices differed in these ways:

teachers working individually, or on their own initiative	teachers working as a team or whole-school
teachers working as part of a pilot or experimental project	teachers working to agreed policy
targets set for all subjects	targets set for core subjects or a few chosen subjects only
teachers set the targets	pupils are involved in setting the targets.

Headteachers gave the impression that they were working towards the practices in the right-hand column. They reported no grand scheme for the use of targets. They were encouraging classroom experimentation while setting statutory targets for cohorts' attainment, without necessarily connecting individual pupils' targets in any way with whole-school targets. In none of the nine schools I visited had there been a decision to use targets in order to shift classroom practice and a school's ethos away from didacticism and pupils' dependence on teachers, towards pupils' greater involvement in the setting and assessment of the tasks for themselves or in negotiation with their teachers. Nor have I elsewhere yet come across targets being used in this way: with the intention of creating a more transparent or collaborative teaching and learning style, and of raising pupils' motivation and sense of achievement specifically by involving them in setting and reviewing targets within subjects and/or in cross- and extra-curricular activities.

In the autumn 2000 performance management was introduced in schools. Policy had to be in place by December of that year, and during the first two terms of 2001 most teachers began their first cycle of performance reviewing and objectives setting. This is treated to more detailed discussion in Chapter 9, but here we can note that it is now possible for teachers and managers to make vital links between their own performance management objectives, teaching and care teams' targets, individual pupils' targets, and whole-school targets.

How would you characterise your school's development of the use of targets? These are questions you can ask when auditing the use of whole-school targets:

At what stage is the whole staff in using whole-school targets?	awareness?
At what stage are subject, management and year teams in using targets?	understanding? commitment?
At what stage are individual managers and teachers in using objectives within performance management?	implementation? evaluation?
At what stage is the whole staff in using targets for individual pupils?	development? dissemination?
At what stage is the whole staff in linking their use of targets in these different contexts?	

The visits by your school's threshold assessor will have given some feedback on your implementation of performance management. And others, including your governors, will be interested in the answers to those questions.

Why are monitoring and evaluation vital?

Using targets does not of itself guarantee the desired improvement. Referring to case studies of schools that have improved their performance, Ofsted, in *Strategies to Promote Inclusion: Improving City Schools*, states that:

> There is no single, or peculiar, recipe for improvement in these schools, but some common ingredients are essential to the mix: strong management, a well-focused curriculum, good teaching, close monitoring and effective personal support, together with clear communication with parents. Essentially what make the difference are the clarity, intensity and persistence of the school's work and the rigour with which it is scrutinised. At best, all the energy of the school serves the same end: raising standards.
>
> (Ofsted, 2000b, p. 7)

You can use targets as a spur to being committed to monitoring and evaluating the efforts you make. The intention to change your school for the better has to be accompanied by a commitment to checking whether or not changes to systems, provision or ethos really make any difference to the pupils' learning, bearing in mind that their learning may be apparent in their attitudes and behaviour, as well as in their academic performance.

In its report *Raising the Attainment of Minority Ethnic Pupils: School and LEA Responses*, for example, Ofsted records that 'A longstanding obstacle to progress is the reluctance of schools and LEAs to monitor pupils' performance by ethnic groups' (Ofsted, 1999b, p. 54). You have to begin with monitoring, collecting testimony, asking questions, forming hypotheses, making and implementing plans, in order to be able to monitor and evaluate effects.

You have first to be consistent in your assessment of your pupils' attainment and progress. You have to collect the data, analyse the strengths and weaknesses in the pupils' learning, and focus on the aspects of performance that you want to change. You have then to follow the rigorous processes of planning, monitoring and evaluating effects. Without this, there is a real danger that good intentions and valiant efforts will be unfocused and not be learned from. You need to monitor and evaluate your policy and practice in the use of assessment and targets in order to be assured that data and decisions validly serve the purposes you have for them.

What makes a good target – part 1: evidence you might look for as an indication of how, and how well, targets are being used to promote individual pupils' learning

A range of colleagues in different roles can monitor teachers' practice and, in so doing, seek evidence of pupils' using targets. Any occasion when one colleague considers the quality of one another's work is an opportunity for monitoring. It is important, though, that everyone concerned understands what is proposed, and agrees to what will happen as a result of the monitoring. You might, for example, use activities arising from initial teacher training or continuing professional development work, school improvement, or occasions of performance management monitoring. (See Chapter 9, p. 96–9, for a discussion of lesson observation protocol.)

You can ask about individual pupils' targets:

- Do the pupils know what targets they are working on?
- Do the targets express what the pupils are expected to learn?
- Does the pupils' use of targets help them understand what they have to do to be successful in their tasks?
- Are the targets positively worded, that is, omitting all negatives, such as *not*, *never*, and so on?
- Are the targets so worded that, when pupils review them, they can say whether or not, or to what extent, they have succeeded?
- Does the way the targets are used make it possible to locate appropriate evidence to support the review?
- What do teachers and pupils feel is helpful about their use of targets?
- What do teachers and pupils feel is not so helpful about their use of targets?
- How might the use of individual pupils' targets be improved in teachers' and pupils' opinion?

Governors too might have access to such information in order to help them see how individual pupils' targets are used. Parents and carers might learn about how targets are used through reports on their children's progress and achievements, and through newsletters and other forms of communication, explaining the school's ways of working. Inspectors and other quality assurers might have access to any of the above, when they examine the use of targets in the school.

Let us consider what makes a good target. Are some kinds of individual pupils' target better than others?

You might use the taxonomy of targets for individual pupils given at the start of Chapter 3 as a basis for surveying the kinds of target that are being used by individual pupils in your school. Discussion with colleagues about this might centre on the different proportions found in each category. Do some pupils benefit from symbolic targets more than from others? Would you be satisfied if 90 per cent of targets were basic? Are there any implications for curriculum planning, if you have many examples of generic targets? Do any teachers enable pupils to use meta-cognitive targets; if so, how did they come to do so? Would you expect the majority of targets to be partial? Are any meta-cognitive targets used – and with what effect? Would you expect to see many definitive targets? Do pupils graduate from one type of target to another? Do certain subjects tend to use one target type? Do the subject files that your subject leaders annually update contain examples of targets used by pupils in different year groups? (See Chapter 8, concerning subject reviews.)

You might also use Shirley Clarke's concepts of learning intention, success criteria, and aside (Clarke, 2001a) as a basis for analysing pupils' targets. (See Chapter 3, pp. 41–3.) In a sample of current practice evident in your classroom or school, do the pupils' targets reveal their learning intentions? Do the targets refer to their success criteria? If they do not, how do the pupils come to understand their success criteria? Do the targets give a rationale for the activity and the learning? If not, how do the pupils come to understand the reasons why the work is important?

The acronym SMART has become a clichéd definition of qualities to look for in targets. The elements seem desirable enough: **s**pecific; **m**easurable; **a**chievable; **r**ealistic; **t**ime-scaled. But perhaps the ultimate definition of a good target is a pragmatic one: a good target helps the learner learn. In the research I carried out into pupils' perceptions of targets, reported in Chapter 2, I was impressed when pupils remembered past targets and the learning that those targets involved. This is an important feature too in the Gillingham Partnership Project that Clarke reports (Clarke, 2001b).

A good target is likely to bring success, not without a struggle perhaps, but contributing to the individual pupil's self-confidence and desire to learn and achieve more. Above all, you need to ask the pupils about their targets, for they will indicate how good their targets are.

In a different kind of sense, a target is a good one if it reflects integrity between the different kinds of target that belong to the key fields of educational activity: individual pupils' and teachers' work; teams' work; and whole-school improvement.

What makes a good target – part 2: evidence you might look for as an indication of how, and how well, targets are being used to promote the effectiveness of teaching and care teams and of the school as a whole

Senior managers work with subject leaders, section heads and co-ordinators to review teams' performance: to set, monitor and evaluate teams' use of targets. A main source of information about teaching and care teams' use of targets is their own regular self-reviewing of their performance. (Chapter 8 discusses this in detail.) The main source of information about whole-school development is the school-improvement plan. (You can use the taxonomy given at the end of Chapter 5 to analyse the kind of team and whole-school targets being used in your school.)

Of the targets that were set by teams and by the school you can ask:

* What was the evidence that the targets were hit, or not hit?
* What were thought to be the main contributing factors to the success, or lack of success?
* What was learned from the process?
* Is that chapter of development now closed, or are there further useful steps to take; if so, what?

The debates that ensue take place in the contexts of teams' reviews and of whole-school-improvement planning and evaluation.

It is also the responsibility of senior managers to monitor and evaluate the effectiveness of performance management and the contribution of targets ('objectives') in that context to teaching and care teams' and the whole-school's achievement and improvement. What the senior management team is looking for is correspondence between the targets that are used at the different levels of individual pupil and teacher, team, and institution. Governors too, responsible for strategy and accountability, in their role as critical friends, will seek evidence of the contribution that performance management objectives are making to teams' and the whole school's effectiveness. And inspectors and other quality assurers might have access to any of the above, when they examine the use of targets in the school.

Coherence between whole-school targets and individual pupils' targets should not be thought of as coming from one determining the other. Whole-school targets cannot be the mere aggregate of individual pupils' targets. And individual pupils' targets cannot be worked out from whole-school targets. Integrity in a school's use of targets, in all their various contexts, comes rather from thoughtful cross-checking between them.

Target activity	*Quality evidenced by*
the individual pupil's use of targets	talking with pupils individually and in groups, both in and out of lessons; in-house and/or commissioned research into pupils' perceptions; questionnaires; outcomes . . .
the use of targets by teaching, pastoral, and management teams	talking with teams; their policies, records, reports, files; monitoring, evaluation and inspection reports; research; outcomes . . .
the use of targets ('objectives') by managers and teachers in their performance management	talking with managers, teachers, and Team Leaders; performance management records, with permission; continuing professional development activities and records; outcomes . . .
the use of whole-school targets	discussion with managers, teachers and governors; the school-improvement plan; research; surveys of public opinion; LEA/diocese/finance partners' judgements; outcomes . . .

(Refer also to the discussion and matrix in the final two pages of the Introduction.)

Achieving integrity between these fields means tackling anomalies. If, for example, whole-school targets refer to literacy, you should find evidence of efforts to improve literacy in individual pupils' targets, in teaching teams' planning and development work, and in some teachers' performance management objectives. If a significant number of pupils' individual targets refer to ICT, then you should look for ICT as a target area in school-improvement planning and activity, in teachers' performance management objectives, and in teams' targets.

Furthermore, you have to create, and then find confirmed in practice, integrity in the levels of challenge that targets contain. For example, if significant numbers of pupils are aiming to increase their performance above what would be expected for pupils of their age in schools similar to yours, you must seek its equivalent in teams' targets, performance management, and whole-school-improvement work. You have to work towards, and then expect to see, an equivalent level of challenge in targets across all the different fields of activity. You need to be alert to discrepancies between the levels of challenge in different fields. Very demanding whole-school targets have to be supported by high expectations in the pupils' targets, in teachers' performance-management objectives, and in teams' efforts to raise standards.

A good target is one which works well in its own terms, and which has a productive resonance with targets in other fields. A good target, then, serves well the educational interest of its user, whether that be the individual pupil, the teaching, pastoral or management team, the individual teacher, or the whole school. And it serves also to reinforce targets that are being used at other levels – individual, team, or whole school.

Key questions concerning the use of targets in school self-evaluation

Some kinds of evaluation involve making judgements about performance at a given moment in time. The approach to self-review conventionally recommended to schools, for example, by some LEAs, concentrates attention on a single year group of pupils' performance. Schools are encouraged to select a cohort of pupils, set one or more targets, plan strategy, monitor progress and draw conclusions from the outcome. This is a kind of managerial action research, usually focused on just one year group at a time. What you may gain from this is intensity, both of purpose and learning from the experience. What you may lose, however, is breadth of vision and participation of the whole school.

The Ofsted inspection handbook (Ofsted, 2000a) contains an instructive section on self-evaluation. It identifies four questions at the heart of evaluation: Are all the pupils in your school learning as much as they are capable of learning? What can you do to find out? When you answer the first question, how do you know you are right? What do you do about it when you have the answer? It guides you in considering what stage you have reached in a process of developing self evaluation as a school. It provides a range of starting points, and offers advice on using the CD-ROM that accompanies the handbook.

The approach suggested here is different in that it takes as a premise that what you are monitoring or evaluating is a dynamic. We are concerned with monitoring and evaluating the impact of targets on the school's effectiveness and improvement. Our focus is the extent and quality of change.

First, how is your school changing? In terms of any changes in recent years to your:

- catchment area
- pupils' socio-economic background (e.g. parental occupation and higher education; FSM)
- pupils' baseline or prior attainment
- comparisons with schools like yours
- pupils' achievements after leaving
- SEN
- attendance rates
- exclusion rates
- inclusivity
- curriculum initiatives and developments in the school,

have changes to your school's context had the evident effect of:
- raising standards?
- lowering standards?

This encourages you to begin to explore contextual reasons for any changes in your school's performance.

Second, how is your school's performance changing? When you consider a range of indicators over three or more years, such as:

- your school's performance against national and local targets
- your school's performance against targets negotiated with your LEA or governing authority
- your school's PANDA report for core subjects
- differences between boys' and girls' performance
- differences between ethnic groups of pupils' performance
- differences between high-, mid- and low-attaining pupils' performance
- progress measures
- value-added indicators
- pupils' attitudes and behaviour
- the range of opportunities provided for pupils
- how inclusive your school is
- any other features of school life that are valued or thought significant
- perceptions of pupils, parents and carers, those to whom your pupils go to continue their education or training, and possibly employers,

is your school's performance:

- improving?
- unchanging?
- declining?

This encourages you to consider a range of data for and changes in the school's performance: quantitative and qualitative, across the board, as well as homing in on subjects, based on your own values and priorities as well as those of government and media.

Third, how are comparisons between your school's performance and other schools' performance changing? Is your school's performance:

- following the trends of other schools in the country as a whole, of other schools in your locality, and of schools similar to yours?
- making improvements at an exceptional rate?
- falling behind the rate of improvement elsewhere?

This encourages you to consider comparisons, drawing on as wide a range of benchmark data as possible, including the PANDA, Autumn Package, and material supplied by your LEA or governing authority.

Fourth, what changes do you expect in your school's performance in the future? Taking account of changes in:

- what is known about the pupils
- what is known about the staff
- available resources
- the school-improvement plan and strategic vision for the future of the school,

what targets and time-scales do you have for:

- the whole school?
- individual subjects?
- year groups?

This encourages you to examine your strategic use of whole-school targets.

Using targets, whether for whole-school development or for individual pupils' learning, implies processes of monitoring and evaluation. Seeing your efforts through to the discussion, recording, reporting, and celebrating of achievement is vital, and sometimes neglected in schools. Monitoring and evaluation can fall by the wayside, because schools are such busy places whose resources are barely adequate to meet the demands made of them. Probably the most important step is to build monitoring and evaluation into timetables and calendars, and to expect to use monitoring and evaluation to decide how better to serve pupils' welfare, learning and achievement.

Appendix 1

Pupils' responses to my questions about their activities, learning and targets

I sometimes tape-recorded the pupils, and sometimes wrote down what they said. As far as possible, what is written below is what the pupils actually said. As an abbreviation, 'g' stands for girl, and 'b' for boy, appearing immediately after the quotation.

January School – first, 4–8, town and surrounding area

I interviewed four pupils, usually two girls and two boys, from each class.

What have you learned recently in school?

YR   Sheets: like Letterland (g). Sounds (for letters) (g).
          Writing (g). Numbers (up to 100, forwards and backwards) (b).
          Play soft gym: we bash it and jump it (b).
          Special books: for English, maths, literacy . . . (b, g).

Y1/2i   Spellings (g). About money (g). Change (b).
          Dictation, rotation, symmetry (b).

Y1/2ii   How to write joined up writing (b).
          In maths we have to add nine and take away nine; number bonds, 20 and 10 (g). In English we've been writing letters (g).
          In maths I've learned my two times table (b).
          In maths I've learned my two, five and ten times tables (b).

Y1/2iii   How to share (b). How to take turns (g). To let people borrow stuff (b).
          To do the Golden Rules (b).

Y3/4i   About Ancient Greece in ICT. (bs) Fractions in maths (b).
          To do things quicker on the computer; to keep fingers on the middle keys (bs). In literacy, stories and fables (g). Money: taking away (g).
          In maths, teacher writes some numbers up and you've got to guess what they're going up in – work out the missing numbers (g).

Y3/4ii   Ancient Greece (b). Times tables (b). Spelling (g).
          Division (b). Fractions (g).

Y3/4iii   Project – Ancient Greece (b). Doing technical design things of Ancient Greece (g). Using the computer we write it in our own words and draw pictures (g).

What has helped you learn (those things) in school?

YR The teachers; we watch Numbertime and Letterland on video (b).
We have sheets to learn the numbers (b).
Writing – the teachers write on the board so we can copy it (b).
Sheets: drawing (g).
Video. When we watch Numbertime video we shout (g).

Y1/2i The teachers come round and help me with my work (g).
If I fell over, my golden play pals would help and wash my knee off (g).
Spellings (b).
Miss A helps by coming round and checking spellings (g).
Golden Time helps me sew (g).

Y1/2ii Other people (b). My brain (b). Teachers (g).

Y1/2iii If we're doing maths, we always look at a number line (b).
If we're stuck, you can use your fingers (g).
You can do number different ways – add nine, take one, is add ten (b).
If you're stuck, write an answer and do it backwards (b).

Y3/4i They make it easy – they help us, if we get stuck (b).
We get the chance to ask and say 'I don't understand' (b).
If the teacher's busy, we have to talk to our friend (gs).
And Miss's helpers help (g).

Y3/4ii Talking to friends (b).
Sometimes they write what we're meant to do on the board (and you don't have to remember everything) (b).
When they come and talk about what we're doing (g).
In maths we're allowed a sheet with numbers up to a hundred. In maths little cards (b).

Y3/4iii Teachers (b).
For spelling I read a lot (g). It helps me to learn spelling if I read it (b).
Learning difficult spellings, e.g. for long words, by making up rhymes and songs (gs, b).

What ways do you have of knowing what you are going to learn?

YR Don't know (bs, gs). We learn the alphabet (g).

Y1/2i We do Golden Time on a Friday (g).
PE every Monday (b).
(They kindly listed all the subjects they do, plus assembly and so on, including 'plan, do, review time', hand skills, construction . . . [g, b].)

Y1/2ii Teachers normally tell you (b).
We get Golden Time every Friday (b).
When it's special . . . (g).

Y1/2iii They tell you what you might be doing next day (b).
If you don't know, the teacher tells you (g).

Y3/4i We have timetables (g).
They say now then this is what we're doing next week (b).
She tells us stuff a little bit about what we're doing (g).

We have certain things on certain days (b). We carry on with some work (g).

Y3/4ii   Timetable (g). Letters (b). Sometimes we have to remember (b). We know the routine (b).

Y3/4iii Teachers tell us (b). In literacy she says 'Next week we're going to be working on this . . .' (b).

What ways do you have of knowing how well you are doing?

YR   The teacher writes down how well we read (b). Team points (b). In assembly. The class cup (g).

Y1/2i   Teacher tells us (b). When you're doing sums, you know if you're doing well (g). Team points (b). When I go through my book, I see well done (g). Lunchtime awards (b).

Y1/2ii   When it's school meeting (b). Our teachers read our maths or literacy whether it's right or wrong (g). Team points (b).

Y1/2iii Teacher tells you (b). She marks our books (b). You could ask a friend (b).

Y3/4i   There's three different groups (what group you're in tells you how you're doing) (b). If we do pieces of work, teacher writes comments on what we need to practice, and spelling mistakes (g). Team points which means it's good (g). A couple of months ago we had these little cards – red if you miss your target and yellow if you're good (b). You go down to Mrs R and the Special Book (g).

Y3/4ii   My mum tells me on my report (g). They put down little messages, like if we've done good or need more practice (b). When they give you the class cup (g). Team points (b).

Y3/4iii Teachers tell us or write in our books, and give ticks (g, b). Team points (b). Class cup. Headteacher's award (b, g).

What are you good at?

YR   Putting names on the board, counting numbers, soft gym (b). Joined up writing (b). Drawing a house (g). Writing for our alphabet book (g).

Y1/2i   Football, writing a story (b). Skipping, drawing (g). Spellings (b). Writing a story (g).

Y1/2ii   Taking away, adding nine or ten (g). Spelling (b). Handwriting (b).

Maths, all of maths, my brain goes crazy at maths, it quickly calculates everything like a little computer (b).

Y1/2iii Maths – I get all my sums right (g).
Maths – all of it (b). Maths – number bonds to 20 (b).
Literacy, handwriting (b).

Y3/4i Maths: fractions, money, times, divide and all the sums (b).
Spelling and literacy (g).
Maths: guess the number (g).
Maths: long division (b).

Y3/4ii Maths generally and literacy generally (b).
History – Ancient Greece (b).
Maths – fractions, adding – and history (g).
Maths – the three times table (g).

Y3/4iii Reading – I like all reading (g).
Maths – it's hard – and literacy – I like writing (b).
Times tables (g). All maths (b).
I like playtime – I'm good at football (b).

What are you trying to get better at in your school work? Tell me about that in a little more detail.

YR Letters. Learning (g).
Writing (b).
Everything (b).

Y1/2i I forget spaces, don't put capital letter (b, seeming quite proud of being different.).
Writing sentences (g).
I don't put full stops. Spellings (b).
Learning the time (g).
Football (b).

Y1/2ii My topic (b). Handwriting (g). Taking away (b). Nothing really (b).

Y1/2iii Handwriting (b). Reading (b).
Literacy (g). Literacy, writing stories and letters (b).

Y3/4i My little targets are my seven and eight times tables (g).
ICT: all of it (b).
My seven times table (b).
Full stops and punctuation in the right places (g).
We write our targets down and stick them on the wall (b).

Y3/4ii Spelling (g). The four times table (g).
Presentation – every report says use a ruler (b). Presentation (b).

Y3/4iii Behaviour – generally (b).
I'm trying to improve my handwriting – it goes up unless I've got guidelines to use (g).
My targets (b). Golden rules (b).
In the playground (g).
Handwriting (g).

(They explained a system of putting pupil's names on the board if they're silly, and ticks or crosses can improve or worsen your situation.)

Do you have targets? Can you tell me about them? (What do you think about them?)

YR   No.

Y1/2i   Golden Rules (b). Everything (b).

(They told me some of the Golden Rules and the penalties for breaking them.)

Y1/2ii   Not allowed swearing (g). Not allowed fighting (b).

No punching, no kicking (b).

Walk away from people being unkind and tell a teacher. If you break it, you get a red card (g).

Y1/2iii   When we have circle time, we have targets. If you fall out, try and make friends (g). If someone's being horrible, walk away (b).

In maths our targets are to use five and a bit (b).

Targets are what you get happy and sad faces for (b).

Y3/4i   On Wednesdays, but not every week, we meet up after lunch in the art area and clever people go to Miss B's group, and we get a target and write it in a book (bs).

In every group, if we don't understand and we thought we did, we get a target and 'See me' from the teacher (b).

We have a ladder and we draw ourselves going up the ladder for when we have a target (g).

Two months ago we had our Ancient Greece wall with targets (b, g).

Team points, and planet groups (g).

Class cup for somebody who's improved (b).

Y3/4ii   We used to have targets: on the wall, paper stuck up, with stars. *Why did it stop?* It was an old display (b).

Golden Rules (b). Class targets like don't shout out (g).

Y3/4iii We've got one in the class and one for the group (walk in without being noisy) (b). We have circle time targets and base targets and our own ones up on the wall (g).

We can say what we want to do as a target (g).

In our classroom we have two targets for at school, and two for at home (g).

I remember mine – not to torment my cat, and keep the computer tidy (b).

Mine are finish work in time, and get better at times tables (g).

Mine are to remember to dust my room each Saturday, and improve my handwriting and spelling (b).

Mine are not be horrible to my sister, and help out (g).

Mine are not to torment my two big foster brothers, and keep my room tidy (b).

February School – primary, 4–11, town

For all but one class, I interviewed four pupils from the class, usually two girls and two boys; for Class 6 we used a circle-time format.

What have you learned recently in school?

YR   'K' sounds (g). Letters, s, e, m (b). Reading (b).

Y1   Not to run down the corridor: a rule (b).

Writing (g).

Not to shout out (b).

How to use dictionaries, using letters and the alphabet (g).

Y2   Computers: boxes, computer voice, borders, writing size . . . (bs, gs).

Y3   All about the Egyptians: Tutenkhamen, mummies, the sphinx, Howard Carter, Lord Caernarfon . . . (bs, gs).

Birds: size, weight, what they eat, where they nest . . . (bs, gs).

Y4   Weather: different kinds of weather in different places (g).

Division: it's complicated (b).

Painting: making it not so blobby (g).

Fractions and times tables (b).

Y5   Sex education: 'Where did I come from?' – it was funny but serious as well (gs, bs).

How to write a poem (g).

Using the computer: punctuation (b).

Human body – learned more than in Year 3. Space (gs, bs).

Ancient Greece: children, clothes, how they lived, toys; Athens, Sparta, Trojan War (gs, bs).

Long division; fractions; adding; taking away . . . (gs, bs).

On a school trip: Streetwise – really fun, it was so real . . . (g).

We've done a lot this year – we've got some files . . . (g).

Y6   (thirteen girls and eleven boys answered; five girls and five boys passed.)

How to set out time (b).

About how the heart works (b).

That violence doesn't solve everything (b).

How to use speech marks properly (g, b).

To use 24 hours (g).

How to set out an argument for and against (g).

How to use protractors (g).

Angles (g).

Forces (g).

How to turn fractions into improper fractions and back again (b).

How to turn 24 hours into the twelve hour clock (b).

How to do a good short story (b).

To weigh in kilograms (b).

To write a short story in a certain time (g).

Times tables and the 24 hour clock (g).

What has helped you learn (those things)?

YR   Writing; doing it (bs). Seeing the alphabet; doing the alphabet (g).

Y1   The rule: being told off (b).
     Writing: the teacher and writing (practice; doing it) (gs).

Y2   The teacher. Charts on the wall (for times tables) (bs, gs).

Y3   Big books; literacy books; dictionary (bs, gs).
     Teachers when we get stuck (b).
     Maths books, times tables books (g).
     Big blue squares and a pen each; on the back there's a magnet thing,
     and you write the answers, and then if you get it right you can write it
     on your sheet – it rubs off: they're very useful actually (bs, gs).

Y4   Weather: atlases and books (b).
     Division: the teacher told me how to use the calculator (g).
     Painting: the teacher helped me and showed me how to do it (b).
     Fractions etc.: cubes and multilink (g).

Y5   The teacher. Books. Pictures. Videos. Computers. Your mum and dad;
     relations, your family. Yourself. Memory (gs, bs). The doctors (g).

Y6   (sixteen girls and fourteen boys answered; two girls and two boys passed.)
     Mr T does fun things and that helps you remember; having a good-
     humoured teacher; Mr T jokes; having a nice/good/not too strict
     teacher; enjoyable/funny lessons (seven gs, five bs).
     Through mistakes (two bs).
     Through story (b).
     Having text books which are fun and have cartoons (g).
     To write an action story, watching a video and reading other writers (g).
     Books (g).
     Having one teacher right through school (g).
     Diagrams (b).
     My Toe by Toe reading book (b).
     Calculators (b).
     Computers (two bs, g).
     Friends to help you (g).
     Posters on the wall (g).
     Experience: (on football field I hacked someone and he hacked me
     back) (b).
     I enjoy helping people and not bullying (g).

What are you going to learn today or soon in school?

YR   Not sure.

Y1   The rest of our folk dance in PE (g).

Y2   Handwriting. How to turn the computer on (bs, gs).

Y3   About the Celts. The Tudors: Queen Elizabeth and Henry VIII (bs, gs).

Y4   Hurricanes (b).
     For the clarinet: more notes (g).
     For the guitar: when I finish Book 4 I have a test (g).

In division and multiplication: big sums (b).

For a concert coming up: learn new tunes (b).

Y5   She tells us. We stay on a subject for about a month, or a term (gs).

In Year 6 we do the Second World War (g).

Y6   (The class was not asked this question.)

What ways do you have of knowing what you are going to learn?

YR   Not sure.

Y1   Mrs Y tells us, e.g. when we sit on the carpet, e.g. 'Tomorrow we're going to do addings and take-aways' (g).

Y2   Mrs X tells us what we're going to do next week (b). Not always (g).

Y3   Mr A tells us (b). We also know from books (g).

We see displays of what older classes have done (and know we'll do that) (g).

Mr A has this big book thing to show the term stuff – it's very useful (g).

Y4   The teacher tells us (b, g).

We have this white homework maths book, look at the next page; it helps to know what you're going to do (b).

At home I have a tutor to help me with my maths and she works in a school and whatever we're doing someone else is doing it, so I know what we're actually going to do (g).

Y5   I've got a brother older than me, and he tells me. Mrs S tells us at the beginning or end of the term (g).

We have a focus for each subject: it's a letter that tells us our homework, our spellings, what we're doing in English and maths . . . (bs, gs).

Y6   (twelve girls and seven boys answered; six girls and nine boys passed.)

We have a rota/timetable for lessons posted on the wall/door (two gs, three bs).

We get told (two girls, b).

If something different from the routine is going to happen, or there will be a special lesson, we are told (two gs).

On a certain day we have a certain thing, like RE Tuesdays (g).

Newsletter (g).

For football Mr A gives us a letter (b).

For cross country Mr E gives a letter to take home (b).

For netball, we are told about practice (g).

What ways do you have of knowing how well you are doing?

YR   Mrs V says 'You've done really really well' and you get a smiley face (b).

When you're first for PE you get a big smiley face (g).

Mrs U writes 'Excellent writing' (g).

Then you go to the good book (g).

He beed really good and went to the good book (g).

Y1   Miss comes and tells like 'good boy' and 'good girl' (b).

Team points; go to the good book (b, g).

Y2   Stars; ticks; team points; happy faces; 'excellent' (bs, gs).

Using the 'good book'; class cup; reports to Mummy and Daddy (bs, gs).

Y3   Spelling tests (g).

Mr A tells our mums how well we're getting on at consultation evenings, and if we ask our mums, they'll tell us (g).

There are some people who go in groups called ALS groups and they're the ones that are having trouble with spellings (g). They have easy things like monsters (b).

Mr A marks our work and gives it back to us (b). He writes ticks, 'Good work', 'Excellent', 'Terrific' . . . (gs, bs).

On worksheets it sometimes says 'I can . . .' (eg 'add') and Mr A ticks it or puts a cross (g, b).

We have homework books and Mr A sometimes gives us A, or B or C: three As and you go to the good book; three Cs and you see Mrs H (b, g). Stickers (g).

Gold standard for handwriting. Purple books. Yellow (and different coloured, blue, pink . . .) cards (gs, bs).

Y4   In clarinet we have units and however high you get you know you're getting better (g).

In numeracy we have these big tests – marks; and in history too (b).

At home I have a file for rewards (b).

In numeracy we have different coloured tables and they're all different grades; like the blue table is for really hard sums, the red table is for medium grades . . . (g, b). I used to be on yellow table and I knew I was getting better because I was better than everyone else and everybody knew I was getting better, so Mrs Z swapped me round the tables for numeracy and we all got good grades (g).

Y5   We get a report. 'Well done.' Mrs S writes a comment or a tick. Team point. Good book. Certificate. At the end of two weeks, we count up our team points . . . Class cup (gs, bs).

Y6   (fourteen boys and thirteen girls answered; two boys and five girls passed.)

The compliments board (a place to write up a confidential compliment to anyone) (b, g).

Marks in our book/Mr T writes in your book (two bs, g). Ticks in your book (g).

The teacher says/writes 'Well done' (b). He tells us (b).

Mr T working with you (b).

Through tests (g).

Reports (three gs, two bs).

A stamp in your book (g).

Parents evening (g, b).

Yellow card warning (three yellow cards means . . .) (g).

You go to the good book (g).

Team points (g).

The class cup (g).
Homework grades: A, B and C (b).
Table of the week (b).
When your mum comes in (b).
Results of SATs tests (b).
Reading book star (g).

How do you know you have done well personally, for yourself, without anyone telling you? (Only Years 1 and 2 were asked this question.)

Y1   If you write a story and you go on to four pages or two pages (b).
Y2   If you look at your work and see if it looks good (g).
      If I'm doing handwriting and I concentrate really hard and look at my work at the end and say 'That looks quite good', I think 'That's quite good for me' (b).
      Sometimes my slippers can help me. (g: she had teddy bear slippers because she had a bandage on her 'injured' foot.)

What are you good at? (Only Years 3 and 5 were asked this question.)

Y3   Maths (b). English (b). Reading (g). English (g).
Y5   Maths, adding, IT, literacy, English (b). ['You're good at everything really' (g).]
      English, IT (b).
      Dance, PE, English, maths (g).
      Handwriting, literacy, reading and art (g).

What are you trying to get better at in your school work? Tell me about that in a little more detail. (Only Years 3 and 5 were asked this question.)

Y3   Drawing pictures: people and animals (b).
      Art: painting patterns on stones (b).
      Times tables: the 12 times table (g).
      Maths: take aways (g).
Y5   Maths; fractions. Mrs S knows about it (g).
      Climbing the rope in PE. I think Mrs S knows about it. Maths: take-aways, tables (g).
      Maths: learning my tables. My mum and my dad know about it. Art: drawing (b).
      Being tidier: everyone knows what I'm like. Drawing but that is my own idea to improve on (b).

Do you have targets? Can you tell me about them?

YR   She tells us what to do (g).
      Sometimes she gives us different worksheets (g).
      Sometimes badgers get hard work, because badgers are so clever, they get the hardest work (g).
Y1   No (bs, gs).

If you're reading a book, then you can think and read it in your head –
I thinked it by myself (b).

To stop whining – my mummy (b).

Like you've got 'read them', 'spell them', and if you can spell them you
might be able to go to the good book (g).

Y2 No.

Y3 I want my English to improve at the same rate as my maths which is
better (b).

To draw straight lines (b).

We all do work – that's our target (gs).

Sometimes different tables have different work to do (b).

Y4 Mrs Z in the autumn did some targets (for) what she wanted us to get
better at and today we're going to see if we've actually achieved them.
One of my ones for numeracy was learn by heart my two, three, four,
five, six and ten multiply tables (g).

Learn two to ten times tables (g).

We had between ten and twenty targets. Mrs Z wrote them down on a
sheet. So I have them at home and I know what they are. One of my
main targets was to stop talking during . . . (g).

We had targets for the year, numeracy and literacy targets (b).

My target was to get my writing much, much bigger. (b)

In literacy every time we have group reading with the teacher, that
helps me to read my book (g).

Y5 Geography: I don't like it; it goes on and on and on (b).

My reading: I haven't been reading as much as I should be, so I need to
catch up on it (b).

My target's probably to find out where the next Harry Potter book's
coming from; and then to read a chapter a night (g).

Climbing the rope in PE. Choosing more non-fiction books from the
library.

Choosing more poetry and plays as well (g).

Y6 When the whole class does well, we get a class stamp; eighty stamps
means a class reward (g).

In our books, Mr T says like 'Aim to write neatly . . .' (g).

To become a brain surgeon: my mum works in hospital and . . . (b).

To be good in the playground (b).

To keep on improving in maths. And to try to live with people who get
on my nerves (b).

Checking through my story, spotting mistakes (g).

Getting not too many yellow cards (two gs, b).

Try and finish work in time (g).

Do better work, improving my handwriting. And improving my
football for the school (b).

Be a professional snooker player (b).

To be good in class and go to a good secondary school, get a good education, and do the job I want to do (b).

Be a footballer: I want money (b).

Be a professional formula one driver (b).

Grasp new maths topics (b).

My ways of knowing my targets are that Mr T writes them in my book and asks us in lessons, and gives us our target for the lesson (b).

In the spring, summer and winter terms we have 'what we've done best' and 'what to improve' – written down and Mr T keeps it in a file which we see (g).

Get neater (g).

Finish my times tables cards (g).

Stop talking (g).

Be better at football (b).

Aim for handwriting. Finish my homework. Work harder. Be nice to everybody (g).

March School, primary, 4–11, town

I interviewed four pupils, usually two girls and two boys, from classes 3 to 6 in the library, tape-recording the conversation.

What have you learned recently in school?

Y3i   About seeds; iris bulbs; cress; experimenting with carnations and celery to make dyes (gs, bs).

Y3ii   Three puzzles (b). Cereal, manufacture, names and types (bs, g).
          Working in partner (g). Plants growing (b).
          Maths – test, homework, a sheet with numbers like 5, 10, 15, 20 . . . (b).

Y4i   Maths – adding 2s (g). Literacy – about similes (b) Art – plants (b).
          Science – plants, food dye, carnations and celery. (g)

Y4ii   In music, singing a song, to go to the Wintergardens and McDonald's. (g)
          In maths, tally charts; thinking back on what we've been doing. (b)

Y5i   Weather, climate (b).
          In literacy, lots of different things – homophones, antonyms (g).
          In science, light, sound (g).

Y5ii   Weather; the Dome; about the body (g).
          About history – Henry VIII, the Tudors (b)
          King Arthur, myths and legends (g).
          Taking notes (g).
          Music – how to compose; computer work (b).

Y6i   Weather; parts of flowers (b).
          Literacy (b). Timed stories (g).

Y6ii   Parts of flowers (g). Topic – weather, Andy Goldworthy, natural things (g).

What has helped you learn (those things) in school?

Y3i Teachers (g).

When you're at the table, if you don't understand, she lets you ask and she explains (b).

Targets cards (for example, my times tables and joined up handwriting are my targets) (g).

Y3ii A teacher. You can ask friends too (b).

Sometimes easy words. If something's hard you get easy work first, then you get used to it and then go on to harder. You can get the teacher to help you, and friends (g).

I get ALS and she helps us when we do our test, and with maths (gs).

Dictionaries, thesauruses (bs).

Spelling test on Friday – we practise and get them right (b).

Y4i We have targets so we can look at the front of the book and see them (g).

Y4ii Dictionary; books (b). Thesaurus (b).

Spellings (g). Writing (b).

Listening to tapes; listening to the teacher (b).

Y5i Ears; looking (b).

Diagrams that Mrs H does on the board (g).

Talking about it (g).

Asking questions if you're not sure (b). Putting hand up for help (b).

Y5ii Spelling – homophonaire.

Listening (b). Having fun lessons (b). The two-second box (b).

The star box (b). The suggestions box (g).

Y6i Treats when we work hard (b).

Helpers (b).

Y6ii Examples of things; acting out; choral stories, reading plays and taking turns to take parts (g).

Teachers (b). Support staff (b). Books (g).

What ways do you have of knowing what you are going to learn?

Y3i Mrs B tells us in the morning (g).

Y3ii The teacher might tell you (b). Sometimes she doesn't and keeps it a secret (g).

Y4i Teacher has a programme (b). She tells us (g).

I look and see, when I'm on the carpet (b).

There's a timetable – I look at it (b).

Y4ii We've got a chart by the door (b).

We know what we're doing on certain days (b).

Targets – new ones each week (b).

Y5i We have a timetable up on the wall (b).

Mrs H tells us sometimes what we have in the afternoon (g).

Y5ii We don't (b).

Mr T tells us (g).

We've got a list. I have a bad brain day on Monday, Tuesday and Friday (b).

Y6i   We've got SATs (b).

We used to have a timetable and fill it in each week; now we have a different teacher and she tells us (b, g).

Y6ii   A timetable in the past, but we swapped (g). Weekly timetable (g). Literacy between 11 and 12 each day (b). Number work after assembly (b). We've got used to the timetable (g).

Teachers give us a clue, for example, they hand out books, and set tests (g).

What ways do you have of knowing how well you are doing?

Y3i   Mrs B writes it (g) Once a term she writes a report, and all teachers give marks 3 to 1 (b).

Y3ii   We get marks on spelling and the teachers marks with a tick, cross . . . (b). Spelling and underlining (g).

By the group you're in – the yellow group don't get underlining (g). Comments; homework award, merits and vouchers (b).

In maths we write down answers, at the end we swap books, teacher tells us the answers, we give ticks and there's a box for the total score (g).

Each week or month we have a look at our books and read through and see if we've got spelling mistakes or anything else (b).

Parents' evening (g).

Y4i   You have a report (g).

She tells you that was a good piece of work. You get hard work awards and 'getting better' (g).

Teacher writes comments (b). You always get 'good' or not and something to improve on (b). I know when I'm doing well when I read the comment at the end of my work (g).

If you enjoy a lesson, you're good at it (b).

We're in different groups – if the teacher thinks we're in the group that's too easy she'll move us up (b).

Y4ii   He says well done (b).

Hard work award – certificate – class book – pen – voucher (b, g).

Reports, parents evening (g).

Y5i   Mrs H marks our work (g).

Recently we've had reports (g).

Hard work award – merits – token . . . (g, b).

Y5ii   We've got target cards – he writes down like a warning; if you've been good, you get a blue card (g).

Mr B is kind; he says we're the best class ever (b). We have fun with him; he's like a friend to us (g).

Y6i   We get levels; and comments (b). On how you can improve (g).

Target cards (b). When we achieve, we tick and move on. And the teachers test you (g).

Y6ii   Teachers mark our books (g). They don't just tick them; they write
        targets, and reports twice a year. And there are consultation evenings (g).
        If you're totally dropping, they pull you aside and say (g).
        There are special needs groups and special tutoring groups (g).

What are you good at in your school work?
Y3i   Language (b). Maths (g). Topic (g). Science (b).
Y3ii   Maths (g). Most things – topic, literacy, maths (b).
        Spelling – I'm nearly in the top group (g).
        Maths and spelling – but some words I can't spell (b).
Y4i   (Question omitted.)
Y4ii   Maths (b). Drawing, maths, literacy (b). Computer work, maths (b).
        Literacy, maths (g).
Y5i   Literacy, PE (b). Literacy (two gs).
        Comprehension; can be good at art, sketching (b).
Y5ii   Mr B says – but I don't think so – reading, but I don't do enough at
        home at the minute (g).
        Art; others say literacy because I'm a consultant; technology; all right
        at maths; I'm good at talking and being dopey (b).
        Nothing. Literacy – creative writing; not handwriting; in maths I'm
        going to move up a set (b).
        Creative writing about horses (g).
Y6i   Maths – it's sometimes hard but still fun (g). Maths (g).
        Timed stories, but I don't like them (b).
        PE, hockey (b). Playing rugby – we're New Zealand (b).
Y6ii   English (g). Numeracy (b). Art – drawing (b).
        Learning. PSE – in circle time you get asked and the teachers push out
        your opinion (draw out what you think even when you didn't know
        you thought it) (g).

*What are you trying to get better at in your school work? Tell me about that in a little
more detail.*
Y3i   Maths – times tables (b, g). Topic (g). Literacy (b).
Y3ii   Spelling (b). Science and maths (g). Words I can't spell and maths (b).
        Don't know (g).
Y4i   Maths, writing stories (g). My drawing, using speech marks (g).
        Maths, drawing, literacy and science (b). Capital letters (b).
Y4ii   Singing; writing a book (b).
        Times tables (b).
        Poetry (b).
        Reading and spelling (g).
Y5i   Maths – long division (b, g). Maths (g, b).
Y5ii   Literacy and handwriting (b).
        Keep handwriting all the same – I have lazy days (g).
        Keep handwriting neat; start reading at home more (g).

Handwriting; reading at home (b).
Y6i   Literacy – timed stories (g).
Science – the difference between mass and weight, newtons (b).
Grams and kilograms in maths (g).
Topic in science (b).
Y6ii   Maths (g).
Science – I'm trying to like it; I don't like saying the hypothesis (g).
Science – there's a lot of information (two bs).

Do you have targets? Can you tell me about them? (What do you think about them?)
Y3i   Speech marks and commas (g). Full stops and capital letters (b).
To use capital letters and full stops and commas (g).
To spell 'they' and 'could' – these are targets already hit; to use commas and speech marks – these are being worked on now (b).

Those are literacy targets – do you have others?
Use more dividing and times (g). Times tables (g).
Learn my 2, 3, 4, 5, 10 times tables (b). Can't quite remember (b).

How do you know you've hit your target, or not?
Mrs B looks through the book at the end of the day and ticks it off (b).
When we've done something right, she puts 'see me' or puts eyes and an arrow (g).

Why only targets in literacy and maths?
They are to remind us what to do – it means what you're heading for (gs, bs).
I look through my whole story with the target card to see if I've done it right (b).
Y3ii   My target used to be put letters round the right way, now it's don't sit against the cabinet and don't put capitals in any old where (b).
Write the date in five minutes and not copy other people (g).
Use adjectives in story time (b). Use adjectives, nouns and verbs (b).
Do not join my gs and fs (g).
Y4i   Literacy: join my handwriting, add on the end of letters. Maths: add two different numbers (b).
Maths: learn 4, 3, and 2 times tables. Literacy: not put capital letters in the middle of sentences (g).
Literacy: not put capital letters in the middle of sentences; only use speech marks when you should (b).
Literacy: I've got to make my writing bigger (g).
Targets help you improve (g).

Can you remember past targets?

In literacy I succeeded with speech marks; in maths, to be able to write numbers in one box (b).

Last year in maths I learned all my times tables (g).

I did not putting capitals in the middle of sentences (g).

I can add 2 to nearly any two-digit number (b).

Y4ii   Learn to add up to 1000 (g).

Cannot remember present targets but my last target was find a word quickly in the dictionary (b).

Convert decimals to fractions (b).

Learn to do graphs (b).

Y5i   Continue to use paragraphs (b). Continue joining letters (b).

Use paragraphs (g).

To work quickly but neatly, use apostrophes and commas (g).

Those are all literacy – do you have any other targets?

Work on long division and multiplication (g, b).

Work on long division (g).

No (b).

We have targets every month (g).

If we think we've completed it, we set another one (b).

Can you tell me a target you hit recently?

Use paragraphs (g). I've done joining letters (b).

Improved presentation – *how?* – I switched pens (b).

Have shorter sentences (g).

Y5ii   Spelling; personal targets also – to join handwriting and remember to do homework (g).

Handwriting and reading at home (b).

Keep handwriting neat; read at home; don't go to sleep (b).

Read at home; spelling (g).

Y6i   Timed stories; brackets, dashes, colons, semicolons (b).

To use semicolons and colons (g). Punctuation and paragraphs (g).

Joining handwriting (b).

Other than literacy?

Consolidate division, multiplication, addition and subtraction (b).

Learn all the tables (g).

Get better at equivalent fractions (g).

Learn all tables (b).

Do they help?

Yes, you know what you've got to improve (g).

Y6ii   Capital letters (g). Join writing (g).

Make my writing bigger (two bs).

Teacher writes them at the back of the book. Once a month we look and see if we've done it. I like my own personal targets (g). I prefer the teacher's (b).

We have numeracy targets once a week; we don't look at them, they're pinned on the wall. We also have group ones (two gs). I forget mine (g). I think mine was times tables (b).

April School – primary, 4–11, town

I put my questions to each class as a whole and wrote down the pupils' answers as we went round, as in circle time.

What have you learned recently in school?

YR   Words (g). Pictures (b). Books (b). Reading (a book) (two bs).
        Making dinosaurs (b) Jigsaws (b) Doing fish (b). Rats (b).

Y1/2   Fiction books. Spelling new words. Time. Some flowers give fruit.
        Material (bs, gs).

Y2   Shapes. Pentagon, hexagon, octagon. Time (bs).
        Numbers. Greater and less than: >, < (gs).

Y3   [Choosing to 'pass' = 7]
        English. Non-fiction/fiction. Listening. Spelling.
        Maths. Angles: right, obscure, acute. Ir/Regular shapes.
        Plants: what they eat. Habitat. Mountains. Water. Beans: how to grow them.
        The Pied Piper. Romans.
        Pop-up books. North, south, east and west.
        Assembly (bs, gs).

Y5/6   Some writing about when we feel jealous. About people's feelings.
        About novels. Poems. Songs. Making up our own riddles.
        Solving riddles.
        Maths: percentages. Fractions. Decimals.
        Science: electricity.
        Acting for the school play. Art. Cooking (gs, bs).

What has helped you learn (those things) in school? [Numbers of pupils nominating subject or activity shown in brackets where the number is greater than one. Distinguishing between boys and girls was not always possible from my notes or the tape.]

YR   Teachers (b). You get a name card (b). Put your name on and get a sticker (b).
        Do 'choosing' (two bs).

Y1/2   Our minds. Our brains [5]. The ideas make us think.
        Our teachers [2].
        Our dictionaries. Thesaurus. Word cards. Spelling [2].
        The hundred squares.

Y2   In maths, the number line.
      Our teachers: they tell us things. Our Support Assistants.
      When stuck, my word bank.
      When working something out, I look at the questions again.
      When stuck on a word on a sheet, I put my hand up.
      For spelling, a dictionary.
      I think again.
Y3   [Choosing to 'pass' = 5]
      When we go in pairs. When I work by myself: it gives me more time.
      When I have support from my group.
      My brain [4].
      The support assistant and teacher [5]. Explaining work on the board.
      My ALS group [3].
      Index/Contents/Glossary. Splitting words up [2]. Adverbs and link words.
      Blocks for counting. The multiplication square.
Y5/6 Teachers (g). Having a teacher I like (b). People explain (g).
      Special people who work with your special needs (g).
      My brain (b). Finding out different methods of working things out (b).
      Working in groups (b). Working with partners (b).
      When we do research (b). When I make mistakes (b).
      Understanding what to do (g).
      Friends (b). Sitting where you want to, and pen and paper (b).
      All the books, and what's writ on the board (b).

What ways do you have of knowing what you are going to learn? [Numbers of pupils nominating subject or activity shown in brackets where the number is greater than one. Distinguishing between boys and girls was not always possible from my notes or the tape.]

YR   It's Mothers' Day soon.
Y1/2 It's nearly Easter (so we do lots to do with Easter, and Mothers' Day).
      Miss Y tells us.
Y2   Teacher tells us.
      We're working on shape and I just know.
      At home time we get a letter.
Y3   [Choosing to 'pass' = 3]
      It's wrote up on the board [12].
      Mrs Z tells us [2].
      Miss S (student) writes it as a surprise.
      I look around.
      Clues, and I ask the teacher.
      After first play we always have numeracy or literacy.
      Spelling and times table tests on Friday.
      Routines like Gymnastics on Monday.
Y5/6 Our teacher tells us (4 pupils). She writes it on the board (g).

Sometimes we get told what our next topic is (b).
A friend tells you (b). Newsletter (b). Assemblies (b).
In a minute we'll do work (b). I don't know (b).

What ways do you have of knowing how well you are doing? [Numbers of pupils nominating subject or activity shown in brackets where the number is greater than one. Distinguishing between boys and girls was not always possible from my notes or the tape.]

YR   We work (g). We take our name off and play and read a book . . . (b).
        I'm always completing.
Y1/2   By going to my targets in my book [2].
        By reading the work through [4].
        Listen to Mrs Y [2].
        For maths I use my fingers.
        We can check it. Use 'have-a-go paper' and see if it's right.
Y2   When you get the work, the teacher tells you. The star chart.
        We look at our work when we get it back: look for star, smiley face, tick.
        If it's wrong or has a line underneath, we work it out again.
        Mrs X comes and tells us.
        To do painting, she tells us what to do so we know (the success criteria).
        I always check. When we see our spelling, we see if they're right.
        Marking – she takes our work to the staffroom.
Y3   [Choosing to 'pass' = 2]
        Get a smiley face [7]. Teachers write in the back of your book.
        Teachers tell you in your book [9]; e.g. 'check this' [2].
        Teacher calls me up.
        Open evening – my mum tells me.
        In maths, if I get the question right, I'm quick at it.
        If I try my best.
        I look back in my book. I check when I think it's not right.
        Work goes on display. You get a coloured star.
Y5/6   Spelling shows how we're progressing (b).
        Comments in our book (four bs). Teacher tells you or writes it down
        (four gs).
        Go to the teacher, marking and stickers (b). Ticks and dots on work (b).
        Teacher compliments (b).
        SATs practice and marks (g). Times tables test of Fridays (b).
        My brain (g). Targets (g, b). Merit points (three bs).
        Friends tell you (b). Reports and parents evening (b).
        Assistants in maths, sheets and marks (b).

What are you good at? [Numbers of pupils nominating subject or activity shown in brackets where the number is greater than one. Distinguishing between boys and girls was not always possible from my notes or the tape.]

YR   Playing the games (g). Reading books (b).

Computers (b). Completing computers (b).
Crocodile puzzles (two bs). Drawing (g).
Choosing (g). Milk time (b).
Tidying up (b).

Y1/2   Writing in my diary [2]. Literacy. Spelling [2]. Talking.
Maths [4].
Art [5]. Colouring.
Making models. Puzzles.
Football [2].
Playing monsters.

Y2   [All responded]
English [2]. Reading. Spelling [2]. Spaces (leaving them between
words). Maths [4]. Science [2].
Art [5]. Drawing [2]. Painting [2]. Colouring.
DT. Making houses. RE [2]. History.
Sheets. PE. Games.
Getting class stars. Tests. Tasks. Challenges.

Y3   [Choosing to 'pass' = 1]
Reading [4]. Reading and writing. English [4]. Literacy.
Maths [14] Sums. Science [2].
Art [13]. PE and Dance.
Playing. Football [3]. Chatting [2].

Y5/6   English (g). Spelling (two bs). Handwriting (b). Story writing (g).
Maths (four gs, five bs). Art (four gs, four bs).

*What are you trying to get better at in your school work? Tell me about that in a little
more detail.* [Numbers of pupils nominating subject or activity shown in brackets
where the number is greater than one. Distinguishing between boys and girls was
not always possible from my notes or the tape.]

YR   Writing *j* (b). Reading books (five pupils).
Reading folder (b). Finishing computers (b).
Drawing (b). Work (b).
Sore knee (b).

Y1/2   Capital letters and full stops [2]. Full stops [2].
Writing [3]. Spelling. Reading through my work. Literacy.
Doing my *ds* and *es* properly.
Maths.
Shoelaces. Football.

Y2   [Numbers of pupils nominating subject or activity shown in brackets;
total responding = 18]
English. Reading. Spelling. Writing [2]. Doing *b* and *d*.
Putting capitals to start sentences. Neater writing. Keep full stops at
the end.
Time [2]. Technology. Making stuff. History.
Running. Work neater. Tasks.

Do my targets. Getting more class stars.

Y3   Stories [3]. Joining my writing. Handwriting [2]. Writing [2].
Spelling.
Poems. Reading. Knowing words' meaning.
Maths [6]. Times tables. Science [4].
Art. Drawing.
Cutting out cows. Pass the ball.
Targets.
Sitting quietly. Stop being naughty. Be (more) good(er) [2].
Stop tormenting my sister. Eating. Tidying my bedroom. Cleaning up.
Stop fighting my brother [2]. Riding my bike downstairs.

Y5/6   English (three bs, two gs). Spelling (two gs).
Handwriting (g, b). Writing bigger (b). Remembering spellings (b).
Maths (three bs, two gs).
Science (four gs, b).
Presentation (b). Art (two bs, g). Cooking (g).
Handling my behaviour (b).

Do you have targets? Can you tell me about them? (What do you think about them?)
[Numbers of pupils nominating subject or activity shown in brackets where the
number is greater than one. Distinguishing between boys and girls was not always
possible from my notes or the tape.]

YR   (The class has been playing football as part of their 'outside work' and
practising by using targets for the goal.)
Playing football (6 pupils). Always scoring a goal (b).
Go on stage (g).

Y1/2   [Not able to recall or respond = 4]
Full stops [6]. Commas (and doing well). Capital letters [2].
Use finger spaces [3]. Make sure it makes sense. Use describing words.
Form letters the right way round. Press lighter on my pencil.

Y2   [Total responding = 24]
Put capitals in the right places: [4]. Full stops: [4].
Neater handwriting: [4]. Spelling: [5]. Leave more spaces between
words: [3].
Stop putting capital letters in the wrong places: [1]. Joined up writing: [1].
Use more interesting words in my writing: [1]. Get my writing right: [1].

Y3   [Not able to recall or respond = 3]
Get my handwriting small. Keep the margin. Keep writing on the line.
Join up handwriting [2]. Write neater (with a pen) [2]. Even
handwriting.
Use capital letters [2]. Commas [2]. Full stops. Capital letters and full
stops [3]. Learn spelling patterns.
Use interesting words. Use spelling thesaurus. Avoid repetition.
Improve my story plans. Use more adjectives [3]. Link words.
Don't think so much.

Y5/6   [Pupils 'passing' = 9]
        Not to draw on the front and back of books (b).
        How to do as well in a test as normally (g).
        Write in paragraphs (four gs). Keep to the same tense (g).
        Writing 'and' (g). Write bigger (b). Ascenders and descenders (b).
        Punctuation (two bs). Spelling (b). Full stops and capital letters (b).
        Punctuation, paragraphs, and not making silly mistakes in maths (b).
        Writing longer stories (b). Better ideas in my writing (b).
        Presentation (g). Stop rushing (b).
        Finger spaces (b).
        Everything (b).

May School – middle 9–14, town and surrounding area

I interviewed four pupils, usually two girls and two boys, chosen by the teachers of classes from each year group, tape-recording the conversations.

What have you learned recently in school?
Y5   Paragraphs, commas, speech, spelling (g).
       Complex sentences, syllables (b).
       Onomatopoeia, metaphors, similes, idioms, alliteration (g, b).
       Why those things? Because they're the main things, the most useful skills for the future. We go over them (g).
Y6   Volume, area, perimeter in maths (g).
       Kenya, types of animal (g).
       Listening, discussion texts (b).
       DT, electric circuits, cooking (b, g).
Y7   In history: about medieval life (b).
       In maths: about fractions (g).
       In English: persuasive writing, like in holiday brochures (g).
       In science: about animal and plant kingdoms (g, b).
Y8   Human biology in science (b). Corfe Castle, the Civil War (g).
       Voyage of Discovery: in groups chosen by the teacher, creative problem-solving (g).

What has helped you learn (those things) in school?
Y5   We have labels up on the board for all the things we learn as we do them, like onomatopoeia, etc (b).
       When we're writing a story, Miss tells us to include those things (g).
       The teacher does photocopies for people with different abilities: if you're not so talented, you get simpler sheets (g).
       We have different groups, like 'Roald Dahl' for not so good, and 'Dick King Smith': the groups help because like 'Roald Dahl' wouldn't be able to complete 'Jenny Dale's' work in the time (g).
       When we work in pairs (g).

When Mrs X gives us levels and effort grades (g).

It could be our targets help us: she gives us them with a date in our book: you can see what to improve on (gs).

You can have it in your head when you're working (b).

She says like you've achieved two targets (g).

Examples of targets, all taken from Literacy exercise books, appearing once every few weeks:

- Think carefully about your paragraphing – they can be rather long at times
- Be sure to keep your handwriting the same throughout a piece of work
- Remember new speaker, new line when writing speech
- Remember that all stage directions begin with a capital letter
- Indent all paragraphs
- Read through your work when you have finished: double check your spelling and punctuation
- Copy carefully from the board
- Double check your spelling and punctuation
- Make sure that capital letters, especially the letter I, do not creep into your work in the wrong places
- You are going to have to work on the quality of your work: you are making too many mistakes – you're still using the capital B
- Remember that proper nouns always have a capital letter.

Sometimes the pupils write the targets themselves in their books when the teacher has spoken to them.

We're reminded of what we need to do. Like nagging: you have to do them – making your work more quality (g).

Targets and written comments in our reading records and in our 'first of the month book' also help (b).

Y6   Help from the teachers (g).

In science experiments. In maths sometimes the teacher shows you, and usually gives you extra help, if you get stuck (b).

Teachers explaining (g).

You (the other girl) have a red folder – like extra help (g). Yes, it's quite easy (g).

Y7   Text books (g).

Having it explained (b).

Things written on the board (g).

Sheets sometimes are useful, but not necessarily; helpful when you get the information right in front of you, and some are more exciting than others (g, b).

Y8   When it's fun you want to learn (b).

Something to look at, models (g). Books (g).

If the teacher is good, not really strict; if you get on with the teacher (b, g).

Things on the board, like not making us remember it all (g).
Less writing: learning it without having to write everything down (b).

What ways do you have of knowing what you are going to learn?
Y5   At the beginning of the lesson the teacher tells us (g).
        Sometimes she tells us what we're going to be doing tomorrow (g).
        Sometimes we have to finish off work from the last lesson (g).
Y6   The teacher sometimes tells you, or if she doesn't, you just wait till the
        lesson. Or you just ask (b).
Y7   Timetable (g). Sometimes they tell us, like a week before, like to bring
        in certain things (g). Homework is quite often related to the next
        lesson (g).
        Sometimes things are mentioned in assembly that other classes have
        got on and we haven't (b).
Y8   They usually say the lesson before (g).

What ways do you have of knowing how well you are doing?
Y5   Targets: if you haven't got many, you know you're doing really well (g).
        Effort grades, all the time (g). Merits. Parents evening (g).
        In science tests we have levels at the top (b).
        Sometimes on the work you've done she writes little comments. (g)
Y6   They give us marks (g). 'G' or merit (b).
        Scale of 'M', 'G', 'S', 'D', 'U' (gs, bs).
        If you're doing really well in maths or something, you have to do a
        separate test. And in science you do an older test that no-one else
        does. To see how good you are (b).
Y7   Summatives (g).
        Writing in books (g).
        Parents evenings; sometimes we're allowed, sometimes we're not (g). I
        think it's up to the key stage co-ordinators (b).
        Sometimes they tell us in class (b).
Y8   Teachers tell you (g). We get grades – for each piece of work (b).
        Merits: and then you get a merit award as well, that's really really
        brilliant. You can't get merit awards for just one piece of work (gs).
        And for a certain amount of awards you get a commendation, a
        certificate (b).
        Summatives: at the end of every term they do a comment on how
        you're getting on. They tick boxes, and we have to write in what we
        think (gs).
        Sometimes you get certain tasks to do, set tasks for bigger grades (b).

What are you good at?
Y5   Writing stories (b). Art: drawing (b). Reading (g). Maths, but I don't
        like it: all my family are really good at it, but I hate it (g).
Y6   Spelling, reading out loud (g).

Art, because I like doing sketching. Also DT because we get to make cakes and stuff (b).

Drama, plays (g).

Science, generally (b).

Y7   Art: drawing (g).

Sports: athletics, running; English: spelling (b).

IT, maths, science, generally overall in those (b).

DT: making stuff (g).

Y8   Maths: all of it, especially investigations at home (b).

Science: at the moment, experiments (g).

English, Voyage of Discovery project: to find out things in books and the internet – you don't get much guidance and work at your own speed (b).

Maths: sums (g).

What are you trying to get better at in your school work? Tell me about that in a little more detail.

Y5   That's what our targets tell us (b).

I've got (as a target) new speaker, new paragraph; complex sentences; handwriting because mine's getting too small; paragraphs (g).

Sometimes I rush at the end of my work, so it goes to a close too quickly, so I need to pace my work better (b).

Neat handwriting (g).

My letters have all got to be the same size when I'm writing (b).

Y6   Maths, generally (g).

Maths, generally (g).

Spelling, reading (b).

Maths, generally (b).

Y7   Maths: fractions (g).

English: improve reading, not sure in what way (b).

English: handwriting – it's not quite perfect; tidiness; and creative writing (b).

French: I don't think it's that I'm not very good at it, it's just that I have to concentrate hard in the lessons. It's because it's a different language. It's not any particular bits of French, it's the whole (g).

Y8   Joined up writing: they're always going on about it, because at the upper school it's got to be joined up or you lose marks in your English test, but I find it quicker to print (g). They say it's quicker joined up, but it's not for me (g).

Make my handwriting bigger: everyone's always complaining, and for the upper school. (g)

Writing: slow down – I scribble it out too fast (g).

General English work: we have sets and I'm in a middle set and I'm just trying to get better generally in writing and that (b).

Do you have targets? Can you tell me about them? (What do you think about them?)

Y5 Targets are really useful (b). They're quite good because they tell you what you need to improve on (g).

So you can think 'Right today I'm really going to try and keep my – and once Miss made us write at the top of our work what target we were improving on and, yeah, then she'd look at our work and see if we'd done it and then write a comment on it at the end. So it tells you how your work's been (bs).

Y6 Spellings: Miss tells us to look through some of our books to see if we have spellings to do – for literacy (g).

In literacy we have two pages for targets (g).

In creative writing she writes like 'Put in commas' (b).

Start a new sentence (g).

Before we go to literacy we have handwriting practice. She writes words on the board and we have to copy them – like letters that are difficult to join up (g).

Y7 Keep on doing well – get good results. That's my decision, to get a good job and do what I want (b).

Get better at my reading and try and get better at spelling. I do a red folder: my spelling is not the greatest; my reading's ok. But they say I need to be improved a bit more and I think I do as well (b).

Concentrate: I don't work really hard. You have to work hard some of the time on the more important things (g).

Spelling: which is my decision (g).

We get targets on our summatives, but we don't always see the comments – sometimes we write our comment before we see the teacher' comment (g).

But in maths we get graded: there's four boxes, like investigating, for our levels (bs, gs).

Y8 On our summatives they ask us to put 'I'd like to improve in . . .': they put pointers like things you're good at and things you enjoyed and things you want to improve on (g).

This time I put 'to listen more' because I'm always talking (g).

I put about my handwriting (g).

Does that get followed up by anyone; does anyone pick that up later?

I don't think so (g). Well the teachers put a comment too (g). But then sometimes they write their comment first; and sometimes they don't, so we don't get to read what they've written (g).

Can you remember your targets from the last time? No.

This time round, does anyone look at what you wrote last time? I expect so – they don't always tell us (g).

June School – secondary, 12–16, suburban estates

Year 9 History: I spoke to four girls and two boys.

What have you enjoyed most in history this year?
> Looking at old newspapers (b).
> Going on computers (g).
> The world wars (b, g).
> Unable to say (two gs).

Tell me something that have you learned in history this year.
> About wars and how they're fought (b).
> About evidence (g).
> About war in the trenches, and evidence (g).
> Unable to say (two gs, b).

What are you best at in history?
> Finding information (b).
> Everything (g). Quite a lot (b).
> Nothing. Oh, talking (discussing in class) (g).
> Unable to say (two gs).

What have you tried to get better at this year in history?
> Writing neater (g).
> Not dominating discussions (b).
> Listening (g).
> Co-operating: putting my hand up (g).
> Not getting into trouble (g).
> Unable to say (b).

What targets have you had in history?
> Co-operating; answering and thinking about questions more;
> confidence (g).
> Trying not to rush work, and neater work (b).
> Writing neater (g).
> Getting a good level in my project (g).
> Unable to say (g, b).
> *Did you hit your target?*
> Sometimes (g, b).
> Yes (g).
> Unable to say (two gs, one b).

What helps you learn?
> Writing stuff down (g).
> Unable to say (three gs, two bs).

Do you have targets in other subjects?
> Yes (three gs, b).
> No, or unable to say (g, b).

Can you give an example?
> In maths, my target was level 6 and I got a level 7 (g).
> Confidence (g).
> No answer (two gs, two bs).

Year 10 History: I spoke to five girls and five boys.

What have you enjoyed most in history this year?
> Coal-mining (b).
> Roads (g). Railways (b). Transport (two bs).
> Agriculture (g).
> Population (g).
> Factories (b).
> Everything (g).
> Only just arrived, so cannot say (g: so I did not ask her anything else).

Tell me something that have you learned in history this year.
> Different revision methods, e.g. spider diagrams (b).
> How to revise and answer questions (g).
> Evidence (b). How to use secondary evidence (b).
> How to write good essays (b).
> Loads: agriculture improvers, steam, iron (g).
> About different types of transport (b, g).
> About agriculture (g).

What are you best at in history?
> Skills: putting across my ideas to the class (b). Class discussion (g).
> Essay writing, when I get started; and talking in class (g).
> Finding out evidence (b, g).
> Looking at pictures and working things out from them (g).
> Getting on with my work quickly (b).
> Everything (g).
> Railways (b).

What have you tried to get better at this year in history?
> Revising (b, g).
> Giving longer answers with more detail (g). Trying to remember details in essays (g).
> Essay-writing (b).
> Being more consistent in my work (b).
> Getting most of the work done (b).
> Presentation (b).

What targets have you had in history?
> Improving detail in answers; keeping organised; if I don't do something well, I improve it (g).
> Wider reading (g). Wider reading; start revising earlier (b).
> Essay-writing (g).
> Do more work; improve presentation (b).
> Be more consistent (b).
> Better grade (b).
> Unable to say (g, b).

Did you hit your target?
> Yes (three bs, one g).
> No (b).
> Unable to say (three gs, b).

What helps you learn?
> Revision: Miss introduces the lesson with revision (g). Revision sheets (g).
> Talking things over with friends (two bs, one g).
> Enjoyment (b).
> My dad (b). My mum (b).
> Unable to say (g).

Do you have targets in other subjects?
> All said yes.

Can you give an example?
> Maths – grade C; science – grade B, and a higher set (b).
> Art; science – resistant materials (b).
> English – presentation and behaviour (b).
> Science – concentrate more (g).
> Maths – revise, and concentrate more (g).
> Geography – learn more skills (b).
> Revise earlier (g).
> Ask for help when I need it (b).
> To keep up good work (g).

Do targets help you learn?
> Yes, if test results are below your target, you work harder (b).
> Sometimes: if I've been told I have to do it, I work harder (g).
> Yes, they push you (g).
> Yes, you know what to concentrate on (b).
> Yes (three bs).
> Sometimes (g).
> No (g).

July School – secondary, 11–18, town outskirts and villages

Year 10 English

What are you good at in this subject?   *How do you know?*

g Nothing; presentation and handwriting.   Mum tells me; friends tell me.
b Thinking up ideas.   I find it easiest, and quite enjoy it.
b Speaking and listening.   I get high marks for it.
b Writing non-fiction.   Same as the two above.
g Writing stories and poetry.   I can do it, and I enjoy it.
g Poetry.   I get high marks.
b Not sure; language analysis.   I find it easy.
b Summary.   Ditto.
g I like writing.
g I like poster work.

What are you trying to get better at?

g Writing in general; spelling; making things up.
b Use of words, being compact; spelling (words with suffixes).
b Spelling, grammar, punctuation.
b Spelling, grammar, punctuation.
two gs   I don't know.
two bs   I don't know.
g Essay writing; listening more.
g Essay writing; paying more attention.

What is your focus for the work you're doing now?

g It's too big for a focus, but I'm working on how I say things.
g Overall structure.
two bs   Full stops.
two gs   Not using joining words.

What methods/routines do you have for improving your work/raising your standards?

b Look back and go over the mistakes.
two bs   I don't know.
two bs   Practise.

What have you got better at?

g Writing more slowly; I used to avoid big words because of the spelling, but now I ask for help.
b I used not to be good at poems; I practised rhythm.
b Descriptive writing – using synonyms, metaphor, personification . . .
g Handwriting.
g I don't know.
b Spelling; using paragraphs.
b Full stops; punctuation.

Please, tell me about targets.

b   We get set them – on some projects, e.g. use more full stops, use less slang.

g   I don't find them helpful.

b   I haven't got one now; I don't get many; so I just concentrate on this task.

b   My target is sentence layout, getting meanings right, and putting across my points.

b   My target is punctuation and spelling.

g   Paragraphing, full stops, spelling, and I'm not good at reading.

g   Capital letters.

Several pupils said the target pages in their planners were not used much and not useful.

What is the key to your making progress?

g   One-to-one time with the teacher.

two gs   I don't know.

three bs   Atmosphere – relaxed is better.

g   In Year 9 we didn't do much. Books went unmarked. It was games and videos.

g   Not all teachers help.

g   We need more poetry and essays and pre-twentieth century prose.

What is your aim? What do you want to achieve? What will make the difference?

g   Push myself to a B.

b   I came down from the top set, so I aim to go back up.

b   I'm predicted a B, and I aim to get an A. Use of language.

g   C (predicted E).

g   C (predicted C but I don't think that's right.) What we're practising now.

b   C or B.

C or high C.

Year 8 English: I asked as many pupils as many of my questions as I could.

What are the good points about the targets you have?

b   Every time you open your folder and look at them, they remind you to keep up.

b   Miss tells us every now and then and it gets into your head.

g   If you achieve them, you know you're improving.

b   They show you what you're to do, as an aim.

g   Otherwise you'd forget.

g   Otherwise you'd make the same mistakes.

b   If you aim to improve, you're more likely to remember.

g   If she tells you about the problem you can do something about it.

b   I agree with that view.

g   It's good when you achieve your target.

g   They help.

b   If you've made a mistake beforehand, you correct it.

What are the negative aspects of having targets?
b   They can make you feel bad and not good enough; but I feel they motivate you.
b and g   You've got to keep writing them down.
g   If you've got too many, you can't do them.
g   You can feel dippy.
b   You feel bad if she says them in front of the class.
g and b   Sometimes you forget them.
b   You don't make the effort.

What targets have you hit in the past?
b   I achieved spelling 'd-e-c-i-e-v-i-n-g' (oh!). I'm better at not repeating myself and stating the obvious.
b   Spelling 'b-u-s-i-n-e-s-s'.
b   Change '-y' to '-ies'.
b   'coming' not 'comeing'.
g   Mostly my spelling is better.
g   Story writing.
b   Something in literature essays, but I can't remember.
g   About who speaks in a story.
b   Present tense.
b   Commas (for parenthesis).
two gs   Paragraphs.

Have you any comments on using targets?
g   There should be an exercise made up so that you can try to achieve the target.
g   We never seem to write our target at the top of the work.
b   We need to have targets.
b   We only have them for English and science.
g   We get more for homework.
g   I don't use them always.
b   I don't always bother with mine.
g   They don't help very much. You go through the stage when all the teachers go on about them.

Are some targets better or cleverer than others? No.

Year 9 Science: I asked as many pupils as many of my questions as I could.

What is good about using targets?
b   They remind you of what to do.
g   They make you get more in the test – you have to go up a mark.
b   They can help writing.
g   You know what you've got to get.
g   They make you want to work hard; sometimes you get a merit.

b They give you something to aim at, make you motivated – but they don't really work.

What bad points are there?
b If the student doesn't get the target, they can be disappointed.
g I don't look at them much – they're in the back of my head.
two bs   You don't remember them.
b They're not of value, e.g. handwriting – that is not such a big deal.
g If you don't get it.
g If you're not good, you get no reward.

What is your present target?
All mentioned the score they were aiming for, e.g. 39 out of 50. The following were responses to my asking whether there were non-score targets. Several pupils referred to their planners for these, and couldn't otherwise remember them.
g Sometimes underlining headings, behaviour in class.
g and b Underlining.
g Copying up, spelling, giving scientific explanation.
b Try to slow down.
b Keep writing neater.
g Complete tasks.
b Writing, spelling.
g Scientific explanation.

Why do you have targets in science (but not in some other subjects)?
Most did not offer an answer to this question. Others' answers were:
g and b It helps you improve learning.
b It's a core subject.
b Because the headmaster told them to.
g We do a lot of tests – it shows what you can do if you think about it.
g It's to do with module tests.

Do your parents know your targets?
Some had no answer to this. Others did:
two gs   Yes.
b Yes, they look at the homework diary.
g Mum looks sometimes.
g At parents' evenings.
b It's up to you.
g They don't look but know you get them.
b I don't inform them.

Why are you learning about this/doing this work?
Some pupils were not sure. Others said:
g It's about food tests and energy, diet and health.

b   About foods and how they affect our bodies and health.
b   Seeing how much energy there is in foods – why we eat certain foods.
g   Balanced diet.
b   It's the build-up to GCSE.
    I wondered whether the teacher would have liked them to refer to scientific processes.

August School: secondary, 13–18, rural and small towns

Year 10 Religious Studies: the pupils' answers as a class are reported in Chapter 2, pp. 21–3.

Year 10 Science: I asked as many pupils as many of my questions as I could.

What helps you learn best?
> Having a good teacher (b). This is the best teacher we've had for science (b).
> Miss helps (g). She comes to answer questions and gives ideas of what to do (b).
> Help from the teacher: she doesn't give you the answer – she makes you think (g).
> She makes it interesting (b).
> You get attention from the teacher: if there's a problem, she'll help you (g).
> Good instructions from the teacher (b).
> Miss explains very well (g, b). She does not just get us to copy (g).
> Demonstrations (b, g).
> Loads of information, so you know exactly what to do (g).
> The teacher is quite friendly (g).
> Very good equipment (g).
> Doing practicals (b).
> Books (two bs, g).
> Sheets/Revision guides (two gs).

Do you have targets; if so, what do you have to do to achieve your target?
All pupils I spoke to knew their target which they expressed in terms of a GCSE grade (B, C or D). Their 'recipes for success' were:
* Revising (b)
* Better planning (two bs, g).
* Better coursework (two gs, two bs).
* Writing for coursework (g).
* Writing in more detail (g).
* Padding coursework out; doing more research (g).
* Analysis (g).
* Following the sheets (g).

- Producing quality work (b).
- Doing homework (b).
- Working hard (three bs).

Why does it help you to have targets?

You know what you have to do (b). The teacher shows you where you are now and how far to work to get a result (b). (Clarity.)

You know what to aim for (four bs, g). I can do better (g). It makes you aim higher (g). You can work yourself up (g). It's something to aim for – a challenge. (Purpose/motivation.)

When I was told I could get a D, I was proud (g). If you think you can do it, you can (g). (Self-esteem/confidence.)

September School – special, 3–18, town and surrounding area

Year 5: I asked the class my questions and wrote down the answers of those pupils who volunteered.

What are you good at in school?

Maths, number work (b).

Swimming 400 metres (b).

Handwriting (b).

Maths – counting (g).

Being good, listening to the teacher (b).

Swimming 10 metres (b).

Swimming tests – I've got Water Skills One (g).

Maths – sums (b).

What have you been trying to get better at?

Swimming, backstroke (b)

Behaviour – stop being silly (b).

Being good (b).

Getting merits (g).

Swimming on my back (b).

Writing (b).

Finishing the chart (g).

Be good – be in a happy mood (b).

What targets do you have?

In my blue book, to get four stars, then a treat (b).

They are on the chart at the back of the room (b).

Controlling temper – take tablets to calm down. (b).

Remember my glasses (g).

Little book – four gets a treat (b).

Don't know (two bs).

What helps you learn in school?
> The teacher (two bs). Teachers (b). Mrs M (g).
> Ritalin tablets – two whole and one half (b).
> Reading (b).
> Handwriting (g).
> Getting on (b).

What would help you even more?
> School books (b).
> Listening (b).
> Working hard (g).
> Miss G (b).
> Not being silly (g).
> Don't know (two bs, one g).

Year 6: I sat alongside pupils and asked as many of my questions as I could.

What are you good at in school?
> Maths – numbers (b, g).
> Maths – counting in twos and fives (b).
> Maths – adding up (b).
> Maths and computers (b).
> Reading – Treehouse (g).

What have you been trying to get better at?
> Reading (two bs).
> Reading and writing (b).
> Computers (g).
> Football – tripping up (b).
> Maths – numberwork (g).

What targets do you have?
> Homework (g).
> Don't know (four bs, one g).

What helps you learn in school?
> Adults (b).
> Reading (b).
> Friends (two bs).
> Mum (g).
> Dayday (g): I couldn't understand this reply (JB).

What would help you even more?
> Learning at home (b).
> Teachers (b, g).

The little ones (b): I think he meant he could help them more (JB).
Harder (g): not clear (JB).
Don't know (b).

[I was unable to strike up a conversation with one boy.]

Year 7/8: I asked the class my questions and wrote down the answers of those pupils who volunteered.

What are you good at in school?
Food tech – jam tarts (two gs). Food tech – cakes (g). Food tech – biscuits (two bs).
Maths – writing down sums (b). Maths – guessing the name (g).
Swimming lengths (b).
RE – prayer wheel (b).

What have you been trying to get better at?
Maths – listening carefully, numbers, adding (b).
Swimming – backstroke (two gs).
Handwriting – joined (g). Handwriting (b).
Behaviour (b).
When my brother beats me up, I try to go away (b).

What targets do you have?
Uncle Mike (b).
Short arrows (g).
SATs test (two gs).
A real target out there for shooting (b).

What helps you learn in school?
Teachers (two gs). When Mrs M does reading (b).
Where you read to the teacher and AA (g).
Giving out biscuits (g).
English (b).
Reading (two bs).
Don't know (b).

Year 9: I sat alongside pupils and asked as many of my questions as I could.

What are you good at in school?
Maths – sums (b).
Completing science tests (b).
French tests (b).
Computer skills (b).
Don't know (two gs).

What have you been trying to get better at?
>Science (b).
>English – joined-up writing (b). Writing neater (b). Clear handwriting (b).
>PE (g).
>Drawing in art (b).

What targets do you have?
>Science certificate (b).
>Football (two bs). Cricket (b). Tennis (b). Dancing (g).

Do you have behaviour targets?
>Control temper (b). Keep calm (b).

What helps you learn in school?
>Remembering back (b).
>Maths – counting money (b). Using calculator (b).
>English (b).
>Text book (b).
>If I'm stuck I look in the dictionary (b).
>Pictures (b).
>Computers (b).
>First aiders (b).

Year 10: I interviewed five boys and three girls in ones or twos outside the classroom, in a library area.

What are you good at in school?
>Getting on with my work: I got three AAs in a row. (b).
>Materials in science (b). Science (g).
>History – writing about videos on World War II (b).
>PE (g).
>English tests, media reviews (g).
>Art – I got a certificate (b).
>When I first came here, I was terrified; then I got my first AA; I was really chuffed; then I got my first commendation; Mrs N was really happy; I have got bronze, silver and gold awards for athletics (b).

What have you been trying to get better at?
>Saying the right things (b).
>English – handwriting (b). Handwriting (g). Spelling – by practising (b).
>PSD – sex education: knowing about the baby (b).
>Maths (two gs).
>Maths, science, English, writing, spelling, reading, food technology, history; NEAB award units (b).

What targets do you have?

> Year 11 will be different –working on the Youth Award Scheme (b).
> Just to do well (b).
> EAP: Mr H has it and ticks things off and writes comments (g).
> IT work; working with others; communication; handling numbers (b).
> Reading (g).
> Don't know (two bs, one g).

What helps you learn in school?

> When the teacher talks a lot about the stuff or gives you sheets (b).
> Teacher (g).
> When the teacher is nice and you are back (b). Mr H – he's funny (g).
> Trying to get better at writing, keeping it neat (b).
> When you get certificates (b).
> Maths – because things are better at home, I can learn in school: I'm slowly learning my tables (b).
> Not sure (g).

What would help you learn even better?

> When stuck on writing, calling the teacher over (b).
> Getting more certificates (b).
> The teachers are really nice; we need more helpers in school (b).
> Maths – calculator (g).
> Cannot think of anything (two bs, two gs).

Appendix 2
Marking policy

You may use the following suggested principles as a way of checking and revising your policy for marking. Alternatively, you may use the checklist as a starting point for discussion: delete items that do not accord with your approach; amend items that are close to your practice; add items that are missing and vital to your school's quality of marking.

- Marking can mean responding to pupils' work, whether in conversation or through writing.
- The purpose of individual pieces of work is made clear to the pupils.
- How work is to be assessed is made clear to the pupils; i.e. the success criteria are explicit.
- Teachers make clear whether they are focusing on subject knowledge and understanding, or on literacy and presentation.
- Teachers let pupils know when they can expect their work to be commented on and returned.
- Pupils understand the meaning of any score, grade, or level used.
- Teachers' comments are linked to lesson objectives and individual pupils' targets. They focus on the success criteria, are positive in overall tone, and are personalised, e.g. using the pupil's name.
- More often than not, the pupils are given time to do something with the marking they receive.
- Pupils know what the follow-up is to any piece of work: e.g. *finish it off, practise certain skills, develop the work in certain ways, do corrections.*
- Teachers sometimes correct single errors, but they routinely look for opportunities to teach patterns, and they do this through having the pupils do follow-up work. E.g. the pupils use special notebooks or pages in their exercise books to collect word-families or patterns.
- Teachers use a routine to correct or proof-read, such as this:
  > in the margin means *look along this line to find an error;*
  underlining means *here is the error* and *you must put the error right (because you can manage that);*
  teacher's correction in the margin means *I have put the error right (and you can learn from that).*

Further advice is available in *Pupils' Learning from Teachers' Responses*, published by the Association of Assessment Inspectors and Advisers South West Region (2001).

Appendix 3

Consistency in assessment

Valid targets depend on valid assessments. Teachers' own assessments provide crucial information about pupils' performance. The consistency of the information is vital to schools' self-evaluation and improvement. What follows here sets out what can be done to promote consistency in teachers' assessment of pupils' progress and achievement.

Many colleagues in primary schools call the process of developing consistency agreement trialing; colleagues in secondary schools tend to call it moderation; and colleagues in further education call it verification. We will use a neutral term – standardisation.

Standardisation of assessments is not necessarily a smooth or straightforward process. People, for example, interpret marking schemes, level descriptions, and grade criteria differently. However much you think the task is to agree marks, levels or grades, you are likely to find yourself considering more fundamental things, such as how to teach a certain concept or skill, or how pupils learn, or how individual criteria reflect the nature of the subject as a whole. Indeed, this may be the greatest value of standardisation meetings. You will find, though, despite the best will in the world, your systems will be stretched, e.g. through illness or absence, and through sheer pressure of time.

We will approach consistency in assessment through these questions:

- Why do you need to be consistent as an individual teacher?
- Why do you need to be consistent as a team of teachers?
- What can you do to develop your consistency as an individual teacher?
- What can you do to develop your consistency as a team of teachers?
- How can you make standardisation meetings benefit your pupils' learning?

Why do you need to be consistent as an individual teacher?

Consistency is a part of fair and effective teaching. You need to have a consistent understanding of quality if you are to help pupils learn.

If you were not consistent, pupils might, for example:

- receive conflicting advice about learning from you;

- become resentful that a piece of their work was not praised, but similar work by other pupils was praised;
- be confused and put off that today you say *good* and tomorrow *not good enough*, when pupils have made the same effort and produced, in their eyes, comparable work.

Your consistency reflects your relatively stable grasp of essential concepts and skills in the subject, your sense of how individuals progress in their learning, and your sense of justice between learners.

Why do you need to be consistent as a team of teachers?

What applies to the individual teacher applies equally well to a team of teachers. Pupils should not get different judgements from different teachers. You need to understand how one another judge pupils' work. The best way of developing understanding of one another's methods and criteria is to listen to one another's explanations of what pupils' work means, for example, at standardisation meetings.

You are accountable to one another in the school as much as you are to external authorities. You must justify your assessments to one another; then you may be in a position to justify them to others. The more consistent feeder schools are, the more their information will be relied on at transfer.

Neither teaching the same subject and scheme of work, nor using the same materials, guarantees consistency in assessment. This you have to tackle directly by discussing pupils' work and debating its merits against explicit criteria. However, the more you rush to the final question of what level or grade it is, the more you short-circuit those vital discussions about learning, teaching strategies and your subject.

The more you understand how one another see learning, the more you understand about the results one another get, the stronger you are as a team, and the more able you are to help one another and show others what your pupils have achieved. Consistency means shared understanding, and that is a powerful resource, particularly in times of great change, pressure and accountability.

What can you do to develop your consistency as an individual teacher?

There is no salvation in external moderators' imposing standards on teachers. If teachers leave it to others to decide, their own capacity to make consistent judgements is undermined. These are things you can do to develop your consistency in assessment:

- work with another teacher on developing a unit of work and agree with her/him the assessment criteria, and share outcomes;
- collect as wide a range as possible of pupils' work showing how differently they can demonstrate their capabilities;

- attend courses or exam board standardisation meetings that provide opportunities to consider judgements about pupils' learning;
- attend pyramid, cluster or interschool standardisation meetings;
- study and discuss published exemplar benchmark materials, e.g. QCA's books of pupils' assessed work;
- with colleagues in other feeder or receiving schools, devise work for pupils to take on transfer to their new school or college.

What can you do to develop your consistency as a team of teachers?

Here are some possibilities, depending on your situation and needs. Concentrating on specific roles:
- work together on assessment, recording and reporting to help trainee, part-time and non-specialist teachers;
- expect a co-ordinator, deputy headteacher, or headteacher to monitor pupils' work and colleagues' marking on a regular sampling basis; expect them to feed back perceptions to individuals and to follow up their reports at subject meetings;
- regard the teachers of a key stage as a team, and expect a key stage co-ordinator to develop consistency within the team.

Encouraging a co-operative approach to the teaching itself:
- engage in team teaching where possible;
- arrange for certain teachers to take responsibility for certain things, so that others have the opportunity to observe and learn.

Focusing on marking (see also Appendix 2):
- develop paired and consensual marking: pairs of teachers mark the same pieces of work independently, exchange marks, and negotiate a resolution of differences; pairs rotate and mix through the team;
- discuss exemplar materials as a team in order to clarify shared understandings of criteria;
- as a team, agree the marking scheme for work to be undertaken across a year group, paying special attention to the range of response that would be looked for, and share or display outcomes;
- compile a portfolio of pupils' work that has been agreed by the team as illustrating achievement against particular criteria.

Overcoming tensions that arise in discussions between colleagues when levels or grades have to be awarded:

- follow an agreed and explicit procedure for standardisation meetings, e.g. with a chairperson and someone to note conclusions and decisions (see below);

- develop a climate for meetings whereby colleagues understand that reflection and debate belong to a process of refining judgements and promoting consistency: feel free to express uncertainty, free to be honest and critical without rancour;
- choose awkward and contentious level descriptions or grade criteria deliberately, and recognise that argument can be constructive.

Establishing commonality through various types of practice and documentation used by the team:
- devise and use schemes of work so that learning objectives, content and assessments are common across the teaching team;
- devise and use units of work which relate to specific criteria and are marked according to agreed procedures and values;
- agree the use of common documentation for recording pupils' achievements, e.g. a *Can do* statement list;
- develop a common approach to pupils' setting their own targets;
- agree approaches to the display of pupils' work;
- have a marking policy. (See Appendix 2.)

Involving and informing pupils:
- as a team, develop ways of enabling pupils to understand and apply assessment criteria;
- consult pupils and gather their perceptions when as a team you review policies and practices;
- agree how pupils' work is to be kept and made accessible.

How can you make standardisation meetings benefit your pupils' learning?

You can try to make standardisation meetings focus on learning. It helps to build in the following steps, and to be quite deliberate about this.

- Agree beforehand what levels or grades will be the focus of the meeting; agree also the year groups, and agree who will bring what to the meeting. Make sure enough copies are available of everything that is needed.
- Take it in turns to act as chair. The chair's role is to make sure everyone has the opportunity to contribute, and to make sure the meeting addresses its purpose and finishes on time.
- Take it in turns to act as record-keeper. A basic record of who met, when, and with what focus, can be kept in the subject file, along with examples of pupils' work illustrating agreed levels or grades. (See also Chapter 8, referring to subject leadership.)
- Check what opportunities the pupils have had to develop the capabilities under discussion. Share teaching experiences.
- Discuss the capabilities to be assessed and seek common understanding of

them. Say what you think the words mean in level or grade descriptions. Say what pupils would have to do in order to match the descriptions.

- When you discuss particular pieces of work, invite the teacher concerned to explain the context, the task, conditions, and so on.
- Match the work to levels or grades. Find evidence for the pupils having attained a certain level or grade; explore how the work falls short of and exceeds other levels or grades.
- Consider putting the work in a portfolio of assessed work or the subject file; consider providing additional commentary or annotation that might be helpful to other readers, such as new teachers, supply teachers, senior managers, governors and inspectors.
- Consider how the pupils' learning might be taken further.
- Sum up what has been learned from the discussion.

This appendix is an updated version of an unpublished paper written in 1995 by Fran Ashworth, Les Cowling and myself with the help of a group of English, mathematics and science teachers from primary, middle, secondary, and special schools in Dorset.

Appendix 4

Statistical techniques

This appendix illustrates some of the ways in which assessment data can be used to inform target-setting. We shall consider these technical terms and the processes of using them:

- input and output measures;
- line of best fit;
- value added;
- upper and lower quartiles;
- chances graphs.

I am indebted to Les Cowling for the material contained here. A much fuller and very helpful treatment of this topic is provided by Schagen (2000) who carefully points out that statistics do not give good answers to our important questions about why pupils and schools perform as they do. We want to know why pupils in this school do better than pupils in that school. We want to know whether this teaching strategy or material helps pupils make better progress than that strategy or material. We want to know why our pupils behave as they do. Schagen (2000) tells us:

> statistics always refuse to say anything about causality . . . [G]ood statistical analysis can give us the crucial insights to develop theories, to support them, and to reject the ones that are out of line with the data . . . [A]ny educational theory or suggested intervention whose results cannot be measured in some way should be regarded with scepticism. If it really works, it should be possible to see the results in the numbers – somehow or some-where.
>
> (Schagen, 2000, p. 97)

Input and output measures

Input and output measures can be used to show pupils' attainment and progress in the form of a graph.

An input measure indicates a pupil's level of attainment at a given stage in her/his schooling. This might be Baseline Assessment, made in the first term of Reception. It might be the pupil's average National Curriculum points score for tests at the end of Key Stage 1, 2 or 3. It might be the average point score at GCSE. It can be any relatively early assessment information on a scale. Figure 1 shows one pupil who first scored 15 (input) and then scored 30 (output). Figures 2 plots inputs and outputs from forty-nine pupils – a cohort, or a pair of classes.

An output measure indicates a pupil's level of attainment at a later stage. This might be end-of-key-stage results, GCSE or A/AS level points, for example. This is used as the vertical axis of the graph.

The reason for collecting and focusing on input and output is that the difference between them provides an indication of how far a pupil is judged to have progressed over time. The measures can be collected year by year. They can be studied for single years, and trends can be shown over several years.

The more valid and reliable the measures, the truer the portrayal of progress

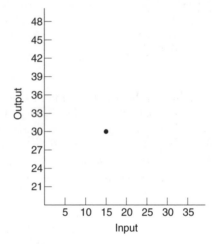

Figure 1 Input and output – a single pupil.

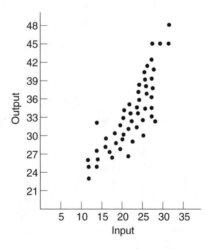

Figure 2 Input and output – forty-nine pupils.

between them. When data are collected for a school, a graph showing input and output correlation can be used as an indicator of how effective the school is. The data from any given school can be compared with data from other schools. And averages can be used, so that judgements can be made about whether a school is performing at above or below average levels.

Line of best fit and value added

The line of best fit shows the average rate of progress between the input and output measures. The line divides a population into two, though a small number of pupils appear on the line itself, having made precisely average progress. Pupils who appear above the line can be seen to have made better than average progress. And pupils who appear below the line can be seen to have made below average progress. (See Figure 3.)

Pupils who appear above the line can be said to have value added to their educational experience.

The line of best fit can be used to show what a pupil with a given measure of attainment according to one assessment might be expected to attain in the later assessment. You find the appropriate point on the horizontal axis, and read up to the line of best fit and across to the vertical axis to see what result the average pupil would expect to achieve. This might be taken as a minimum expected result or target. If for any reason you would expect the pupil to exceed average expectation, you would adjust your target upwards. Similarly, if there were known reasons for anticipating that the pupil would struggle to meet the average expectation, you would adjust the target accordingly. Figure 3 shows the line of best fit for many pupils.

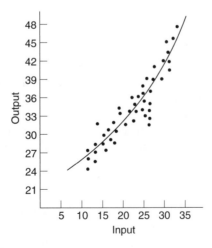

Figure 3 Line of best fit.

Upper and lower quartiles

It is just about half of the population that falls above the line, and just about half the population falls below the line. Further calculations can be done to draw more lines.

For example, a line can be drawn to show the highest performing 25 per cent of pupils. And a line can be drawn to show the lowest performing 25 per cent of pupils. We can call these lines, respectively, the upper and lower quartiles. The band in the middle shows the 50 per cent of pupils between the upper and lower quartiles. (See Figure 4.)

These calculations can be used to inform the choice of target for a pupil. If you would expect the pupil to make a high rate of progress, you would use the upper quartile marker. Figure 4 plots an upper-quartile (UQ) and a lower-quartile (LQ) line.

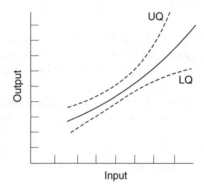

Figure 4 Upper and lower quartile lines.

Chances charts

We can also slice down through the graph. Using the horizontal axis as our reference, we can draw a column to include all of the pupils who are around point 15, point 25, point 35, and so on. Let us call those columns, respectively, A, B and C . . . . This is shown in Figure 5.

In other words, pupils in column A had the lowest prior attainment of the three groups. Pupils in column C had the highest prior attainment of the three groups.

Within a column we can see that, though the pupils attained a similar level in their first assessment, there is a spread of results according to the later assessment measure. Column A, for example, shows that pupils who scored between 11 and 20 points on the horizontal axis went on to score between 21 and 29 on the vertical axis. Column B shows that pupils who scored between 21 and 30 points on the horizontal axis went on to score between 27 and 37 on the vertical axis. Column C shows that pupils who scored between 31 and 40 points on the horizontal axis went on to score between 32 to 48 on the vertical axis.

Now let us look more closely at one of the columns. In column A, for example, we can calculate what percentage of pupils, from their common starting point around 15 on the horizontal axis, went on to attain 24 on the vertical axis. Let us say it was 17 per cent. We can calculate what percentage of pupils, from their common starting point around 15 on the horizontal axis, went on to attain 27 on the vertical axis. Let us say it was 40 per cent. We can calculate what percentage of pupils, from their common starting point around 15 on the horizontal axis,

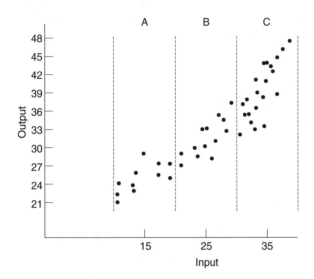

Figure 5 Columns for common inputs.

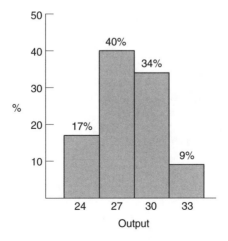

Figure 6 Chances chart.

went on to attain 30 on the vertical axis. Let us say it was 34 per cent. We can calculate what percentage of pupils, from their common starting point around 15 on
the horizontal axis, went on to attain 33 on the vertical axis. Let us say it was 9 per
cent.

On the basis of those results, we can predict that a pupil who scored around 15
in the early assessment would have a 17 per cent chance of scoring 24 in the later
assessment. S/he would have a 40 per cent chance of scoring 27. S/he would have
a 34 per cent chance of scoring 30, and a 9 per cent chance of scoring 33.

Similar calculations can be done for the other columns. The chances that are
worked out in this way might inform the choice of target for a pupil. A chances
chart shows this graphically. Figure 6 shows a chances chart for pupils with the
same input score of around 15, drawn as Column A in Figure 5.

Appendix 5

Case study of developing targets in a primary school

December School, 4–11, serves a town and surrounding rural area which includes a military base.

This school has a history of commitment to certain principles and practices in teaching and learning. The teachers use 'conferencing' (see Graves, 1983, setting aside regular time for the teacher and pupil to discuss progress and next steps), and 'collaboration' (strategies developed, for example, in the Inner London Education Authority, emphasising that teacher and pupil work together, that the teacher does not merely tell the pupil what to do). The school has developed its own way of involving the pupils in their assessment, called Record Breakers. This system, still a cornerstone of teaching and assessment practice throughout the school, so impressed LEA advisers when it was first set up in the 1980s that they used the school as a model of good practice in the promotion of records of achievement. Another powerful development in the school around this time was the Western Australian model of First Steps, providing a foundation in literacy.

Each pupil also has a special book or folder in which each term s/he keeps three pieces of work, over the year representing achievement across the curriculum. This work provides a reference point for the pupil as much as for the teacher: both look back at what was achieved last autumn, say, and notice how much, or how little, progress has been made. The school's leadership team also samples the special books or folders on a termly basis, as part of its monitoring of standards throughout the school. The leadership team writes letters to all of the pupils whose work they see, thanking them and complimenting them on specific aspects of their achievements. They write, for example, *I was very impressed by your use of vivid vocabulary, I noticed how much clearer you are now about fractions*, and so on.

A week is planned into every term to allow for the conferencing to take place between pupils and teacher. Built into this practice is the setting of targets. The value of the pupils' taking responsibility for their own learning is emphasised: the more the child says, the more successful will be their learning journey. When a pupil has shown on three occasions that s/he can do what was required by a target, the target is signed off by both pupil and teacher. Targets for the core subjects are kept at the front of the exercise books, serving as working documents for pupil and teacher. A pupil will say, for example, *Can we sign off my percentages target today?* signalling confidence that the target has been achieved.

All of this work, it was realised very early on, has definite implications for assessment and marking policy. The teachers use pencil to allow the pupils to erase their marking when redrafting. The marking comments focus specifically on the teaching and learning objectives, praise the positive, and make suggestions about how further learning or improvement might be achieved.

The school's culture emphasises the celebration of achievement. At the end of each week, circle time is used as a way of sharing good things that have been done. The pupils choose the three pieces of work they are most pleased with for that week. 'Golden dots' are awarded, and everyone says, *Well done*. At school assembly, once a week, there is a presentation to 'writer of the week', 'mathematician of the week' and 'friend of the week'.

At the heart of the school's approach lie the celebration of achievement and a desire to learn. As the year unfolds, teacher and pupil from time to time have a conversation which focuses on the work that has been done. Together they select pieces of work to go in each pupil's Record Breaker folder which will illustrate and represent the pupil's achievements. The work is annotated, explaining how the work was done, who was involved, what was pleasing about the work, and how the pupil would improve it if s/he had the chance to do it again. Pieces of work are also given National Curriculum levels, and the pupil sets targets.

At the end of each term the teacher and the pupils put together a class topic book, showing what has been achieved, from the planning through to typical outcomes. This work is used in the teachers' assessment-standardisation meetings, and is a focus for colleagues' learning from one another. It also is a focus for the work that is done by way of induction to the school for every new member of staff.

The school's Baseline Assessments give a clear picture of each new intake's range of abilities and needs. Increasingly, pupils are grouped in different ways for different purposes, and a careful eye is kept on giving each pupil a range of experiences with a range of peers to work with. The Baseline Assessments indicate the pupils' potential. It is possible to predict on the basis of the available statistical information, for example, that 60 per cent of the Reception class will go on to attain level 2 in reading, and that 40 per cent are likely to attain level 2c in writing. These informed expectations prompt further tracking of pupils' progress, and the provision of special support or challenge where that appears appropriate.

In the early 1990s during the first years of using Baseline Assessments and tracking pupils' progress through to the end of Key Stage 1, the staff at December School found that their own judgements were being confirmed. Then league tables struck, and there was panic! The school's achievements were not immediately apparent to the casual newspaper reader.

The staff went back to their core beliefs, determined to use assessment data to enrich their teaching and the lives of their pupils. Using the National Curriculum levels, the teachers began to see patterns in the progress that their pupils were making. Typically, for example, a pupil attaining 2b in writing in Year 2 was going on to attain 3b in the optional National Curriculum writing test in Year 4. The teachers developed a detailed sense of what normal progress was looking like.

They were able to describe the steps that the pupils needed to take, and to work out the implications for planning, long, medium and short term.

The headteacher believes it was essential that colleagues saw all of this as a shared responsibility. They chose not to leave the pressure chiefly on Years 2 and 6, but to engage in the debate together and to accept the challenge for the whole school to raise standards as far as possible. As time has gone on, different initiatives have contributed to the school's evolution of teaching approaches, use of assessment and performance data, and use of targets. Not least amongst these is Performance Management. December School's approach is for each teacher once a year to have a morning when they meet with their Team Leader to check their job description, look at their pupils' progress, look back at their records and assessments, to review and set new targets for the pupils. The focus is emphatically on the pupils' learning: *where we'd like her to be next summer is . . .; we can safely say she will be at this level, but, if she can have a really good year, she'll be able to . . .*

Each class list then represents the pupils' past attainments and their targets in terms of National Curriculum or P-scale levels. When the results are available, the lists are colour coded. This has had a powerful effect on colleagues' perceptions. When they first did this, they saw a class list of twenty-nine pupils, twenty-six of whom were highlighted green, meaning they had achieved their targets. Yellow indicated the pupils had made some progress, while falling below the targets. And blue showed the pupil had gone adrift, failing to register progress. In the case of individuals who had not achieved their targets, the background was explored. One child had, for example, returned to India for a long period.

The work on individual pupils makes the building-blocks for the work on cohorts. The headteacher and senior management team work with the LEA adviser to track the pupils' progress and to set targets based on statistical prediction, leavened with a degree of challenge. Pupils' mobility can be accounted for. The process is rational enough to support the teachers' planning and to inform their sense of achievement. The teachers still use pencil and paper records, but the school also makes good use of software, supported by the LEA, allowing them to carry out sophisticated analyses of the data.

Crucial to all of this is a sense of congruity: the values that inform the teachers' work with the pupils have also to inform the managers' work with the teachers and all of the adults' work with one another. The adults need to experience the principles and practices they are expected to model for the pupils. Continuing Professional Development has a high profile in December School, therefore. Teachers and pupils alike use the languages of reflecting, dialogue, planning, targets, activities and review. Teachers and pupils alike need to have language which allows them to describe what they are going to be doing, to express what they are aiming to achieve, to see what success will look like, and to define the steps they will be taking. Everyday conversation revolves around these matters because they are at the centre of everyone's interest.

Appendix 6

Case study of developing targets in a secondary school

Spring School, 11–16, is one of a number of secondary schools serving a large town. Its senior management team recently allocated some time to reviewing assessment arrangements and systems in the school. They decided to introduce a proposal to change policy and practice. The second training day of the school year was chosen as the occasion to put the plan to the staff, discuss amendments and launch the new policy. The aspects of policy and practice that the management team wanted to improve were as follows:

- the roles and scope of responsibility of tutors and heads of year should be enhanced so that they might contribute more effectively to the monitoring of pupils' progress and motivation of pupils;
- the system for interim reporting of pupils' work by subject teachers needed to be more informative: the four assessment-categories (Impressive, Good, Reasonable, Unsatisfactory) did not allow understanding of pupils' *particular* strengths and weaknesses;
- the burden of report-writing needed to be eased.

The review and development of assessment and reporting policy were prompted by recent changes. These included:

- incoming Year 7 pupils now familiar from their primary education with 'levels';
- greater concentration than ever on pupils' *progress* as an educational goal and performance indicator;
- greater awareness that reporting *within* key stages requires a finer measure than whole levels (e.g. bands within level 4: 4a, 4b, 4c);
- awareness that there are cross-curricular or non-subject-specific dimensions to pupils' progress which tend to be underrepresented in assessment, recording and reporting: e.g. Homework, Organisation, Classroom Performance;
- awareness that parents want to be given information about how their child is doing compared with others: e.g. useful concepts here are Exceeds Expectation, Meets Expectation, Disappoints Expectation;
- the statutory requirement to record teacher assessments in all subjects at the end of Key Stage 3;

- the fact that Key Stage 3 assessments can provide a benchmark for progress to Key Stage 4;
- the availability of technology (including optical mark reading systems);
- the governing body's role in monitoring the curriculum and performance.

As a consequence, a system was proposed whereby every pupil would on two occasions in the year have a one-to-one consultation with her/his tutor about progress, needs and targets. The actions proposed were as follows:

- introduce twice-yearly whole-school review days (November and May): closure to allow tutor–pupil one-to-one reviews lasting ten minutes each (a 'review' looks at the last targets set, considers strengths and weaknesses of performance and sets new targets);
- present pupils' progress three times a year (at the end of first, third and fifth half terms), referring to the different priorities of different year groups, e.g. Homework;
- retain annual reporting to parents, with revised format, informed by the new interim reporting and including NC levels/GCSE grades;
- introduce an annual meeting of the head of year with each pupil in the year group on a flexible basis, funded by 'protected' lesson time every week.

Some existing practices were to be given fresh impetus or emphasis in the new arrangements:

- day-to-day marking of pupils' work would no longer include levels or grades;
- teachers' comments to pupils would focus very specifically on learning objectives and individual targets;
- there would be consistency in teachers' use of assessment and reporting systems;
- a determined focus on positive feedback to, and the motivation of, the pupils would be maintained.

On the training day, teachers worked in cross-curricular groups to share views, experiences and aspirations. In a final plenary session the groups' responses were brought together in an agreed statement, as follows:

We have these ways of enabling our pupils to know their learning objectives:

- at Key Stage 3, unit outlines and key words;
- for GCSE, topic outlines, lists of the knowledge, skills and understanding to be developed;
- design briefs;
- verbal and video-recorded demonstrations;
- showing the opposite of what is required;
- making the marking criteria clear;
- giving the pupils choices.

We have these ways of enabling our pupils to influence how they set about their learning objectives:
- carousels of activities;
- trial runs;
- giving them time;
- establishing a baseline of capability;
- being open to negotiation;
- rewards;
- encouraging awareness of preferred learning styles;
- being aware ourselves of our pupils' preferred learning styles;
- continual evaluation.

We have these ways of increasing consistency in our marking:
- remembering pupils with learning difficulties especially in writing;
- departmental moderating;
- providing demonstrations of good practice;
- agreeing focuses of attention;
- thinking about the clarity of the codes and comments we use;
- returning work to pupils within agreed time-spans;
- being clear that there are different kinds of marking.

We have these ways of enabling our pupils to focus on their personal targets:
- using comments following homework;
- giving individual tutorials;
- inviting the pupils to write their reflections on progress;
- using a folder checklist with comments from the pupil and targets set;
- reminders that they have targets;
- keeping a balance with praise and celebration of achievement: sometimes simply compliment the pupil;
- contributions by classroom assistants.

We see these benefits in one-to-one conversations between tutor and pupil:
- We get to know our pupils better.
- Their self-esteem is raised.
- We show them we value them.
- Our pupils have a voice.
- We gain from the feedback.
- We might be the only adults they can talk to in this way.
- We tap into their sensitivity, tackling issues that concern them.
- Pupils' taking responsibility is encouraged.
- The more it happens, the more normal it becomes.
- It picks up the middle-of-the-road pupil.

A provisional structure for one-to-one conversations

- Preparation, and remember there are other opportunities to have this kind of conversation.
- Set the scene.
- Focus on successes.
- Discuss areas for development.
- Select priorities.
- Consider strategies, steps to take, ways ahead.
- Consider, *How will I know when I've got there?*
- Consider rewards and monitoring of progress.
- Make a record.
- Consider parental involvement.

The resources, skills and qualities we need in helping our pupils get the most out of their one-to-one conversations:

- Take a non-judgmental approach.
- Use a tape-recorder? (Perhaps not necessary given the record-format and pad.)
- Let the pupil speak.
- Interpret what the pupil says.
- Be sensitive.
- Summarise what has been said.
- Ask questions.
- Have time to follow up and share information between staff.
- Encourage the pupils to prepare, especially in their minds.
- Have a positive emphasis.
- Encourage the pupils to look out for the effects of these sessions.
- Encourage the pupils to believe we believe.
- Subsequently, reinforce the 'one-liners' that emerge as outcome targets.

Appendix 7

Annual cycle of school self-review and target-setting

Your timings may differ from what appears below, but do you cover the same ground?

Sept.
Analyse summer results.

Confirm new SIP.

Set minimum target grades.

Governors' AGM for parents.

SMT/subject leaders' monitoring of planning.

Performance management appointed governors and external adviser for HT.

Oct.
SEN audit.

Begin performance management review and objectives setting.

Meetings: staff and team leaders.

Preparation for whole-school target-setting.

Analyse benchmark data: including Autumn Package.

Evaluation of performance by GB Curriculum Committee.

Nov.
Check pupils are using targets.

LEA consultant visits to agree whole-school target setting.

Record minimum target levels/grades for each pupil.

Dec.
Update individual pupil records/database.

Jan.
Review progress of each SIP priority.

Begin monitoring of lessons, with feedback, and scrutiny of pupils' work.

SMT/subject leaders' monitoring of planning in selected areas.

Feb.
Evaluate some pupils' views about using targets.

Consider implications of PANDA report.

Take account of new budget and SF provision. Consider resource needs and cost implications for the coming year.

Mar.
Review progress towards individual minimum target grades.

Review progress towards whole-school targets.

Apr.
Update individual pupil records/database.

Complete performance management review and objectives setting meetings: staff and team leaders.

May
Complete monitoring of lessons, with feedback, and scrutiny of pupils' work.

Subject leaders draft action plans to inform SIP.

Incorporate SF and EDP priorities into new SIP draft.

June
Transfer information to the next school/college/ . . .

Draft and circulate for discussion new SIP.

July
Update individual pupil records/database.

Internal transfer of pupil information.

Review curriculum planning.

Note: There is another calendar for all pupils' assessments, NC testing, TA deadlines, reporting times, and parents'/ parents' and carers' consultation times. This includes the making and reviewing of IEPs and annual reviews of statements. Some items would appear in both calendars.

Appendix 8

Assessment policy guidance for schools: show how you put assessment and target policy into practice

Do you agree with these statements? Do they describe your school? If so, what methods do you have for putting them into practice? If not, do you have alternative principles and practices?

1   We strive to develop an ethos which encourages all of our pupils to celebrate their own and others' achievements.

> For example: we use a consistent class merit and headteacher's commendation system.
> We display a wide variety of pupils' work in the foyer and social areas.
> We make presentations at assemblies.

2   The assessment calendar for every year group fulfils statutory, local and school requirements.

> For example: we have a timetable for all statutory assessments including baseline, NC tests/tasks, TA deadlines, optional NC tests, subject assessments, standardisation meetings, transfer deadlines, parents' consultations, reporting deadlines, subject review and target meetings.

3   We have a calendar for school self-review and target-setting.

> For example: see the example in Appendix 5 of this book.

4   Our curriculum planning shows when and how the pupils' progress and achievement are assessed.

For example: our medium-term (topic/unit) planning for every subject shows which main tasks will be assessed, and how.

Key investigations are shown for AT1 in English, maths and science, and for ICT. Day-to-day assessments influence decisions about how to take the teaching and learning forward, i.e. our short-term planning.

Ongoing, specific, constructive feedback to pupils is a vital part of our teaching and learning processes.

5   Our teaching makes use of methods which allow our pupils to show what knowledge, skills and understandings they bring with them to learning situations.

For example: concept-mapping and key-question-raising often start a topic/unit.

We use round-the-class sharing of experiences relevant to the issue at hand. Circle time.

6   The true breadth of our pupils' learning and achievement is assessed, through a range of teaching and learning styles, involving:

- every curriculum subject;
- personal, social, health, and, where appropriate, work-related, education;
- cross-curricular skills and qualities;
- extra-curricular activities;
- unanticipated and unplanned successes;
- understanding of how to learn.

For example: pupils have regular opportunities to share learning and achievement.

Each pupil keeps a folder as an ongoing and comprehensive record of achievement.

We particularly value the successes which were nor predicted or planned for – giving attention to these in lessons, assemblies, and pupils' records of achievement.

We set aside a number of days through the year for whole school projects when younger and older pupils work together, as in health/arts week.

7   Our use of personnel, time and resources gives all our pupils opportunities to grow and learn in all the respects listed immediately above.

> For example: we set aside a number of half days in the autumn and spring terms and a week in the summer for projects and activities which the pupils opt into and help to design.
>
> Led by the class teacher or tutor, voluntary activities and field trips are reflected on so that personal, social, and other experiences and achievements can be recognised.

8   Our teachers confidently use a range of performance indicators, including statutory and teacher assessment results and local and national comparative data:

- to plan the curriculum and set appropriately challenging targets for individual pupils;
- to evaluate the teaching and plan curriculum development;
- set and review targets for cohorts of pupils.

> For example: we use baseline assessments to group pupils and plan next steps in learning.
>
> We analyse NC test information to identify strengths and weaknesses in our pupils' performance and inform future action.
>
> Our own teacher assessments give us feedback on successful features of the curriculum and areas for development, particularly in our medium-term planning. Using three main sources of information (NC results, our teacher assessments and surveys of pupils' perceptions of materials, teaching styles, tasks, challenge, and assessment feedback, and rewards), each subject leader conducts an annual subject review, identifying: strengths and areas for development in pupils' progress and attainment; priorities for improvement; persons responsible; time-scale; resource implications; and success criteria.

9   Our teachers confidently use a range of performance indicators, including local and national comparative data, to evaluate their own effectiveness in their performance management.

> For example: using the pupil data base.
>
> Also used in the context of threshold application.

10   Our pupils say they are usually clear about what it is they are aiming to learn or achieve in lessons, topics, units or courses.

> For example: monitoring of teaching by subject leaders and senior management usually includes some questioning of pupils about the purpose of their work; this is collated and reported on by the assessment co-ordinator to the whole staff in the annual assessment review.

11   We use a variety of methods to make lesson objectives and assessment criteria clear to our pupils.

> For example: frequently used are: theme focuses and topic objectives in English, science, ICT, DT, creative and performing arts, posted on display boards; skills shown in booklets and topic materials for maths, humanities and RE; skills shown on charts in PE; unit objectives leading to certification in modern foreign languages.
>
> Sometimes we stop and share ongoing work which meets or approaches success criteria. When working too, we stop and remind pupils of objectives, asking *What will make good work today?*
>
> Sometimes we show pupils' work produced by peers on previous occasions. We commonly recap at the beginnings and ends of lessons, where possible, involving the pupils in identifying key concepts and skills.

12   We use a variety of methods to agree personal targets with our pupils.

> For example: twice a year the class teacher or tutor has a one-to-one contact with each pupil to discuss successes and areas for improvement, leading to the choice of no more than three priority targets.
>
> At some stage in every topic or unit we try to ensure every pupil is aware of a personal focus of attention in addition to the overall learning objectives for the class or group; the more experienced the pupils, the greater the voice they have in determining their goals.
>
> Pupils sometimes have cards on which to record:

Goal	Date	Progress/Achievement

13   We use a variety of methods to enable our pupils to share in decision making about how they will set about achieving their lesson objectives and targets.

> For example: at its simplest the pupils are invited to choose between two ways of tackling the task. A more sophisticated method is helping the pupils to come up with a selection of approaches to cover part of a topic or unit, and agreeing time-scale, deadlines, resources, help needed, etc. The most open-ended method used with our most experienced pupils is to challenge them to design the project which will demonstrate their specific capabilities in the required respects.
>
> We encourage pupils to identify three pieces of work which show a target achieved and to contribute to discussion about the next target which might be achieved.

14   We use a variety of methods to enable our pupils to express how well they think they are doing, and how they might do even better.

> For example: midway through a topic/unit, we try to give the pupils a short reflection time when they are encouraged to identify a success so far and an area to develop.
>
> During the literacy hour, the teacher sometimes leads a work review focusing on individual targets; and this is used to guide the teacher's subsequent marking.

15   We use a variety of methods to enable our pupils to develop the skills to comment constructively on one another's work, and help one another learn.

For example: we use response partners in English and the humanities.
In most subjects it is common for at least one piece of work per term to be a group effort – groups comment on one another's work by giving two points of praise and one way it could be improved.
Sometimes we model the language and criteria: *I like this because . . ., My favourite bit was . . ., Next time I would like to see . . .*

16   We use individual plans, assessments and reviews to address the special needs of pupils on our SEN register.

For example: each pupil on the SEN register has an individual education plan which records specific assessments, both formal or standardised and informal, including observations by classroom assistants; these are fed into the pupil's annual review by the SENCo or class teacher.

17   Our teachers consult classroom assistants and others, such as therapists, who can provide information about pupils' progress and achievement and work in partnership with us.

For example: we use a loose-leaf file on the teacher's desk for classroom assistants to note special achievements and observations for individual pupils.
We incorporate classroom assistants', pre-school providers' and parents' and carers' contributions when making our Baseline Assessments.

18   Parents and carers are encouraged to contribute to assessments of their child's progress and achievement.

For example: we use a home–school book for two-way communication.
At the spring parents' consultation meeting, there is discussion about how the parents and carers can support the pupil in tackling their goals, such as wider reading.

19   Our teachers use an agreed and consistent approach to marking and responding to pupils' work.

> For example: our marking relates to the learning objectives for the tasks set.
> We use a code which pupils should understand: For example: in the margin,
> > means *look along this line to find a correction*; an underlining means *here is
> the error for you to put right*.
> Our written comments avoid the deflating use of *but*, i.e. praise followed by
> *but* and a criticism; we prefer praise followed by *now . . .* or *next time*.
> We use a smiley face on a spring to mean *big step forward* or *real progress* or
> *concept understood* or *skill achieved . . .*

20   Our pupils know that sometimes our marking asks them to do corrections
or extension work, whereas at other times we acknowledge their work with a
tick.

> For example: setting a task, we check pupils understand their objectives or
> targets and realise whether *this work will receive a comment and guidance
> about how to correct, improve or extend* it, as opposed *to this work will be read
> through and ticked, and only if something vital is missing or misleading for revision
> will the teacher add anything*.
> We give time in lessons for pupils to follow up the marking, when the fuller
> kind of marking has been used.
> We have class posters displaying our marking symbols.

21   Our pupils have ways of recording their progress and achievements within,
across and beyond the curriculum, and value doing so.

> For example: pupils have regular sharing times to do a variety of self assess-
> ment activities, not all of which are recorded or paper-based.
> The pupils are encouraged to express pride in their work and to use the 'traf-
> fic light' system of self-assessment: green for *all going well*, amber for *some
> difficulties, but overall success*, and red for *problems stopping progress*.
> The pupils are encouraged to take pride in and personalise their record of
> achievement folders.

22   Our teachers are confident that their ways of recording pupils' progress and
achievements fit their purposes, and adhere to agreed principles and deadlines.

For example: subject leaders include in their annual subject reviews a question about whether records are really doing their job.

In late September we have a staff meeting to review how our records are being used and to share further information about our pupils before setting group or class targets.

23   Our records are manageable, accessible and useful.

For example: we update our records throughout the year so that they inform planning.

We have a chart as part of our policy which allows us to check:

Record   Location   Responsibility   Purpose   Audience   Destination

24   We efficiently carry out statutory assessments, tests and tasks, and, where appropriate, examinations for public qualifications.

For example: subject leaders record quality-assurance visits by the head-teacher, LEA inspectors and QCA.

25   We standardise our statutory National Curriculum end-of-key-stage Teacher Assessments.

For example: we focus on pupils' work which we think is a strong example of a given level, a fair example of the given level, and a borderline example of the given level.

26   We have meetings to study examples of pupils' work, to learn from one another's teaching, and to agree interpretations of level descriptions or grade criteria.

> For example: the teachers for each subject have an annual meeting to look at examples of pupils' work, share good practice, discuss level and grade descriptions, and record lessons learned.
> In standardising our own teacher assessments this year we have been concentrating on pupils' use of imagination; last year we focused on writing skills.
> We have developed subject-based portfolios of pupils' work in which each piece has notes on where to go next with the pupils' learning.

27   We fulfil statutory requirements for transferring information about pupils' needs, progress and attainment when they leave our school.

> For example: liaison with our feeder and/or next schools has led to a combination of locally agreed practice and use of the national form.
> We have built into our induction programme a meeting with pre-school providers to share information about individual pupils' experiences and achievements.

28   Colleagues in school who receive pupils' assessment data and records find them concise, informative and constructive.

> For example: towards the end of the summer term, after the initial transfer of information about pupils, we have a brief meeting to iron out any snags for the next time around.
> We send the pupils' last targets to the next teacher or form tutor or school.

29   Our pupils are pleased with the advice and support they receive when they apply for voluntary activities, grants, courses of further or higher education, or employment.

> For example: we survey pupils' perceptions of the guidance they receive relating to personal matters and choices; we feed back what we learn into our recording of achievement practices.

30   Our annual reports to parents conform to statutory requirements.

> For example: we use LEA updates to cross-check requirements.
> We have invited our LEA link inspector to check this whenever there has
> been a change to the legislation and prior to Ofsted inspection.

31   Parents and carers, and other people who receive them, find reports informative and constructive.

> For example: every two years we sample parents' and carers' opinions about
> reports and consultation meetings.
> Parents have a comment box on the annual report which they can complete
> at home or at the consultation meeting.

32   Our senior managers consult subject leaders and teachers in order to compare perceptions of strengths, weaknesses, and areas for development in our assessment practice, and use that information in coherent strategic planning to improve the teaching and learning in our school.

> For example: key stage co-ordinators use the QCA Standards Reports to discuss teaching and learning implications, and report these to senior management meetings.
> Each subject leader's annual review contains an analysis of strengths and areas for development in pupils' performance, with suggested implications for whole-school improvement and targets; these are discussed at a meeting in the spring term as part of a whole-school curriculum review.

33   Our annual governors' report to parents fulfils statutory requirements and provides a commentary on our results and targets, when that is thought helpful.

> For example: this was confirmed in our last Ofsted inspection.
> We have taken advice from our governor services officer on this and been
> given a seal of approval.

34   We have clearly designated, agreed and understood responsibilities for head-teacher, co-ordinator and staff in relation to assessment, recording, reporting, and the use of targets.

> For example: this is contained in the job descriptions we introduced three years ago, and is reviewed as part of our performance management process.

35   We have an effective programme for monitoring and evaluating our assessment policy and practices.

> For example: this is part of the assessment co-ordinator's remit who draws together the work of the subject leaders.
>
> As part of our monitoring process, teachers swap classes for a session and discuss with the pupils topics, lesson objectives, attitudes to learning, marking of work etc., having prepared a list of questions or prompts together as a staff beforehand. Our assessment co-ordinator develops an action plan which informs our school-improvement plan.
>
> We use our surveys of pupils' and parents' and carers' perceptions to focus our reviews.

36   We have a view of how our assessment policy and practices have developed over recent years.

> For example: major changes have been in: the annual use of performance data and use of targets; use of IT for reporting to parents; agreement of a whole-school marking policy; the use of self- and peer-assessment by pupils; clarifying the difference between lesson objectives and pupils' individual targets.

37   We use our school improvement plan as a way of developing our assessment and target policy and practices further.

> For example: at least one of the items in our assessment and target policy always features in the school-improvement plan, either because of statutory requirement, or because pupils' and parents' and carers' views encourage it, or because our subject reviews recommend it.

Bibliography

Ainscow, Mel (1999) *Understanding the Development of Inclusive Schools*. Brighton, Falmer Press.

Ashton, Patricia, Hunt, Pamela, Jones, Stephanie and Watson, Gillian (1980) *Curriculum in Action: An Approach to Evaluation*. Milton Keynes, Open University Press.

Askew, M., Rhodes, V., Brown, M., Wiliam, D. and Johnson, D. (1997) *Effective Teachers of Numeracy. Report of a Study Carried Out for the Teacher Training Agency*. London: King's College London, School of Education.

Association of Assessment Inspectors and Advisers South-West Region (2001) *Pupils' Learning from Teachers' Responses*. Contact: *http://www.rmplc.co.uk/org/aaia* and email *aaia@rmplc.co.uk*.

Award Scheme Development Accreditation Network (ASDAN): material available from Central Office, 27 Redland Hill, Bristol BS6 6UX, tel. 01179467774.

Bandura, Albert (1997) *Self-Efficacy: The Exercise of Control*. New York, WH Freeman and Co.

Barbiana, The Children of the School of (1970) *Letter to a Teacher*. Harmondsworth, Penguin.

Black, Paul and Wiliam, Dylan (1998) 'Assessment and Classroom Learning'. Abingdon, Carfax Publishing, *Assessment In Education*, vol. 5, no. 1.

BERA (2001) 'Methodological Seminar on Hay/McBer Research into Teacher Effectiveness', *Research Intelligence*. British Educational Research Association Newsletter, no. 75, April 2001. Email: michaelbassey@bera2.demon.co.uk.

Burgess, Tyrrell and Adams, Elizabeth (eds) (1980) *Outcomes of Education*. Basingstoke, Macmillan.

Busher, Hugh and Harris, Alma (2000) *Subject Leadership and School Improvement*. London, Paul Chapman.

Centre for Studies on Inclusive Education (2000) *Index for Inclusion: Developing Learning and Participation in Schools*. CSIE, 1 Redland Close, Elm Lane, Redland, Bristol BS6 6UE.

Clarke, Shirley (1998) *Targeting Assessment in the Primary Classroom: Strategies for Planning, Assessment, Pupil Feedback and Target Setting*. London, Hodder & Stoughton.

Clarke, Shirley (2001a) *Unlocking Formative Assessment: Practical Strategies for Enhancing Pupils' Learning in the Primary Classroom*. London, Hodder & Stoughton.

Clarke, Shirley (2001b) *Gillingham Partnership – Formative Assessment Project 2000–01: Interim Report on the First Term of the Project – Communicating Learning Intentions, Developing Success Criteria and Pupil Self-Evaluation*. London, Institute of Education, University of London. Accessible on the website of the Association of Assessment Inspectors and Advisers: www.aaia.org.uk.

DES [Department of Education and Science and the Welsh Office] (1984) *Records of Achievement: A Statement of Policy*. London, Her Majesty's Stationery Office.

DES [Department of Education and Science and the Welsh Office] (1987) *National Curriculum – Task Group on Assessment and Testing: A Report*. London, King's College London, University of London.

DFE [Department for Education] (1994) *Code of Practice on the Identification and Assessment of Special Educational Needs*. London, Department for Education.

DfEE [Department for Education and Employment] (1997) *From Targets to Action: Guidance to Support Effective Target Setting in Schools*. London, DfEE, QCA and Ofsted.

DfEE [Department for Education and Employment] (1998) *Supporting the Target Setting Process: Guidance for Effective Target Setting for Pupils with Special Educational Needs*. London, Department for Education and Employment.

DfEE [Department for Education and Employment] (1999) *Social Inclusion: Pupil support – The Secretary of State's Guidance on Pupil Attendance, Behaviour, Exclusion and Re-integration*. Circular 10/99. London, Department for Education and Employment.

DfEE [Department for Education and Employment] (2000a) *Performance Management: Guidance for Governors*. London, Department for Education and Employment.

DfEE [Department for Education and Employment] (2000b) *Performance Management in Schools: Model Performance Management Policy*. London, Department for Education and Employment.

DfEE [Department for Education and Employment] (2000c) *Performance Management in Schools: Performance Management Framework*. London, Department for Education and Employment.

DfEE [Department for Education and Employment] (2000d) *Performance Management in Schools: Guidance Note*. London, Department for Education and Employment.

DfEE [Department for Education and Employment] and Folio InfoBase (1998) *Progress File Achievement Planner: Assisting Planning to Introduce the Progress File – a CD-ROM*. London, Department for Education and Employment. Also accessible via website www.dfee.gov.uk/progfile.

DfEE [Department for Education and Employment] and QCA [Qualifications and Curriculum Authority] (1999) *The National Curriculum: Handbook for Primary Teachers in England – Key Stages 1 and 2* and *Handbook for Secondary Teachers – Key Stages 3 and 4*. London, Department for Education and Employment and Qualifications and Curriculum Authority.

Donaldson, Margaret (1978) *Children's Minds*. London, Fontana/Collins.

Dorset County Council (1988) *Report of the Drama Action Group*. Dorchester, Dorset Education Department Advisory Section County Assessment Unit.

Fullan, Michael (1988) 'Managing Curriculum Change', in *The Dynamics of Curriculum Change: Curriculum at the Crossroads*. London, School Curriculum Development Committee.

Galton, Maurice, Hargreaves, Linda, Comber, Chris, Wall, Debbie and Pell, Tony (1999) 'Changes in Patterns of Teacher Interaction in Primary Classrooms: 1976–96'. Abingdon, Carfax Publishing, *British Educational Research Journal*, vol. 25, no. 1.

Goldstein, Harvey (2001) 'Using Pupil Performance Data for Judging Schools and Teachers: Scope and Limitations'. Abingdon, Carfax Publishing, *British Educational Research Journal*, vol. 27, no. 4.

Graves, Donald (1983) *Writing: Teachers and Children at Work*. London, Heinemann.

Harris, Alma (1999) *Effective Subject Leadership: A Handbook of Staff Development Activities*. London, David Fulton.

Harris, Alma (2001) 'Department Improvement and School Improvement: A Missing Link?' Abingdon, Carfax Publishing, *British Educational Research Journal*, vol. 27, no. 4.

Harris, A., Jamieson, I.M. and Russ, J. (1995) 'A Study of Effective Departments in Secondary Schools', *School Organisation*, vol. 15, pp. 283–99.

Hay/McBer (2000) *Research into Teacher effectiveness – Phase II Report: A Model of Teacher Effectiveness*. Hay/McBer, made available via the DfEE to members of the British Educational Research Association attending the seminar held on 9 May 2001 at the Institute of Education, University of London.

Holt, John (1971) *How Children Learn*. Harmondsworth, Penguin.

Humphreys, Keith and Thompson, Michael (1998) *Equals Baseline Assessment Scheme*. PO Box 107, Coach Lane Campus, Newcastle upon Tyne NE7 7WL.

Kent Curriculum Services Agency (1995) *Accreditation for Living and Learning Skills (ALL)*. Kent Local Education Authority.

Kent, Tim and Norwich, Brahm (2000) *Target Setting for Individuals and Schools: How Can it Work with SEN? Guidance for Reflective Practice in Target Setting based on a Development Research Project*. University of Exeter, Partnership Office, School of Education, Heavitree Road, Exeter EX1 2LU.

Keys, Wendy and Fernandes, Cres (1993) *What Do Students Think about School? A Report for the National Commission on Education*. Slough, NFER.

Lambert, L. (1998) *Building Leadership Capacity in Schools*. Alexandria, VA, Association for Supervision and Curriculum Development.

Luria, A.R. and Yudovich, F.I. *Speech and the Development of Mental Processes in the Child* (1959), ed. Joan Simon, transl. Joan Simon and O. Kovasc. London, Staples.

Mosley, Jenny (2001, and earlier) Publications available from Jenny Mosley Consultancies, 8 Westbourne Road, Trowbridge, Wiltshire BA14 0AJ, tel. 44 (0)1225 767157. Positive Press.

O'Connell, Bill (1998) *Solution-Focused Therapy*. London, Sage Publications.

Ofsted [Office for Standards in Education] (1999a) *Principles into Practice: Effective Education for Pupils with Emotional and Behavioural Difficulties*. London, Ofsted.

Ofsted [Office for Standards in Education] (1999b) *Raising the Attainment of Minority Ethnic Pupils: School and LEA Responses*. London, Ofsted.

Ofsted [Office for Standards in Education] (2000a) *Handbook for Inspecting Secondary Schools*. London, The Stationery Office.

Ofsted [Office for Standards in Education] (2000b) *Strategies to Promote Inclusion: Improving City Schools*. London, Ofsted.

Pilot Records of Achievement in Schools (PRAISE) team (1988) *Records of Achievement: Report of the National Evaluation of Pilot Schemes*. London, HMSO.

QCA [Qualifications and Curriculum Authority] (1998) *Target Setting in Special Schools*. London: QCA.

QCA [Qualifications and Curriculum Authority] (1999) *Investing in our Future: Early Learning Goals*. London, QCA.

Ramaprasad, A. (1983) 'On the Definition of Feedback', in *Behavioral Science*, vol. 28, pp. 4–13.

Royal Society for the Arts (1998) *National Skills Profile: Assessment Kit*. Westwood Way, Coventry CV4 8HS.

Sadler, R. (1989) 'Formative Assessment and the Design of Instructional Systems', *Instructional Science*, vol. 18, pp. 119–44.

Schagen, Ian (2000) *Statistics for School Managers*. Westley, Suffolk, Courseware Publications.

TTA [Teacher Training Agency] (1998) *National Standards for Qualified Teacher Status* and *National Standards for Headteachers*. London, Teacher Training Agency. Also available are *National Standards for Subject Leaders* and *National Standards for Special Educational Needs Co-ordinators*.

Torrance, Harry and Pryor, John (1998) *Investigating Formative Assessment: Teaching, Learning and Assessment in the Classroom*. Milton Keynes, Open University Press.

Von Glasersfeld, Ernst (1978) 'Radical Constructivism and Piaget's Concept of Knowledge', in E.B. Murray (ed.) *The Impact of Piagetian Theory*. Baltimore, Johns Hopkins University Press, pp. 109–22.

Vygotsky, Lev (1978) *Mind in Society: The Development of Higher Psychological Processes*. Cambridge, MA, Harvard University Press.

Glossary

AGM Annual General Meeting – for parents, organised by the governing body of a school.

A level and AS level Two-year advanced (A) level and one-year (AS) General Certificate of Education examination qualifications, providing conventional access to higher education; grades are A to E, and for the purpose of calculating averages they score at A level 10 points for grade A, 8 for B, and so on down to 2 for E, and at AS level 5 points for A, and so on down to 1 for E.

Attainment What one or more pupils are assessed to have shown themselves capable of on a single occasion. (See **progress**.)

Autumn package Government booklets published October/November each year since 1998 giving summary national results, benchmarking tables and value-added charts of various assessments, tests and examinations carried out by schools.

Average point score A figure representing the average level of attainment by pupils in a particular test or examination. It is derived by assigning a certain number of points to given levels or grades.

Baseline assessment A method of recording attainment of children during the first weeks of schooling, usually at age 4 years. At the time of writing, there is no single national scheme but a range of registered schemes from which schools must choose.

Benchmarking A process of making comparisons between groups of schools thought to be similar in some way, for example, schools with fewer than 8 per cent of pupils eligible for free school meals.

CATs Cognitive Ability Tests, as available from NFER-Nelson (see **NFER**).

CEA Cambridge Education Associates – a company providing support for schools and other agencies relating to education management; an Ofsted school inspection contractor; and DfES contractor for Performance Management and Threshold Assessment.

Chances chart or **graph** Graphical representation of the percentage of a group of pupils with a similar result in an earlier test predicted to attain each level or grade in a later test.

Circle time A procedure, developed and promoted by Jenny Mosley, whereby pupils discuss matters of concern to their learning.

Cluster   Group of schools, usually in a locality, which co-operate, for example, to share training opportunities, resources, and so on.

Conferencing   Teacher and pupil discussing tasks, learning and targets. This practice was researched and popularised by Donald Graves (1983).

Core   (subjects in the National Curriculum) generally thought to be English, mathematics and science, sometimes also including Information Communication Technology.

DfEE   Department for Education and Employment – now the **DfES**.

DfES   Department for Education and Skills – the central government office responsible for education. Through the 1990s until June 2001 it was the DfEE; previously called the DFE (Department for Education), and before that DES (Department for Education and Science).

EBD   Emotional and Behavioural Difficulties – a particular kind of special educational need.

EDP   Education development plan – for the LEA. The equivalent of a school's **SDP/SIP**.

GB   Governing Body – the group statutorily responsible for a school's strategic direction and accountability.

GCSE   General Certificate of Secondary Education, qualifications for 16 year-olds and others in a range of subjects; grades are A* to G, scoring 8 points down to 1 point for the purpose of calculating averages etc.

HMI   Her Majesty's Inspector(ate) of Schools.

HT   Headteacher.

ICT   Information Communication Technology – a National Curriculum subject and cross-curricular key skill.

IEP   Individual education plan – usually helping to provide appropriate teaching and learning for individual pupils who experience special educational needs.

IiP   Investors in People – a national quality standard which sets a level of good practice for improving an organisation's performance through its people; established in 1991, and initially administered by the DfEE; issues an annual company report, available on www.iipuk.co.uk

Key skills   Relevant to Key Stage 4 and post-16 education, previously called core skills: Communication; Application of Number; Information Technology; Working with Others; Problem-Solving; Improving Own Learning and Performance (all at levels 1 to 4); and Personal Skills Development (at level 5).

Key Stage   A period of two, three or four years covering part of the National Curriculum. The NC consists of: Key Stage 1 from age 5 to 7 years, school years 1 and 2; Key Stage 2 from age 7 to 11, school years 3 to 6; Key Stage 3 from age 11 to 14, school years 7 to 9.

LEA   Local Education Authority – the local government body responsible for the administration of maintained schools.

Median   A measure of an average result. The score for which 50 per cent of the scores lie above and 50 per cent lie below.

Meta-cognition Thinking about thinking. This is activity which enables pupils to stand back and reflect on their learning.

National Curriculum tests/tasks Assessment materials issued by the government for 7-, 11- and 14-year-old pupils' statutory assessments in English, maths and (except for 7-year-olds) science. Optional materials are also available in English and maths for Y3, 4, 5, Y7, and Y8 and in a range of subjects for 14-year-olds in Y9.

NC National Curriculum – the statutory definition of the ten subjects to be taught in state schools from the age of 5 to 14 years.

NFER National Foundation for Educational Research, which in partnership with the publishing company Nelson produces Cognitive Ability Tests, used in schools as a basis for predicting likely academic results.

NLS National Literacy Strategy – government sponsored initiative designed to raise standards of pupils' literacy from Reception to the end of Key Stage 3.

NNS National Numeracy Strategy – government sponsored initiative designed to raise standards of pupils' numeracy from Reception to the end of Key Stage 3.

NQT Newly qualified teacher.

OCR Oxford Cambridge and RSA (Royal Society for the Arts) Examinations – offering qualifications at a variety of levels for a wide range of subjects.

Ofsted Office for Standards in Education – the government agency responsible for school inspection.

PANDA An annual performance and assessment report produced for schools by the government inspection agency Ofsted. Available usually during the spring term.

PM – Performance Management A form of appraisal with potential consequences for salary. For headteachers, two or three appointed school governors conduct a process of review and setting objectives, advised by an External Adviser. For teaching staff, the equivalent process is conducted by the headteacher or team leaders, designated by the headteacher.

PICSI Pre Inspection Context and School Indicator: report issued by Ofsted before a school is inspected, containing data about the school's characteristics, attainment, attendance, exclusions, and so on, helping the inspection team ask questions to inform their time spent in the school.

Progress The gains one or more pupils are assessed to have made between two dates.

P-scales Pre-National-Curriculum or performance scales, devised by QCA to help teachers plan for and assess progress of pupils whose capabilities are not represented by National Curriculum level 1, that is, pupils with particular special educational needs.

Pyramid Schools in a locality representing all phases, from first or infant schools, through junior or primary or middle schools, to secondary or upper schools and sixth forms or further education.

Quartiles A technique of dividing up a set of scores so that relative standings can be compared consistently. The scores are split into four so that 25 per cent of the scores fall below the lower quartile, 50 per cent fall around the median, and 25 per cent fall above the upper quartile.

QCA   Qualifications and Curriculum Authority – the government organisation responsible for the definition and assessment of the National Curriculum and other forms of qualification.

RS   Religious Studies – a subject that can be studied to GCSE or A/AS level.

Residual   The difference between a predicted value and an actual value.

Scaffolding   Providing tasks whose structure supports learning.

SDP   School development plan. (See also **SIP**.)

SEN   Special Educational Needs – we might expect one in five pupils to experience special educational needs at some time in their schooling.

SENCo   Special Educational Needs Co-ordinator – the teacher responsible in a school for bringing together all the assessment and provision arrangements for pupils who experience SEN.

SF   Standards Fund – monies provided to schools by central government and augmented statutorily by the LEA to support initiatives and development work.

SIG   School improvement group – those responsible for steering activities designed to raise standards through the SIP (qv), including, for example, the headteacher, deputy headteacher, chair of governors, vice-chair of governors, chairs of GB committees.

SIP   School improvement plan. (See also **SDP**.)

Standards reports   Government booklets published usually in the spring term which describe particular strengths and weaknesses in pupils' responses to the National Curriculum tests.

Statutory targets   Required by government of schools, predicted results to be published for cohorts of pupils at the end of Year 6, Year 9 and Year 11.

Subject Leader   The teacher responsible for leadership and management of a subject. The Teacher Training Agency sets out national standards for this role.

Success criteria   Explanation of what a pupil will have to do in order to achieve what a task requires.

TA – Teacher Assessment   Judgements made by teachers about the overall level of attainment reached by pupils. Statutorily these must be recorded at the end of each key stage: for the core subjects of English, mathematics and science at Key Stages 1 and 2, and for all National Curriculum subjects at Key Stage 3.

Team Leader   The teacher delegated by a headteacher to be responsible for one or more colleagues' performance management process.

TGAT   Task Group on Assessment and Testing, chaired by Professor Paul Black. See in the bibliography: DES (1987) *National Curriculum – Task Group on Assessment and Testing: A Report*.

UPN   Unique Pupil Number – which allows assessment data to be collected anonymously for every pupil in the country, year on year, as a basis for wide-ranging analyses of results and trends nationally.

Value-Added A statistical comparison of schools' performance in terms of the relative progress made by pupils in relation to attainment in (usually) National Curriculum assessments/GCSE, yielding a regression line; hence schools above and below the average are said to provide positive value-added and negative value-added respectively.

Y Year: a year group of pupils, starting with R for reception class, then Y1, Y2, and so on to Y12 and Y13 in the sixth form.

Index